GULF
IDEOLOGICAL
DYNAMICS

EXPLORING THE QUEST FOR UNITY AND DISCORD

GEW REPORTS & ANALYSES TEAM, HICHEM KAROUI (ED.)

GLOBAL EAST-WEST (LONDON)

CONTENTS

Gulf Ideological Dynamics   1
   Exploring the Quest for Unity and Discord

Foreword   3
   Roadmap

1. Introduction   19
     A. Overview of the Gulf region
     B. Importance of understanding Gulf ideological dynamics
     C. Purpose and structure of the book
     D. Landmarks

2. The Gulf's Ideological System   47
   Understanding its Existence and Functioning

     A. Defining the Gulf's ideological system
     B. Political dimensions of the Gulf's ideological system

C. Economic dimensions of the Gulf ideological system

D. Social dimensions of the Gulf ideological system

E. Cultural dimensions of the Gulf ideological system

F. Determinants and interplay of the Gulf ideological system

G. Landmarks

3. Case Study: The Qatar Crisis of 2017-2020   91

Background and Context

A. Background and context of the crisis

B. Analysis of factors contributing to the crisis

C. The role of the Gulf ideological system in managing or exacerbating the crisis

D. Impact of the crisis on Gulf regional dynamics

E. Lessons learned and implications for the future of Gulf unity

F. Landmarks

4. Historical and Cultural Factors Shaping Gulf   123
Identities

A. Historical legacies influencing Gulf identities

B. Cultural diversity and its impact on Gulf unity

C. Role of religion in shaping Gulf identities

D. Social norms and values in Gulf societies

E. Landmarks

5. Geopolitical Rivalries and Alliances in the Gulf   149
Region

　　A. Historical context of geopolitical rivalries

　　B. Gulf states' alliances and their impact on unity

　　C. The role of external powers in shaping Gulf dynamics

　　D. Implications of rivalries and alliances for Gulf Ideological Unity

　　E. Landmarks

6.　External Influences and Global Dynamics in the Gulf　　179

　　A. The influence of global economic forces on Gulf ideologies

　　B. International relations and their impact on Gulf unity

　　C. The role of international organizations in shaping Gulf ideologies

　　D. Global security challenges and their effects on Gulf ideological dynamics

　　E. Landmarks

7.　Internal Challenges and Contradictions within Gulf Societies　　209

　　A. Socioeconomic disparities within Gulf countries

　　B. Political divisions and their impact on Gulf unity

　　C. Youth, identity, and the quest for change in Gulf societies

　　D. Women's roles and empowerment in Gulf societies

　　E. Landmarks

8. Assessing the Need for and Feasibility of a Unified   243
   Gulf Ideological System

   A. Benefits and challenges of a unified Gulf ideological
   system

   B. Comparative analysis of other regional ideological
   systems

   C. Political and economic implications of Gulf ideological unity

   D. Public opinion and the desire for unity in Gulf
   societies

   E. Landmarks

9. Pathways towards Greater Ideological Conver-   277
   gence

   A. Diplomatic initiatives for fostering Gulf unity

   B. Economic integration and its impact on Gulf ideological dynamics

   C. Cultural exchanges and the promotion of shared
   values

   D. Grassroots movements and civil society initiatives
   for unity

   E. Landmarks

10. Implications for Regional Stability, Security, and   303
    Development

    A. The role of Gulf ideological unity in regional sta-
    bility

    B. Security challenges and the need for coordinated
    approaches

C. Socioeconomic development and the benefits of Gulf unity

D. Environmental sustainability and the quest for shared solutions

E. Conclusion: Reflections on the future of Gulf ideological dynamics

F. Landmarks

Bibliography   347

GULF IDEOLOGICAL DYNAMICS

Exploring the Quest for Unity and Discord

Contribution to the Sociology of the Gulf

Collection: The Gulf
Global East-West

FOREWORD

Within the Gulf region, a myriad of internal challenges and contradictions shape its ideological landscape. These dynamics reflect the complex interplay between tradition and modernity, political divisions, socio-economic disparities, and the quest for change. In this chapter, we delve deeper into these factors, examining their origins, manifestations, and implications for Gulf unity and discord.

Traditionalism vs. Modernity:

Gulf societies have long grappled with the tension between preserving traditional values and embracing modernity. Traditional values, deeply rooted in religious beliefs, cultural heritage, and historical practices, have shaped the region's identity and fostered a sense of continuity. However, rapid modernization, fueled by vast oil wealth and globalization, has introduced new ideas, technologies, and social norms into Gulf societies.

This clash between tradition and modernity creates internal divisions as different segments of society navigate their roles and identities in the changing Gulf landscape. The conservative ideologies associated with traditionalism often emphasize the preservation of cultural and religious values, seeking to maintain social order and stability. These ideologies find support within conservative segments of the population, who fear that rapid modernization may erode their cultural heritage and religious customs.

On the other hand, more progressive segments of society, including women, youth, and intellectuals, champion the adoption of modern values and advocate for greater personal and social freedoms. They perceive modernity as an opportunity for social progress, inclusivity, and economic development. This clash between traditionalism and modernity forms the basis for ongoing debates and discussions, influencing educational systems, cultural practices, and societal norms within Gulf societies.

Political Divisions:

Political divisions present another internal challenge to Gulf unity. Within some Gulf countries, power struggles, ideological differences, and varying visions for governance can lead to political polarization. Rival factions within ruling families or political elites often compete for influence and control, which can manifest in policies that reflect conflicting interests and priorities.

These divisions can hinder efforts towards Gulf cooperation, as different countries may support opposing regional proxies or have diverging priorities in diplomatic relations. Disagreements over regional dominance, regional security alliances, and foreign policy approaches can strain Gulf unity. Furthermore, geopolitical dynamics and external influences can exacerbate these divisions, particularly when external powers exploit existing fault lines to further their own interests.

Moreover, the absence of inclusive political systems, limited civic participation, and restricted political freedoms can contribute to discontent and frustration within Gulf societies. When grievances are not adequately addressed or channeled through peaceful avenues for expression, it can result in social unrest and political turmoil, further undermining unity within the Gulf.

Socio-economic Disparities:

Socio-economic disparities pose another challenge to Gulf unity. While the region boasts immense wealth and prosperity, there are significant wealth inequalities within and between Gulf countries. The distribution of wealth often tilts heavily towards a select few, exacerbating socio-economic gaps and creating marginalized populations.

Gulf societies face the challenge of striking a balance between preserving the benefits of their rentier economies, driven primarily by oil and gas revenues, and addressing social and economic inequalities. These disparities are not limited to income and wealth distribution but also affect access to healthcare, education, housing, and employment opportunities. Marginalized groups, such as the expatriate labor force, migrant workers, and individuals from lower socioeconomic backgrounds, often face limited opportunities for upward mobility, leading to feelings of exclusion and resentment.

Governance structures and policies play a crucial role in ensuring equitable distribution of wealth and opportunities. Gulf governments have initiated socio-economic reforms, including diversification efforts, social welfare programs, and investments in education and infrastructure. However, the pace and effectiveness of these reforms vary between countries, and further efforts are needed to address socio-economic disparities comprehensively. Failure to address these disparities can fuel social unrest and frustration, further straining Gulf unity.

Quest for Change:

Gulf societies are not immune to the desire for political and societal change. This quest for change is driven by various factors, including increasing education levels, access to information through technology, and exposure to global trends and movements. The Arab Spring in 2011 had a profound impact on the region, prompting Gulf countries to reassess their internal dynamics and respond to the aspirations of their citizenry.

These calls for change often stem from a desire for greater political participation, accountability, transparency, and respect for human rights. Citizens, particularly the younger generation, are increasingly vocal about their expectations for responsive governance, social justice, and the protection of individual rights. While Gulf governments have implemented selective reforms and initiatives to address some of these demands, navigating the delicate balance between maintaining stability and addressing citizens' aspirations remains a challenge.

These demands for change often encounter resistance from entrenched power structures and conservative ideologies that resist significant shifts in the status quo. Striking a balance between meeting citizens' legitimate demands and maintaining social order and stability poses an ongoing challenge to Gulf governments. Moreover, external pressures and geopolitical rivalries can further complicate the internal dynamics, as external parties often exploit these demands for change to advance their own interests or destabilize the region.

In summary:

The internal challenges and contradictions within Gulf societies contribute to the complex ideological landscape of the region. The tension between tradition and modernity, political divisions, socio-economic disparities, and the quest for change shape Gulf unity and discord. Understanding and addressing these internal dynamics are crucial for fostering a more inclusive and cohesive Gulf region.

By acknowledging and navigating these challenges, the Gulf can strive towards a more balanced and harmonious ideological system that promotes the wellbeing and aspirations of all its people. While progress has been made in certain areas, such as economic diversification and limited social reforms, continued efforts are necessary to address political divisions, socio-economic disparities, and the evolving aspirations of Gulf citizens. Only through genuine dialogue, inclusive governance, and responsive policies can the region overcome its internal contradictions and harness its potential for sustainable development and unity.

Roadmap

The Gulf region, with its strategic location and abundant resources, attracts attention and engagement from various global actors. This section further explores how external factors and global trends shape the ideological environment of the Gulf region. It examines the impact of global economic forces, international relations, international organizations, and global security challenges on the Gulf ideological system.

I. Influence of Global Economic Forces: The Gulf region's economic prosperity is intricately linked to global economic dynamics. This section explores the effects of global economic forces on Gulf ideologies.

1. Impact of Global Trade and Investment: Gulf economies heavily rely on international trade and foreign direct investment (FDI). The chapter examines the implications of global trade patterns, economic policies, and investment flows on Gulf ideological dynamics:

2. Trade Patterns: The Gulf region serves as a crucial hub for global trade, connecting major economies in Asia,

Europe, and beyond. The diversified trade relations with various regions influence Gulf ideologies as economic interdependence shapes cooperation and common interests.

3. Economic Policies: Global economic policies, including those determined by major trade blocs like the World Trade Organization (WTO) and regional free trade agreements, influence Gulf ideologies. The adoption of liberal economic policies, regulatory frameworks, and market reforms is often influenced by global economic trends and international pressures.

4. Investment Flows: Foreign direct investment (FDI) plays a significant role in the Gulf region's economic development. The influence of global investment flows on Gulf ideologies can be seen in terms of economic liberalization, privatization, technology transfer, and diversification efforts, among others.

5. Role of Energy Markets: As major oil and gas producers, Gulf countries are influenced by global energy markets. The section explores the impact of price fluctuations, energy policies, and efforts towards diversification on Gulf ideological choices:

6. Price Fluctuations: The volatility of global energy markets affects the economic stability and revenues of Gulf states. Fluctuations in oil prices impact Gulf ideologies by influencing fiscal policies, government

spending, and resource allocation.

7. Energy Policy Adaptation: Global calls for sustainable development, renewable energy transition, and decarbonization efforts influence Gulf energy policies. The response to these global trends shapes Gulf ideological choices on environmental sustainability, energy diversification, and the balance between traditional oil-based economies and emerging industries.

8. Diversification Efforts: Gulf countries strive to reduce their reliance on hydrocarbon revenues through economic diversification. Global economic trends and technological advancements impact the choice of sectors for diversification, such as finance, tourism, manufacturing, and technology. These choices carry ideological implications for the region's ambitions and future trajectory.

9. Technological Advancements and Digital Revolution: The rise of digital technologies and the Fourth Industrial Revolution have global implications, including for the Gulf region. This section discusses the influence of digital transformation on Gulf ideologies, including social, economic, and political dimensions:

10. Digitalization and Economic Transformation: The adoption of digital technologies influences Gulf economies, including e-commerce, fintech, smart cities, and digital infrastructure. The integration of

digitalization into economic sectors shapes Gulf ideologies related to digital governance, entrepreneurship, and social empowerment.

11. Social Implications: The digital revolution has profound effects on society, including changes in communication patterns, connectivity, and access to information. These social transformations through technological advancements shape Gulf ideologies on issues like media regulation, privacy, and education.

12. Political Impacts: Digital technologies also influence political dynamics, such as e-governance, citizen participation, and cyber-security. The adoption of digital tools in political processes impacts Gulf ideologies on transparency, government accountability, and citizen engagement.

13. **International Relations and Gulf Ideological Dynamics: The Gulf region's geopolitical standing is shaped by complex relations with international actors. This section explores the impact of international relations on the Gulf ideological system.**

14. Strategic Alliances and Partnerships: Gulf countries maintain relationships with various global powers. The chapter analyzes the implications of strategic alliances and partnerships on Gulf ideological choices, considering factors such as security cooperation, defense agreements, and regional military presence:

15. Security Cooperation: Gulf countries forge alliances to enhance their security capabilities and deter potential threats. These alliances often influence Gulf ideologies related to regional conflicts, counter-terrorism efforts, and the balance of power in the region.

16. Defense Agreements: The Gulf region hosts military bases and installations of foreign powers, which shape the perception of national security. The presence of foreign military forces impacts Gulf ideologies by influencing defense policies, regional stability considerations, and the diversification of security partnerships.

17. Regional Military Presence: The presence of foreign military forces and naval patrols in the Gulf region influences Gulf ideologies on issues such as sovereignty, territorial disputes, and the balance of power. This presence can shape the perception of external threats and influence Gulf states' foreign policy choices.

18. Influence of Major Powers: Global powers, including the United States, China, and Russia, have significant influence in the Gulf region. This section examines how the Gulf ideological system is influenced by the policies, interests, and competition among these major powers:

19. United States: The United States plays a crucial role in Gulf security, political stability, and economic relations. The U.S. foreign policy and military presence

in the region impact Gulf ideologies on issues such as regional conflicts, human rights, democratization, and diplomatic alignments.

20. China: China's economic engagement and growing presence in the Gulf region shape Gulf ideologies. Chinese investments, infrastructure projects, and trade relations influence Gulf economies, regional connectivity, and the perception of shifting global power dynamics.

21. Russia: Russia's involvement in the Gulf region, including military cooperation and engagement in regional conflicts, influence Gulf ideologies on issues such as power balancing, diplomatic alignments, and regional stability considerations.

22. Regional and International Organizations: Gulf countries actively participate in regional and international organizations. The chapter explores the influence of organizations like the Gulf Cooperation Council (GCC), Arab League, United Nations, and others on Gulf ideological dynamics, including decision-making processes, normative frameworks, and collective actions:

23. Gulf Cooperation Council (GCC): The GCC aims to promote regional integration and cooperation. The organization's initiatives, decisions, and policy coordination influence Gulf ideologies related to economic,

political, and security integration.

24. Arab League: As members of the Arab League, Gulf countries participate in collective decision-making and policy coordination with other Arab states. The Arab League's resolutions, positions, and regional initiatives shape Gulf ideologies on Arab identity, regional conflicts, and cooperation.

25. United Nations and International Organizations: Gulf countries participate in international organizations, including the United Nations, IMF, World Bank, and others. The influence of these organizations on Gulf ideologies can be seen in areas such as human rights, sustainable development, global governance, and international norms.

26. **Global Security Challenges and the Gulf: The Gulf region confronts numerous security challenges with global implications. This section investigates the impact of global security dynamics on the Gulf ideological system:**

27. The Role of Conflict and Instability: Conflicts and crises in neighboring regions have significant reverberations in the Gulf. This chapter analyzes how regional conflicts, such as those in Syria, Yemen, and Iraq, shape Gulf ideological choices and security perceptions:

28. Ideological Support: Gulf countries provide ideological, financial, and military support to factions involved

in regional conflicts. These choices reflect the ideological dimensions and considerations in regional power struggles and security interests.

29. Security Perceptions: Regional conflicts and instability influence Gulf states' security perceptions and threat assessments. The impact of these conflicts on Gulf ideologies can be seen in the prioritization of defense capabilities, military spending, and regional security alliances.

30. Non-State Actors and Terrorism: The rise of non-state actors, such as terrorist organizations, poses global security challenges that impact the Gulf region. This section explores the influence of terrorism and extremist ideologies on Gulf state responses and counter-terrorism efforts:

31. Counter-Terrorism Cooperation: Gulf countries collaborate with international partners to counter terrorism and extremist ideologies. The influence of global counter-terrorism initiatives shapes Gulf ideologies on issues such as national security, intelligence-sharing, and ideological confrontations.

32. Ideological Counter-Narratives: The Gulf region actively promotes counter-narratives against extremist ideologies. The influence of global efforts in countering radicalization and promoting moderate ideologies shapes Gulf approaches to education, media, religious

discourse, and social integration.

33. Cybersecurity Challenges: The Gulf region faces growing cybersecurity threats with global implications. This section examines how cybersecurity challenges influence Gulf ideological choices and policies:

34. Digital Threats: Cybersecurity threats, including hacking, cyber espionage, and information warfare, pose risks to Gulf states' critical infrastructure, national security, and public perception. The response to these threats shapes Gulf ideologies on issues like digital governance, privacy, and the role of technology in society.

35. Regional Collaboration: Gulf countries collaborate regionally and internationally to strengthen cybersecurity capabilities and protect against digital threats. The influence of global cybersecurity initiatives and information-sharing platforms shapes Gulf ideologies on issues such as cyber defense, international norms, and cooperation.

In summary: The Gulf region's ideological landscape is influenced by a wide range of external forces and global dynamics. Global economic forces shape Gulf ideologies through trade patterns, investment flows, and technological advancements. International relations, including strategic alliances and partnerships, influence Gulf ideological choices on security, diplomacy, and political alignments. Global security challenges, such as conflicts, terrorism, and cybersecurity threats, have reverberations in the Gulf region and shape its ideological responses. Understanding these external influences and global dynamics is crucial to comprehend the complex ideological system of the Gulf.

INTRODUCTION

T he Gulf region has garnered significant attention and interest due to its unique geopolitical and economic characteristics. Comprising countries such as Saudi Arabia, United Arab Emirates, Qatar, Bahrain, Oman, and Kuwait, the Gulf region is home to a diverse range of ideologies, making it a compelling subject to explore. This book explores the complexities of ideological dynamics in the Gulf region, aiming to comprehend the pursuit of unity and the root causes that may result in discord.

Understanding Gulf ideological dynamics is essential for comprehending the region's complexities and for contextualizing regional events. It allows us to gain insights into the political, economic, social, and cultural dimensions that influence the decision-making processes of Gulf states. By examining these dimensions, we can better analyze the relationships between Gulf nations and the implications for broader regional dynamics.

The Gulf ideological system is shaped by a combination of historical, political, sociocultural, and economic factors. The history of the Gulf region is marked by colonial legacies, tribal affiliations, and geopolitical forces, which have left deep imprints on the region, shaping not only the political systems but also societal norms and values.

Historically, Gulf societies were organized around tribal affiliations, which played a significant role in shaping identities and political structures. Tribal customs and alliances continue to influence the social fabric of Gulf nations, often intersecting with political ideologies and shaping the distribution of power within each state. The dynamics of tribes can either reinforce existing ideological alignments or contribute to shifting political alliances.

The establishment of modern Gulf states was influenced by the colonial legacies of the region. Saudi Arabia, for example, has been deeply shaped by its alliance with the Wahhabi religious movement, which has become the dominant ideology in the country. The UAE, on the other hand, was formed through the amalgamation of different emirates, each with its own governing structure and social norms. These historical factors have contributed to different ideological orientations within Gulf states.

Politically, Gulf states exhibit varying degrees of ideological alignment. While some countries, such as Saudi Arabia and the UAE, adhere to conservative, pan-Islamic ideologies, others, like Qatar and Oman, have pursued more independent and pragmatic approaches. These ideological differences stem from historical alliances, rivalries, and competing visions for the region's future.

Saudi Arabia, as the birthplace of Islam, has positioned itself as a leader of the Muslim world, advocating for a conservative interpretation of Islamic principles. The kingdom's close alliance with Wahhabi clerics has shaped its internal and external policies, influencing its approach to issues such as women's rights, religious freedom, and political reform. This conservative ideology has had an impact on Saudi Arabia's regional alliances, particularly in countering perceived Iranian influence.

The UAE, in contrast, has positioned itself as a modern and progressive nation, embracing elements of global culture and aspiring to be a global hub for business and innovation. Its ideology emphasizes economic diversification, social tolerance, and women's empowerment. This approach has made the UAE a regional leader in terms of attracting foreign investment, developing advanced infrastructure, and promoting cultural diversity. The UAE's ideology has also influenced its foreign policy, with a pragmatic approach to regional affairs and a focus on maintaining stability.

Meanwhile, Qatar has pursued an independent foreign policy and has often found itself at odds with its Gulf neighbors, particularly Saudi Arabia and the UAE. Qatar's ruling family has positioned the country as a mediator on the global stage, facilitating negotiations and supporting non-state actors in conflict zones. This approach, combined with the country's investment in global media outlets, has provided Qatar with a unique platform and influence. Qatar's ideological orientation is characterized by a desire for autonomy, regional influence, and soft power projection.

Oman, under the late Sultan Qaboos, followed a unique path, maintaining a policy of neutrality and non-interference in regional affairs. The Sultan positioned Oman as a mediator and facilitator of dialogues, earning the country a reputation as a trusted partner in regional and international conflicts. Oman's ideology is centered around stability, internal development, and regional collaboration, making it an essential player in Gulf geopolitics.

Economically, the Gulf states share a reliance on hydrocarbon resources. Oil and gas wealth have played a crucial role in shaping economic policies and development strategies within the region. However, different states have taken varying approaches to economic diversification and social welfare.

The UAE and Qatar have been at the forefront of efforts to diversify their economies beyond oil and gas. The UAE, particularly Dubai, has developed a vibrant service sector, attracting international businesses, tourists, and skilled professionals. This diversification has helped the UAE become a regional hub for finance, trade, and logistics. Qatar has also invested in diverse sectors, including finance, real estate, and sports, hosting major international events such as the FIFA World Cup 2022. The country's sovereign wealth fund has made strategic investments around the globe, ensuring long-term economic sustainability.

Saudi Arabia, on the other hand, has recently embarked on an ambitious economic reform program under its Vision 2030 initiative. Recognizing the need to reduce dependence on oil revenues, Saudi Arabia aims to diversify its economy through investments in sectors such as tourism, entertainment, technology, and renewable energy. Vision 2030 also seeks to provide social and economic opportunities for Saudis, including increased employment and enhanced women's empowerment.

Other Gulf states, such as Bahrain, Kuwait, and Oman, have also pursued economic diversification efforts to varying extents. Bahrain has developed a thriving financial sector, while Kuwait has focused on expanding its petrochemical industry. Oman has prioritized tourism and infrastructure development as part of its economic diversification strategy. However, challenges of bureaucracy, governance, and market competitiveness remain for these countries.

Socially and culturally, the Gulf region exhibits a diverse array of identities and aspirations. Traditional tribal affiliations, sectarian divisions, and generational differences contribute to social dynamics within each country. While conservative norms and values remain prevalent in some Gulf societies, others are experiencing significant shifts due to globalization and the influence of a younger, more cosmopolitan generation.

Gulf societies have traditionally been deeply rooted in tribal customs and collectivist values, emphasizing loyalty, honor, and family ties. These social dynamics have influenced political structures, economic decision-making, and cultural practices. Tribal affiliations continue to play a role in shaping social interactions and power dynamics, particularly in rural areas.

Sectarian divisions, particularly between Sunni and Shia Muslims, have also shaped Gulf societies and political alignments. The rivalry between Saudi Arabia and Iran, which extends beyond ideological differences to include geopolitical and religious dimensions, has fueled sectarian tensions and led to proxy conflicts across the wider Middle East. The perception of threats from rival ideologies often reinforces conservative norms and sectarian identities within Gulf states.

However, Gulf societies are not static, and they are experiencing rapid social changes influenced by globalization, urbanization, education, and technology. A growing cosmopolitan youth population, educated both domestically and internationally, is increasingly embracing more liberal values and seeking opportunities for personal growth and self-expression. This generational shift has manifested in various ways, from demands for greater political participation and social reforms to changing cultural practices and attitudes.

The role of women in Gulf societies is another critical dimension. While historically women faced limitations in education, employment, and social mobility, there has been notable progress in recent years. Gulf governments have placed increased emphasis on women's empowerment, recognizing the potential for women's contributions to economic development and social progress. Efforts to increase women include providing access to education and employment opportunities, promoting gender equality and women's rights, and empowering women in leadership positions. For instance, Saudi Arabia lifted the ban on women driving in 2018, allowing greater mobility and independence for women. The UAE has also made significant strides in women's empowerment, with women holding key positions in government and business.

However, challenges and disparities persist in the region. While progress has been made in terms of women's rights and empowerment, traditional gender roles and societal expectations remain prevalent. The pace of change varies across different Gulf states, reflecting the influence of cultural norms and political considerations. Furthermore, migrant labor, which comprises a significant portion of the workforce in Gulf countries, often faces labor rights issues and limited access to social benefits.

The interplay of these various factors - historical, political, economic, and social - creates a complex landscape of Gulf ideological dynamics. The pursuit of unity and stability, combined with the desire for autonomy and influence, has shaped alliances, rivalries, and strategies within the region. These dynamics can either foster cooperation or lead to tensions and conflicts.

Understanding these ideological dynamics is crucial for policymakers, researchers, and anyone interested in the Gulf region. It provides insights into the factors that shape decision-making processes, the implications for regional stability, and the opportunities and challenges for economic and social development.

By examining the historical, political, economic, and social dimensions, this book aims to shed light on the Gulf's ideological dynamics, offering a comprehensive analysis of the region's complexities. It delves into the alignments and tensions between Gulf states, explores the role of tribal affiliations and sectarian divisions, examines economic diversification efforts and their impact on societies, and analyzes the social changes and aspirations of Gulf populations.

Through a nuanced understanding of Gulf ideological dynamics, we can better appreciate the intricate relations between

Gulf states, the motivations behind their actions, and the potential avenues for cooperation and conflict resolution. Only through such understanding can we navigate the complexities of the Gulf region and work towards a more stable and prosperous future for all its inhabitants.

A. Overview of the Gulf region

The Gulf region, also known as the Arabian Gulf, encompasses a vast area in the Middle East that holds significant geopolitical importance. It is surrounded by Iraq to the northwest, Iran to the northeast, and Saudi Arabia to the south. These countries, along with Kuwait, Qatar, Bahrain, and Oman, constitute the Gulf Cooperation Council (GCC), a regional intergovernmental organization aimed at fostering cooperation and integration among its member states.

The history of the Gulf region spans thousands of years, with the Arabian Peninsula being a crossroads of trade and civilization. Throughout the ages, this region experienced the rise and fall of several empires, including the Akkadians, Sumerians, Babylonians, Persians, and Ottomans. These various influences have left indelible marks on the region's culture, architecture, and languages.

However, it was the discovery and exploitation of oil in the early 20th century that transformed the Gulf region into a focal point of global attention. The significant reserves of oil found in the region provided immense wealth and power to the Gulf countries, revolutionizing their economies and shaping their political landscapes.

The oil industry has played a pivotal role in the Gulf's economic development. The region boasts one of the world's largest proven oil reserves, ensuring that it remains a crucial player in the global energy market. The revenue generated from oil exports has facilitated rapid economic growth and infrastructure development, catapulting Gulf countries into the ranks of high-income nations.

Dubai and Abu Dhabi in the United Arab Emirates, for instance, have become vibrant hubs for finance, tourism, and trade. They attract millions of visitors every year, offering luxurious hotels, shopping malls, and world-class entertainment facilities. Qatar has emerged as a global leader in liquefied natural gas, utilizing its resources to enhance its global influence and diversify its economy.

Saudi Arabia, the largest economy in the Gulf, has pursued ambitious economic diversification plans with Vision 2030. This transformative vision aims to reduce the country's dependency on oil and foster innovation and entrepreneurship in sectors such as tourism, entertainment, and technology. The implementation of Vision 2030 represents a paradigm shift in Saudi Arabia's economic policies, signaling a desire to adapt to changing global trends and promote sustainable growth.

In addition to the economic impact, the Gulf region's ideologies have also been shaped by its rich cultural heritage and Islamic history. Islam serves as a unifying factor, with the majority of Gulf citizens practicing Sunni Islam. Historically, many Islamic scholars and philosophers have emerged from the region, contributing to the development and dissemination of Islamic teachings.

However, it is also important to note the religious diversity within the Gulf region. Iran, for example, is predominantly Shia, and this sectarian difference has influenced the geopolitical dynamics of the region. Saudi Arabia and Iran have historically competed for regional influence, viewing each other as rivals and engaged in proxy conflicts in countries such as Yemen, Bahrain, and Syria.

Furthermore, the Gulf region has been impacted by historical and ongoing territorial disputes. One example is the conflict between Iraq and Kuwait, which led to the first Gulf War in 1990 when Iraq invaded Kuwait. The region has also witnessed the influence of outside powers, such as the United States, which has maintained a military presence and strategic alliances with Gulf countries to safeguard its interests and ensure stability in the region.

Internally, the Gulf states have differing governance structures and levels of political openness. Saudi Arabia, for instance, practices an absolute monarchy, where the ruling family holds significant power and influence. Qatar and the UAE have embraced more hybrid systems of governance, combining monarchy with representative institutions. Each country has its unique development trajectory, societal norms, and approach to governance, creating variations in their ideologies and domestic policies.

Challenges exist within the Gulf region as well. The rapid economic growth and urbanization have led to socio-economic disparities, with some segments of society benefiting more than others. This has raised issues of inequality and social cohesion, which Gulf governments are addressing through various social and economic reforms. Efforts are being made to diversify the economies further, enhance education and healthcare systems, and promote inclusive policies that empower all citizens.

In addition, the region faces environmental challenges, including water scarcity and rising temperatures. With its arid climate and limited freshwater sources, the Gulf countries are actively implementing strategies to address these challenges. Desalination plants, for example, provide a substantial portion of the region's freshwater supply, but they also pose environmental concerns due to energy consumption and brine discharge. Sustainable development strategies that promote water conservation, renewable energy, and environmental preservation are essential for the region's long-term viability.

Looking ahead, the Gulf's ideologies will continue to evolve in response to internal and external pressures. Economic diversification efforts, social reforms, and increasing investment in education and innovation are among the steps being taken to create more inclusive and sustainable societies. Regional cooperation, exemplified by the GCC and other initiatives like the Arab League, can help foster greater unity and overcome ideological differences for the mutual benefit of all Gulf countries.

The Gulf region's complex history, economic significance, diverse cultures, and evolving geopolitical dynamics make it a fascinating and critical area to study. Understanding the ideologies that shape the region is essential not only for the people who reside there but also for the global community as a whole. By exploring the past, present, and future of the Gulf region, we can gain insights into the challenges, opportunities, and potential pathways to greater stability and progress.

B. Importance of understanding Gulf ideological dynamics

Understanding the complexities of Gulf ideological dynamics is crucial for comprehending the intricacies of the region's socio-political landscape. With the Gulf region comprising a cluster of nations with distinct political, cultural, and religious backgrounds, the study of ideological dynamics provides valuable insights into the challenges and opportunities that shape the region's future.

The Gulf ideological dynamics not only impact the internal affairs of individual countries but also have significant repercussions for inter-state relations, regional stability, and global dynamics. Therefore, it is important to recognize the importance of gaining a deeper understanding of these dynamics and their implications beyond national borders.

Historical Context

To appreciate the significance of Gulf ideological dynamics, it is essential to delve into the historical context of the region. The formation of modern Gulf states derived from a range of factors, including colonial legacies, tribal histories, and nationalist movements.

During the colonial era, the British exerted significant influence in Bahrain, Kuwait, and the United Arab Emirates (UAE). These British Protectorates, strategically located along the maritime trade routes, became crucial assets for British imperial interests. The British influence in these territories not only shaped the political landscape but also introduced elements of modernization, such as infrastructure development and administrative reforms. However, British intervention also had consequences, fostering dependency on external powers and leaving lasting impacts on the distribution of power and state formation in the region.

Meanwhile, Qatar's historical narrative was intertwined with the Ottoman Empire's weakening control over the Gulf. A Qatari-Ottoman rivalry emerged, as Qatari tribes resisted Ottoman rule and sought alliances with other Gulf powers, such as the Al Khalifa ruling family in Bahrain. This rivalry, in part, contributed to the formation of modern Qatar as a distinct entity.

Geopolitical Significance

The Gulf region holds immense geopolitical importance due to its location and abundant natural resources, particularly oil. Sitting at the intersection of three continents, the Gulf is a crucial thoroughfare for global trade, connecting East and West. Consequently, major global powers such as the United States, Russia, and China have vested interests in the region's stability and resources.

The Gulf's oil reserves have not only fueled economic development but have also attracted external powers seeking to secure their energy interests. These interests have led to the establishment of military bases and the intervention of global powers in Gulf affairs. Hence, the ideological dynamics within the Gulf impact various stakeholders with broader regional and global implications.

Moreover, Gulf states' differing ideological allegiances contribute to rivalry and alliances both within the region and beyond, shaping the broader balance of power. The ongoing competition between Saudi Arabia and Iran for regional influence is a prime example of how Gulf ideological dynamics have broader consequences that transcend borders. Understanding these complexities provides insights into the interconnectedness of Gulf affairs with broader international relations.

Societal Transformations

Gulf societies have undergone rapid transformations in recent decades, driven by technological advancements, globalization, and evolving social norms. These changes have generated diverse aspirations, challenges, and ideological trends within Gulf societies.

The region has witnessed an unprecedented rise in youth populations, bringing forth new ideas, ideologies, and demands for greater participation in shaping their societies. Moreover, increased exposure to global ideas through rapidly expanding media platforms and the influx of foreign migration have contributed to the diversification of ideologies across the Gulf region.

Governments have responded to these societal changes with varying degrees of acceptance, imposing restrictions, or embracing social reforms. For example, Saudi Arabia's Vision 2030 and the UAE's push for economic diversification and social liberalization reflect attempts to navigate the evolving societal landscape. Nevertheless, differential approaches to social change and the interpretation of ideologies contribute to tensions and debates within Gulf societies.

Peace and Stability

Gulf ideological dynamics bear significant implications for regional peace and stability, as the region has experienced various conflicts, territorial disputes, and external interventions throughout history.

Conflicting ideological perspectives often manifest in political rivalries, proxy wars, and religious divisions. The Iran-Saudi Arabia rivalry, sectarian tensions, and the ongoing conflicts in Yemen and Syria exemplify the complex interplay between geopolitical interests, ideological orientations, and regional stability.

Dissecting the underlying ideological underpinnings of these conflicts can provide crucial opportunities for building trust, resolving disputes, and mitigating conflicts. Understanding the motivations behind these conflicts helps identify potential areas for dialogue, negotiation, and peaceful coexistence among Gulf states.

Economic Considerations

Economic factors play a critical role in understanding Gulf ideological dynamics. The region's economies have traditionally been heavily dependent on oil, which brings its own political, social, and economic challenges.

Resource management, economic diversification, and the distribution of wealth influence ideological stances and policy choices of Gulf states. Differing visions for economic development, budget allocations, and foreign investments may reflect divergent ideological priorities among governments.

As Gulf states grapple with the need for economic diversification, sustainable development, and the management of finite resources, understanding the relationship between national economic policies, resource management, and the ideological perspectives of Gulf states becomes crucial. It sheds light on potential areas for cooperation or conflict, as well as the aspirations and challenges faced by Gulf societies.

Human Rights and Social Justice

The examination of Gulf ideological dynamics encompasses an analysis of human rights, social justice, and equality within the region. Evaluating how differing ideological frameworks impact the treatment of marginalized groups, gender equality, religious freedom, political participation, and freedom of speech is vital for understanding the sociopolitical dynamics in the Gulf.

While progress has been made in some areas, challenges persist, and the interpretation of ideological principles often leads to varied approaches. Awareness of these complexities is crucial for identifying potential hurdles to achieving unity and promoting a fair and inclusive society in the Gulf.

In summary

The importance of understanding Gulf ideological dynamics cannot be overstated. It allows for a nuanced understanding of the region's histories, identities, and aspirations, paving the way for comprehensive analyses and informed decision-making. By acknowledging the significance of ideological dynamics, stakeholders can work towards fostering unity, addressing conflicts, and promoting sustainable development while respecting the cultural, religious, and political diversity that shapes the Gulf region. Grounded in historical context, geopolitical significance, societal transformations, peace and stability concerns, economic considerations, and human rights, a thorough understanding of Gulf ideological dynamics provides a foundation for constructive engagement and collaborative efforts toward a prosperous future.

C. Purpose and structure of the book

To gain a thorough understanding of the intricate Gulf ideological framework, it is imperative to conduct an in-depth examination of its political, economic, social, and cultural aspects.

This section seeks to offer a thorough analysis of these facets, investigating the interactions and factors that influence Gulf ideologies.

1. Political Dimension: The political dimension of the Gulf ideological system is primarily influenced by power dynamics and governance structures within each Gulf state. It is characterized by a mix of monarchies, republics, and emirates, each with its own political traditions and ideologies. For instance, Saudi Arabia adheres to a conservative Wahhabi interpretation of Islam, while countries like Bahrain and Kuwait have embraced more inclusive political systems. However, it is important to note that political ideologies in the Gulf are not solely driven by religious beliefs. National interests, regional dynamics, and geopolitical considerations also shape political ideologies. For instance, the rivalry between Qatar and Saudi Arabia is not solely based on religious differences but also has political and regional power dynamics at play.

2. Economic Dimension: Economics plays a significant role in shaping Gulf ideologies. The region's wealth, largely derived from oil and gas reserves, has driven rapid economic development and created distinct economic ideologies within the Gulf. While some states have focused on diversifying their economies through initiatives like Vision 2030 in Saudi Arabia and Qatar National Vision 2030, others remain heavily reliant on oil revenues. Economic ideologies also influence social

policies and the distribution of wealth, leading to varying levels of socioeconomic development within the Gulf. The economic dimension of the Gulf ideological system is also influenced by external factors, such as global economic trends and international trade agreements. For example, the implementation of the Value Added Tax (VAT) across the region reflects attempts to diversify revenue sources and reduce reliance on oil revenue.

3. Social Dimension: The social dimension of the Gulf ideological system is shaped by religion, culture, and societal norms. Islam, as the dominant religion, influences various aspects of social life, contributing to conservative social ideologies in some Gulf countries. However, it is important to recognize that there are variations in the interpretation and practice of Islam across the Gulf. For instance, while Saudi Arabia adheres to a stricter interpretation of Islam, countries like Bahrain and the United Arab Emirates have adopted a more moderate and cosmopolitan approach. Social ideologies go beyond religious beliefs, encompassing issues such as gender roles, family values, and national identity. Traditional Arab values, tribal affiliations, and cultural heritage play a significant role in shaping social ideologies within the Gulf.

4. Cultural Dimension: Cultural factors, including language, heritage, and traditions, have a profound impact on Gulf ideologies. While Arabic is the common

language across the region, dialects and variations exist, creating subtle differences in cultural identities. The Gulf region also has a rich historical legacy, influenced by trade routes, migrations, and interactions with diverse cultures. Historical legacies, such as tribal affiliations and Bedouin traditions, shape cultural ideologies within the Gulf. Furthermore, the promotion of cultural activities, art festivals, and heritage preservation has become an integral part of national ideologies, strengthening national identity and fostering a sense of unity within each Gulf state. The cultural dimension plays a crucial role in shaping Gulf ideologies, facilitating social cohesion and allowing for the expression of shared identity.

The interplay between these dimensions creates a dynamic Gulf ideological system, characterized by both unity and discord. Understanding and analyzing this system requires a nuanced approach that considers the historical, cultural, and socio-economic factors influencing ideologies within each Gulf state. By examining the complex nature of these dimensions, we can gain deeper insights into the quest for unity and the challenges that hinder ideological convergence within the Gulf region.

It is crucial to recognize that the Gulf ideological system is not static, but rather evolving and responsive to internal and external dynamics. Political alliances, economic shifts, social movements, and cultural exchanges all contribute to the continuous transformation of the Gulf ideological landscape. By examining these dimensions, we can unravel the intricate web of Gulf ideologies and gain a comprehensive understanding of the forces at play within the region.

Next, we aim to conduct an in-depth analysis of the Qatar Crisis as a case study to examine the impact of the Gulf ideological framework on regional dynamics and the potential for unity in the Gulf region. Through this examination, we seek to gain valuable insights into how divergent ideologies can affect regional interactions and collaboration, underscoring the importance of a thorough exploration of the intricate factors shaping Gulf cohesion.

D. Landmarks

The Gulf Cooperation Council (GCC) is a political and economic alliance formed in 1981 by six Arab countries in the Arabian Gulf region: Bahrain, Kuwait, Oman, Qatar, Saudi Arabia, and the United Arab Emirates (UAE). Initially established to enhance cooperation and address common challenges, the GCC has evolved into an influential regional organization with wide-ranging implications for the Gulf states and beyond. This chapter explores the politics, policies, and prospects of the GCC, delving into its structure, decision-making processes, areas of cooperation, challenges, and prospects.

The Structure and Objectives of the GCC

The GCC operates through a framework of institutions and decision-making bodies designed to facilitate collaboration among member states. The Supreme Council, composed of the heads of state of each member country, is the highest decision-making authority within the GCC. It meets annually to discuss key issues and set policies. The Ministerial Council, composed of foreign ministers, provides strategic guidance and oversees the implementation of decisions. Additionally, various specialized committees and technical bodies address specific sectors of cooperation, such as defense, economics, social affairs, and health.

The objectives of the GCC include promoting coordination and integration among member states in various areas, such as defense, economy, finance, education, culture, health, and environmental sustainability. The organization aims to foster common policies, enhance economic cooperation, facilitate the movement of goods and services, and strengthen security in the region. Through joint efforts, the GCC seeks to build a unified Gulf identity, promote stability, and project a collective voice in regional and international affairs.

Areas of Cooperation

1. Economic Cooperation: Economic integration is a central pillar of the GCC's agenda. The organization has implemented various measures to enhance inter-GCC trade and investments, such as the establishment of a common market and a customs union. These initiatives have facilitated the removal of trade

barriers, harmonization of regulations, and the creation of a business-friendly environment. Furthermore, the GCC has launched ambitious infrastructure projects, including transportation networks, power grids, and industrial zones, in order to promote economic diversification and integration. Efforts to develop a common currency, similar to the Euro, have been explored, but challenges related to economic disparities and coordination among member states have slowed progress.

2. Security Cooperation: The GCC places great emphasis on regional security and defense cooperation. The Peninsula Shield Force, a joint military force, has been established to address security challenges in the region, such as terrorist threats, border security, and potential external aggression. The organization actively collaborates on intelligence sharing, counterterrorism efforts, and joint military exercises. Additionally, the GCC has engaged in regional diplomacy, mediating conflicts and promoting peaceful resolutions to issues affecting the Arabian Gulf region. The organization has also embarked on naval security initiatives to combat piracy in the Gulf of Aden.

3. Energy Cooperation: Given the Gulf region's significant energy resources, the GCC has prioritized energy cooperation as a means to maximize their collective potential and revenue. Close collaboration in the energy sector has led to joint infrastructure projects, infor-

mation sharing, and coordinated strategies to stabilize global energy markets. The GCC's cooperation extends to oil and gas production, refining, distribution, and investments in alternative and renewable energy sources. By coordinating policies and leveraging their collective bargaining power, the member states of the GCC have significantly influenced global energy markets.

4. Social and Cultural Cooperation: The GCC aims to foster social and cultural integration among member states. Efforts to promote educational exchanges, scientific research, and cultural events have been made to strengthen ties and build a shared Gulf identity. The organization seeks to enhance the quality of education and promote research and development, particularly in areas relevant to the region's future needs. The GCC also addresses social issues, such as labor policies, human rights, and women's empowerment, through collaborative initiatives. Efforts have been made to enhance labor rights, alleviate issues related to migrant labor, and improve health services in member states.

Challenges and Limitations

Despite its notable achievements, the GCC faces various challenges and limitations that potentially hinder its effectiveness and long-term sustainability.

1. Internal Divisions: While the GCC remains committed to cooperation and integration, member states often have differing political, economic, and foreign policy priorities. Inter-state disputes and rivalries occasionally strain the unity and decision-making process of the organization, highlighting the complexity of aligning diverse national interests. For example, differences in approach towards regional issues such as the Arab Spring, conflicts in Yemen, or engagement with Iran have exemplified these divisions.

2. Democratic Deficit: Critics argue that the GCC lacks democratic institutions, as decision-making power predominantly rests with unelected leaders. This undermines the legitimacy and inclusivity of the organization, raising concerns regarding the representation of citizens' interests and the responsiveness of the GCC to societal demands. Calls for greater citizen participation, political reforms, and the development of institutions that promote accountability and transparency have been voiced within and outside the region.

3. External Challenges: External factors, such as regional conflicts, geopolitical rivalries, and global economic fluctuations, impact the GCC's stability and cooperative efforts. The rise of non-state actors, like extremist groups and transnational criminal networks, poses security threats that require joint strategies and collective action by member states. Furthermore, the region's

dependence on oil revenues has exposed the GCC to price volatility, necessitating efforts towards economic diversification and reducing oil dependence.

Prospects for the GCC

1. Enhanced Integration: The GCC seeks to deepen its integration through ambitious projects and initiatives. Considerations for a Gulf single currency, akin to the Euro, continue to be explored. This would require addressing challenges related to economic disparities, coordination of monetary policies, and building consensus among member states. Additionally, the organization recognizes the need for further economic diversification, innovation, and investment in sectors such as technology, renewable energy, and knowledge-based industries.

2. Geopolitical Realities: The changing geopolitical landscape in the Middle East and beyond presents both opportunities and challenges for the GCC. The organization continually adapts its policies to navigate shifting regional dynamics and assert a collective presence on the global stage. With ongoing conflicts, such as in Yemen and Syria, and changing alliances and rivalries, the GCC aims to maintain stability, promote dialogue, and safeguard its member states' interests.

3. Regional Cooperation: The civil uprisings during the

Arab Spring highlighted the need for regional cooperation. The GCC has played a significant role in managing regional crises, providing financial aid to member states facing economic challenges, and contributing to stability in the wider Middle East. The organization has facilitated dialogue and mediated in conflicts, such as the Al-Ula Declaration which resolved a dispute among member states. The GCC also engages with non-GCC countries in the region, including Iraq, Jordan, and Egypt, to foster broader Arab cooperation.

In summary

The Gulf Cooperation Council has emerged as a key player in the Arabian Gulf region, fostering cooperation across diverse sectors and addressing shared challenges. Despite internal divisions and external pressures, the GCC continues to pursue greater integration and bolster its role on the regional and international stage. As the Gulf states navigate evolving geopolitical realities, the future of the GCC hinges on their ability to adapt, strengthen collective decision-making, and align aspirations for economic diversification, security, stability, and enhanced regional cooperation.

THE GULF'S IDEOLOGICAL SYSTEM

UNDERSTANDING ITS EXISTENCE AND FUNCTIONING

The Gulf region is characterized by a rich and complex ideological system that plays a significant role in shaping various aspects of society, governance, and regional dynamics. To fully comprehend and navigate the intricacies of the Gulf, a comprehensive understanding of the existence and functioning of this ideological system is crucial. The objective of this chapter is to provide a comprehensive analysis of the various facets comprising the Gulf ideological framework, investigating its multifaceted characteristics, and investigating how political, economic, social, and cultural ideologies interact within it.

1. **Political Ideologies in the Gulf:** The political dimension of the Gulf ideological system is diverse, encompassing different power structures and governance

models prevalent in the region's states. Gulf countries predominantly consist of absolute monarchies and hereditary rulership, with ruling families playing a central role in decision-making processes. These systems are often justified by ideological frameworks that emphasize stability, continuity, and societal cohesion. Furthermore, political ideologies in the Gulf are sometimes informed by Islamic principles, with states claiming to uphold Islamic governance and values. However, along with traditional political systems, Gulf states have also experimented with elements of parliamentary systems and hybrid models. These efforts often aim to strike a balance between tradition and modernity, responding to demands for increased political participation and representation. Examples include the introduction of elected Shura councils, consultative bodies, and limited political reforms. Consequently, political ideologies in the Gulf strive to maintain stability and legitimacy while responding to evolving societal aspirations.

2. **Economic Ideologies in the Gulf**: Economic ideologies in the Gulf have undergone significant transformations over the years. Historically, oil-rich Gulf countries, such as Saudi Arabia, Kuwait, Qatar, and the United Arab Emirates, heavily relied on oil revenues and adopted state-controlled economies. However, the volatility of oil prices and the desire to diversify revenue sources have prompted a shift toward new

economic ideologies. Various Gulf countries have embarked on ambitious economic diversification plans, focusing on sectors such as tourism, finance, technology, renewable energy, and knowledge-based industries. These new economic ideologies prioritize sustainability, innovation, globalization, and private sector engagement. They seek to build resilient and knowledge-driven economies that can thrive in a post-oil era while ensuring social stability and economic development.

3. **Social Ideologies in the Gulf:** The social dimension of the Gulf ideological system reflects a complex interplay between tradition, modernity, and socio-cultural values. Gulf societies place strong emphasis on family ties, kinship networks, and community cohesion. As a result, social ideologies are often rooted in conservatism, respect for religious norms, and the preservation of cultural heritage. Moreover, gender roles and women's position in society remain important considerations within social ideologies. While traditional gender roles have been prevalent in the past, Gulf societies are witnessing a gradual but steady evolution toward more egalitarian norms. This shift is influenced by global trends, awareness of human rights, and the aspirations of Gulf women who seek greater opportunities and empowerment. Thus, social ideologies in the Gulf reflect a delicate balance between tradition and progressive aspirations.

4. **Cultural Ideologies in the Gulf:** The cultural dimensions of the Gulf ideological system are rich and diverse, reflecting both a shared Islamic heritage and distinct local identities. Islamic culture serves as a unifying factor, influencing various aspects of daily life, rituals, values, and social norms. However, cultural expressions within each Gulf state also exhibit unique nuances and regional variations, shaped by historical, geographical, and ethnic diversity. Gulf societies value literature, arts, music, and various traditions as integral parts of their cultural fabric. Once confined to local audiences, cultural ideologies in the Gulf are increasingly engaging with global audiences, promoting cultural exchanges and fostering dialogue. This interaction allows for the preservation of local traditions while embracing international influences and connectivity.

5. **The Interplay of Gulf Ideologies**: To grasp the complexities of the Gulf ideological system fully, it is crucial to recognize the interplay between these dimensions. Political ideologies influence economic priorities and policies, shaping social values, norms, and cultural expressions. The interplay between these dimensions is both dynamic and complex, influenced by external factors such as globalization, technological advancements, and evolving regional dynamics. Gulf societies face numerous challenges that prompt continuous reevaluation and adaptation of ideologies. De-

mographic shifts, youth aspirations, changing global dynamics, and geopolitical pressures necessitate a constant reassessment of political, economic, social, and cultural ideologies. Thus, the Gulf ideological system is not static but rather adaptive and responsive to the demands of the present and the aspirations for a prosperous future.

Conclusion: Understanding the Gulf ideological system is essential for comprehending the decision-making processes, policies, and societal behaviors within the region. The complexity and multidimensionality of the Gulf ideological landscape highlight the need for cross-cultural understanding, dialogue, and cooperation for the region's progress. By recognizing and appreciating the existence and dynamics of the Gulf ideological system, meaningful engagement and sustainable development can be fostered to ensure a prosperous future for Gulf societies.

A. Defining the Gulf's ideological system

The Gulf region is characterized by a complex and unique ideological system that plays a significant role in shaping the dynamics of the region. Understanding this system is crucial to comprehending the forces at play within the Gulf and their impact on regional politics, economics, society, and culture.

The Gulf ideological system can be broadly defined as a set of interconnected beliefs, values, and principles that govern the political, economic, social, and cultural spheres of the Gulf states. It is a system that combines various ideologies, including religious, nationalist, tribal, pan-Arab, and Islamic fundamentalist ideologies, among others, which exist in a complex and sometimes overlapping manner.

Politically, the Gulf ideological system manifests itself through the dominance of monarchies and the principles of dynastic rule, which are deeply rooted in the region's history and cultural traditions. These monarchies, such as Saudi Arabia, the United Arab Emirates, Bahrain, Oman, Qatar, and Kuwait, are often seen as the embodiment of stability and continuity in a region marked by volatility and change. The concept of monarchical legitimacy is upheld through an ideological framework that emphasizes the role of rulers as custodians of religion, protectors of stability, and providers of welfare. The divine right to rule, rooted in the Islamic faith, is often drawn upon to solidify the rulers' authority and ensure the loyalty of their subjects.

Economically, the Gulf ideological system is strongly influenced by the principles of rentierism, which rely on the abundant revenues generated from the region's natural resources, particularly oil and gas. This ideological framework emphasizes the role of the state as the primary provider of welfare, to ensure social stability through the distribution of economic benefits to citizens. The Gulf states, therefore, adopt a rentier economic model that relies heavily on oil revenues to finance state expenditures and social programs. This economic system creates a social contract between the state and its citizens, where government largesse in the form of generous subsidies, employment opportunities, and public services is exchanged for political loyalty and societal stability.

However, this heavy reliance on oil has also made the Gulf economies vulnerable to fluctuations in global oil prices and exposed the need for diversification and economic reforms. In recent years, several Gulf states have undertaken ambitious economic diversification plans, such as Saudi Arabia's Vision 2030 and the UAE's Economic Vision 2021, aiming to reduce dependence on oil and foster the growth of non-oil sectors. These efforts are driven by the recognition that sustained economic development requires a shift towards knowledge-based economies, entrepreneurship, innovation, and increased private sector participation. These reforms challenge the long-held belief in the Gulf ideological system that the state is the primary driver of economic well-being and force a reimagining of the socio-economic contract between the state and its citizens.

Socially, the Gulf ideological system is characterized by a combination of conservative values rooted in Islamic traditions and increasing influence from globalization. Traditional family structures, gender roles, and social norms are upheld, reflecting the cultural and religious heritage of the region. Yet, Gulf societies are also experiencing significant social transformations driven by rapid urbanization, education, exposure to global trends, and the aspirations of a young and dynamic population. This has led to a delicate balance between preserving traditional practices and embracing the desires of a more cosmopolitan and globally interconnected society.

While traditional values remain influential, especially among the older generation, there is a growing acceptance and adoption of Western lifestyles, consumerism, and social media. Gulf societies are witnessing increased gender empowerment, with women pursuing higher education, joining the workforce, and assuming leadership positions in various sectors. This social change is accompanied by ongoing debates within the Gulf ideological system about striking the right balance between tradition and modernity, and between preserving cultural heritage and embracing global cultural expressions.

Culturally, the Gulf ideological system embraces a diverse range of influences, including Arab, Persian, and Islamic traditions, as well as international cultural exchanges. While efforts are made to preserve and promote local Gulf traditions and heritage, there is also a growing openness to global cultural trends, especially among the younger generations. Gulf states actively invest in cultural initiatives to promote their national identities and establish themselves as cultural hubs within the region. Festivals, museums, galleries, and international art exhibitions are organized to showcase the vibrant cultural scene and foster creativity and expression.

Additionally, the Gulf states have recognized the potential of the creative industries, such as film, music, fashion, and design, as drivers of economic growth and soft power. Initiatives like the Dubai International Film Festival and the Abu Dhabi Art Fair have gained international recognition and provide platforms for local and international artists to connect and showcase their talent. These cultural expressions within the Gulf ideological system represent not only a reflection of identity but also a means of engaging with the global community and contributing to dialogues on art, literature, and intellectual thought.

The Gulf ideological system is not static but evolves in response to internal and external factors. It is shaped by historical legacies, geopolitical rivalries, economic challenges, social transformations, and individual aspirations. The system is also influenced by regional and global contexts, including the interaction with external powers, international organizations, and the impact of globalization. As Gulf societies continue to grapple with the complexities of modernity and tradition, there will be ongoing dialogues and debates that shape the evolution of their ideological system.

Understanding the complexities and nuances of the Gulf ideological system is essential for comprehending the region's dynamics, conflicts, and aspirations. It enables us to navigate the intricacies of Gulf politics, economic policies, social norms, and cultural expressions. By gaining a deeper understanding of the Gulf ideological system, we can better appreciate the forces driving unity and discord in the region and explore the potential for future transformations and developments. This understanding can also contribute to informed analyses and effective policymaking that promotes stability, inclusivity, and prosperity in the Gulf region.

B. Political dimensions of the Gulf's ideological system

The political dimensions of the Gulf ideological system are multifaceted, intricate, and profoundly shaped by a wide range of factors, including historical, cultural, religious, and regional dynamics. Understanding these dimensions is crucial for comprehending the complexities of the Gulf's political landscape and the interplay between ideologies and power dynamics.

- Political systems in the Gulf:

The Gulf countries exhibit diverse political systems, each with its own unique characteristics and governance structures. Monarchies are prevalent in the region, with countries like Saudi Arabia, Bahrain, and Jordan led by royal families. These systems rely on a hereditary line of succession, where the monarch assumes a central role in governance. The ruling families often wield significant power and influence, making key decisions in matters of state. However, some Gulf countries have embraced more progressive political systems. Kuwait and Qatar, for instance, have adopted parliamentary constitutional monarchies, where the ruling families cooperate with elected bodies. These bodies play a crucial role in shaping policies, and legislation, and representing the interests of their constituents. Additionally, the political systems of the United Arab Emirates and Oman feature a mix of traditional leadership structures and modern institutions, combining tribal influences with governmental structures.

- Political ideologies:

Gulf countries represent a variety of political ideologies, each exerting its influence on governance structures, policies, and societal norms. Islamic conservatism, often rooted in Salafism and Wahhabism, is a dominant ideological force, particularly in Saudi Arabia. This ideology emphasizes adherence to a strict interpretation of Islamic principles and social norms, influencing laws related to gender segregation, religious practices, and public morality. However, the level of conservatism varies among Gulf countries, with some nations adopting more moderate interpretations of Islamic principles. Secular nationalism is another ideology present in the Gulf, particularly in countries like Bahrain, Kuwait, and Oman. It promotes the values of national identity, citizenship, and the separation of religion and state. However, Gulf countries often follow a hybrid approach, blending Islamic and nationalist ideologies to varying degrees, creating unique political landscapes.

- Power dynamics:

The distribution of power within the Gulf states plays a significant role in shaping their political dimensions. Power can be concentrated within specific factions or institutions, such as the ruling family, the military, or religious authorities. In Saudi Arabia, power is centralized within the royal family, with the King holding the ultimate authority. The Supreme Council for Islamic Affairs in Kuwait and the Committee for the Promotion of Virtue and the Prevention of Vice in Saudi Arabia wield influence over religious matters, ensuring adherence to conservative Islamic values. Additionally, military and security forces, like the Saudi Arabian National Guard or the Royal Oman Police, contribute to preserving stability and safeguarding the interests of the ruling elites. It is important to note that power dynamics can fluctuate, with internal and external influences shaping political hierarchies and alliances.

- Regional governance structures:

Gulf countries have established various regional governance structures to enhance cooperation and address common challenges. The Gulf Cooperation Council (GCC) has been a driving force in promoting political, economic, and security collaboration among its member states. The GCC provides a platform for collective decision-making, facilitating regional institutionalization and strengthening the Gulf's overall political dimensions. Structures like the Supreme Council, the Ministerial Council, and various specialized committees contribute to policy coordination, economic integration, and defense collaboration. However, the effectiveness of these structures can be influenced by regional rivalries, conflicts, and differing national priorities. The ongoing diplomatic rift between Qatar and some GCC countries serves as an example of how political dimensions can be strained within regional governance structures.

- Foreign policy and alliances:

Gulf countries' foreign policies have a profound impact on their ideological systems and the broader regional dynamics. These policies can be driven by national security concerns, access to resources, regional power dynamics, or historical legacies. For example, Saudi Arabia's foreign policy often reflects its ambition for regional leadership and its rivalry with Iran, shaping its alliances, military involvement, and its stance on regional conflicts. Similarly, the UAE has pursued an assertive foreign policy, seeking to project its influence and diversify its economic interests beyond the region. These foreign policy choices can significantly influence ideological alignments, regional alliances, and the overall stability of the Gulf. It is noteworthy that Gulf countries maintain close ties with various global powers, further shaping their political dimensions and maneuvering in regional power struggles.

- Political movements and activism:

Gulf countries have witnessed various political movements that reflect popular desires for political change and ideological shifts. The Arab Spring uprisings of 2011 brought demands for political reform, social justice, and increased political participation. Bahrain experienced widespread protests calling for democratic reforms and greater equality among its population. Similarly, in Saudi Arabia, various activists have advocated for greater civil liberties, women's rights, and more inclusive governance systems. While these movements have faced significant challenges and repression from authorities, the quest for political change demonstrates the potential for ideological transformations within the Gulf and highlights the complex interplay between grassroots activism, political ideologies, and power structures.

- Influences of historical and cultural factors:

Historical and cultural factors play a crucial role in shaping the political dimensions of the Gulf ideological system. Tribalism, which was historically prominent in the region, continues to exert influence over political affiliations and power dynamics, particularly in countries such as Saudi Arabia and Oman. The legacy of colonialism also influences the region, with countries like Bahrain and Qatar experiencing varying degrees of British influence that shaped their political and economic systems. Moreover, post-independence struggles and ongoing socio-cultural dynamics contribute to the evolution of political ideologies in each state. Balancing the preservation of cultural heritage with modernization and globalization poses a continuous challenge for Gulf societies and institutions.

- Challenges to political unity:

Despite common interests and aspirations for unity, Gulf countries face challenges in achieving political convergence. The region experiences ongoing tensions and conflicts, such as the dispute between Qatar and other GCC countries, differing visions of regional influence, and diverse interpretations of Islamic principles. Economically and politically motivated rivalries, both within and outside the Gulf, can disrupt efforts towards greater unity, as seen in the complexities of the Yemeni political landscape, fragmented Arab Spring movements, or regional responses to Iranian influence. The various historical, ideological, and power dynamics interact, shaping the political dimensions and determining the degree of convergence or divergence within the Gulf ideological system.

Understanding the deep political dimensions of the Gulf ideological system offers valuable insights into the complexities, contradictions, and potential tensions within the region. It enables a more comprehensive analysis of the factors that contribute to unity or discord, providing a nuanced understanding of the Gulf's political landscape. Such an understanding is vital for policymakers, scholars, and observers seeking to navigate the intricate webs of politics, ideologies, and power structures in the Gulf.

C. Economic dimensions of the Gulf ideological system

The economic dimensions of the Gulf ideological system play a significant role in shaping the region's dynamics and relationships. Understanding these dimensions is crucial for comprehending the factors that influence decision-making, resource allocation, and economic policies within Gulf countries. This chapter delves deep into the economic aspects of the Gulf ideological system, highlighting their impact on regional dynamics.

1. Resource Dependency: The Gulf states have primarily relied on oil and gas resources for economic growth and development. These hydrocarbon resources have been the backbone of their economies, accounting for a significant portion of their GDP and government revenues. The Gulf holds approximately 31% of global proven oil reserves and 21% of proven gas reserves, giving it a pivotal role in global energy markets. However, this resource dependency has also made Gulf countries vulnerable to fluctuations in global oil prices and market demand. Over the years, they have experienced significant booms and busts, affecting their economic stability and planning. Moreover, the focus on the oil and gas sector has often stifled innovation and hindered the development of other sectors, contributing to a lack of economic diversification.

2. Rentier State Model: The rentier state model defines the economic structure of many Gulf countries.

This model involves the extraction of resources by the state, followed by the redistribution of wealth to citizens through subsidies, public sector employment, and generous social welfare programs. The rentier nature of Gulf economies has created a social contract between the state and its citizens, where the provision of economic benefits is exchanged for political stability and loyalty. This system has allowed Gulf countries to maintain high levels of social cohesion, as citizens rely on the state for employment opportunities and a comfortable standard of living. However, it has also fostered a sense of entitlement and dependency, with the private sector often lagging in terms of innovation, entrepreneurship, and job creation.

3. Economic Diversification: Over the years, Gulf countries have recognized the need to reduce their dependence on oil and gas revenues and diversify their economies. Economic diversification involves the development of non-oil sectors such as finance, tourism, technology, manufacturing, and renewable energy. While some Gulf nations, such as the United Arab Emirates, Qatar, and Bahrain, have made significant progress in diversifying their economies, others, like Saudi Arabia, Kuwait, and Oman, face challenges in transitioning to non-oil sectors. Bureaucratic hurdles, lack of expertise in emerging industries, and resistance to change have slowed down diversification efforts in these countries. However, with the advent of Vision

2030 in Saudi Arabia and similar initiatives in other Gulf nations, there is a renewed focus on diversification, entrepreneurship, and innovation to build sustainable and resilient economies for the future.

4. Gulf Cooperation Council (GCC): The GCC, comprised of Bahrain, Kuwait, Oman, Qatar, Saudi Arabia, and the United Arab Emirates, plays a significant role in shaping economic dimensions within the Gulf region. The organization promotes economic integration, cooperation, and coordination among its member states. The GCC has launched initiatives like the Gulf Common Market, the Customs Union, and the Gulf Monetary Union to foster economic integration and facilitate trade and investment flows. Additionally, the GCC countries collaborate on matters such as energy policy, infrastructure development, and joint ventures to enhance their competitiveness in global markets. The decisions and policies taken by the GCC influence economic dynamics and relationships within the Gulf. However, despite these efforts, achieving true economic integration and overcoming barriers to trade and investment among member states remains a challenge.

5. Economic Disparities: While the Gulf states boast high levels of wealth, economic disparities exist within their societies. These disparities manifest in income inequality, access to opportunities, and standards of living. The wealth gap between citizens and migrant

workers is evident in Gulf countries due to differences in wages, working conditions, and social benefits. Migrant workers, who form a significant portion of the labor force, often face challenges such as limited rights, exploitation, and inadequate living conditions. Furthermore, disparities exist between regions within each Gulf country, with urban areas reaping the benefits of economic development while rural and remote areas lag in terms of infrastructure, education, and healthcare. Addressing these economic disparities is crucial to ensure social stability and create a more inclusive and balanced economic system.

6. Global Economic Interactions: Gulf states have actively engaged in international economic relations, developing trade links, investment partnerships, and economic agreements with nations worldwide. Leveraging their oil wealth, Gulf countries have sought to diversify their investments, both domestically and internationally. They have established sovereign wealth funds, which invest in various sectors and assets globally, ensuring long-term financial stability and generating additional revenue streams. Gulf states have also positioned themselves as major players in regional and global trade, capitalizing on their strategic geographic location to serve as hubs for trade and logistics. Their ports, airports, and free trade zones attract foreign companies and facilitate the flow of goods and services. However, their dependence on imports for food and

other essential goods exposes them to global supply chain disruptions and price fluctuations, highlighting their vulnerabilities. Efforts to develop local industries, increase self-sufficiency, and enhance resilience against external shocks are ongoing.

7. Impact on Foreign Policy: Economic dimensions play a crucial role in shaping Gulf countries' foreign policies. Economic factors, such as access to markets, investment opportunities, and resource security, drive decision-making in foreign relations. Gulf states strategically establish economic partnerships and alliances to secure their economic interests, enhance market access, and attract foreign investments. For instance, they actively collaborate with major Asian economies like China and India, as these countries offer vast markets for their energy exports and investment opportunities. Gulf countries have also used economic leverage in their diplomatic engagements, offering aid, investment, and trade agreements to strengthen ties with other nations. Additionally, economic considerations influence their regional involvement, as they seek to protect critical infrastructure, secure shipping lanes, and maintain stability in neighboring countries directly affecting their economic interests.

Understanding the economic dimensions of the Gulf ideological system provides insights into the Gulf's development trajectory, policy priorities, and relationships with other countries. By examining these factors, we can better understand the motivations and challenges faced by Gulf countries in their pursuit of economic growth, diversification, and stability. Furthermore, awareness of economic dimensions enables a comprehensive analysis of the Gulf's ideological dynamics and their implications for regional and global interactions.

D. Social dimensions of the Gulf ideological system

The social dimensions of the Gulf ideological system play a significant role in shaping the identity and dynamics of the Gulf region. Social structures, norms, and values within Gulf societies contribute to the formation of distinct ideological perspectives and can either foster unity or exacerbate divisions. Understanding these social dimensions is essential for comprehending the complexities of the region's dynamics.

- Tribal and Clan Structures: Traditional tribal and clan structures have deep historical roots in Gulf societies, and their influence remains significant today. These social structures are characterized by strong familial ties and codes of honor. Tribal affiliations often intersect with political and economic interests, shaping individual and collective identities. Tribal and clan leaders continue to play vital societal roles, mediating conflicts, and providing guidance. However, the effects of modernization and urbanization have led to a gradual transformation of these structures over time.

○ With the growth of cities and the expansion of urban spaces, some traditional tribal and clan structures have become less pronounced. The younger generation, especially those living in urban areas, may prioritize individualism and personal aspirations over tribal affiliations. However, significant segments of the Gulf population still maintain strong ties to their tribes and clans, valuing the sense of community and identity that these structures provide. In some cases, tribes and clans have adapted to the changing times by incorporating modern practices and participating in various aspects of society while still preserving their cultural heritage.

- **Social Hierarchies**: Gulf societies are characterized by various forms of social hierarchies. Wealth, occupation, family background, and education are key determinants of social status. This hierarchical structure often creates inequalities and divisions within society. The distribution of power, resources, and opportunities tends to favor those in higher social positions, leading to resentment and social tensions. These disparities can impact social cohesion and warrant efforts to address inclusivity and social justice.

  ○ While social hierarchies persist, there have been concerted efforts in recent years to address inequality and bridge the gap between different social strata. Governments and civil society organizations have implemented policies and initiatives to promote social mobility and equal opportunities. There is a growing recognition that sustainable development requires the inclusion and empowerment of all members of society. These efforts aim to create a more just and equitable society in which everyone has the opportunity to thrive, regardless of their social background.

- Gender Dynamics: Gender roles and norms play a significant role in shaping the social fabric of Gulf societies. Traditional gender roles often emphasize male dominance, the protection of family honor, and prescribed behavioral expectations for men and women. However, there is an ongoing societal shift challenging these traditional norms. Efforts to empower women, promote gender equality, and broaden opportunities for women in education, employment, and leadership roles have gained momentum. The evolving gender dynamics represent a transformative aspect of the Gulf ideological system.

  ○ Women's empowerment movements have been instrumental in challenging gender stereotypes and advocating for gender equality. Women are now increasingly taking on leadership roles in various sectors, including government, business, and academia. This shift not only benefits women individually but also contributes to the overall development and progress of Gulf societies. However, while significant strides have been made, there is still progress to be made in achieving full gender equality, as cultural norms and societal expectations continue to influence gender dynamics.

- Religion and Cultural Identity: Islam serves as the predominant religion in Gulf societies and provides a strong foundation for cultural identity. Islamic values and practices shape social norms, morality, and governance in the region. Religious institutions and influential religious figures continue to play significant roles in upholding societal values and enforcing moral codes. The integration of cultural practices, traditions, and expressions of identity with religious beliefs reinforces a shared sense of identity within the Gulf societies.

  ○ Cultural identity in the Gulf region is deeply intertwined with religious values, creating a unique blend of Islam and local customs. While Islam provides a common thread, there is also recognition and celebration of the diverse cultural heritage within the Gulf societies. Folklore, traditional arts, music, and cuisine contribute to the richness and diversity of the region's cultural identity. Efforts to preserve cultural heritage and promote cultural exchange contribute to a sense of unity and pride among Gulf communities.

- Social Cohesion and Diversity: Gulf societies are diverse, with significant expatriate populations contributing to multicultural dynamics. While social cohesion is often grounded in shared cultural and religious values, diversity can also lead to tensions and challenges related to inclusivity, integration, and the preservation of cultural heritage. Efforts to promote social cohesion focus on encouraging tolerance, respect, and understanding among diverse populations. Building inclusive societies that value diversity as a strength is essential to strengthen the Gulf ideological system.

○ The Gulf region's rich diversity is an asset that brings together people from various backgrounds, cultures, and nationalities. Efforts to promote social cohesion encompass initiatives such as educational campaigns, cultural exchange programs, and legislation against discrimination. Governments and civil society organizations recognize the importance of fostering an inclusive environment where individuals from different backgrounds can coexist peacefully and contribute to the development of Gulf societies.

• Youth and Generational Shifts: Gulf societies are experiencing generational shifts as younger populations emerge and become more influential. Young people increasingly seek avenues for self-expression, question traditional norms, and advocate for social change. They challenge existing power structures and push for greater participation in decision-making processes. This generational divide can create tensions but also presents opportunities for positive transformation within the Gulf ideological system.

○ The younger generation in the Gulf is more connected to the globalized world, influenced by new ideas, and exposed to diverse cultures and perspectives. They are active participants in social media platforms, which provide them with channels for expression and mobilization. Their voices and demands for change have led to the implementation of policies and initiatives that directly address their aspirations and concerns. Recognizing the importance of youth engagement, governments and organizations in the Gulf are prioritizing youth inclusion, education, employment opportunities, and platforms for dialogue. This focus on youth represents a recognition of their potential as catalysts for societal progress and the future of the Gulf ideological system.

Understanding the social dimensions of the Gulf ideological system provides insight into the complexities of the region's dynamics. These social factors interact with political, economic, and cultural dimensions, shaping ideologies and influencing the quest for unity or discord within the Gulf. Analyzing and addressing these social dimensions is crucial for fostering social cohesion, inclusivity, and a shared sense of identity, ultimately strengthening the Gulf ideological system.

E. Cultural dimensions of the Gulf ideological system

Cultural dynamics play a significant role in shaping the Gulf ideological system. As a region with unique cultural traditions and historical backgrounds, the Gulf countries exhibit a range of cultural dimensions that influence their ideologies and overall societal structures. This chapter delves deeper into the various cultural dimensions that contribute to the Gulf ideological system, shedding light on the complexities and influences shaping Gulf societies.

1. Cultural Identity: Gulf countries have distinct cultural identities rooted in their history, customs, language, and traditions. These identities contribute to the formation of Gulf ideologies, influencing areas such as politics, governance, and social norms. The Gulf Arab countries, including Saudi Arabia, Kuwait, Bahrain, Qatar, Oman, and the United Arab Emirates, share a common Arabian heritage, which includes a strong emphasis on hospitality, honor, and respect. This heritage fosters a sense of unity and a unique Gulf identity, despite the differences among these nations.

2. Religion: Islam plays a central and pervasive role in shaping the cultural dimensions of the Gulf. The interpretation and application of religious principles can heavily influence governance structures, social values, and moral frameworks within each Gulf country.

While all Gulf states adopt Islam as their official religion, there are nuanced differences in religious practices and interpretations. For instance, Saudi Arabia follows a strict interpretation of Sunni Islam, while Oman practices a more moderate form of Ibadi Islam. The role of Islamic law (Sharia) and the level of influence it holds in legislation and societal practices also vary among the Gulf countries.

3. Tribalism and Kinship: Traditional tribal structures continue to influence Gulf ideologies, particularly in areas such as social hierarchy, loyalty, and kinship networks. Tribal affiliations can impact political alliances, resource distribution, and social cohesion within Gulf societies. The notion of honor and loyalty to one's tribe often shapes political decision-making processes and resource allocation. Tribal identity remains essential for many Gulf citizens, and tribal leaders often play a significant role in policymaking and community representation, especially in countries with larger Bedouin populations like Saudi Arabia and the UAE.

4. Arts, Literature, and Media: The arts, literature, and media play crucial roles in reflecting and shaping the cultural dimensions of the Gulf. They provide avenues for self-expression, debate, and the dissemination of cultural values. Traditional art forms such as calligraphy, traditional dance (e.g., Al-Ayyala, Liwa), storytelling, and poetry (e.g., Nabati poetry) hold significant cultural importance in the Gulf. Contemporary

Gulf literature reflects societal issues, historical narratives, and cultural values. Media outlets, both traditional and digital, have gained prominence in shaping public opinion and fostering cultural dialogue. In recent years, Gulf countries have invested heavily in promoting their cultural heritage through museums, festivals, and artistic initiatives, strengthening their national identities while embracing innovation.

5. Education and Knowledge Transmission: Education systems are instrumental in perpetuating cultural values and shaping Gulf ideologies. The curriculum, teaching methodologies, and emphasis on specific subjects all contribute to the inculcation of national and cultural identities, as well as the transmission of ideological perspectives within each Gulf country. Education reforms in the Gulf have aimed at incorporating modern knowledge while preserving traditional values, showcasing a delicate balance between global influences and cultural preservation. Efforts to introduce critical thinking, bilingual education, and scientific research have become integral aspects of Gulf education systems, aligning with the countries' aspirations for knowledge-based economies.

6. Gender Roles and Family Structures: Gender roles and family structures significantly shape Gulf ideologies. Traditional gender norms can influence political participation, legal frameworks, and social expectations within Gulf societies. While progress has been made

towards gender equality in areas such as education and workforce participation, traditional patriarchal systems still persist in some aspects of Gulf societies. Shifts in family structures, such as increased nuclear families, also impact Gulf ideologies, as they influence social dynamics and community support systems. Addressing gender-related challenges and advancing women's rights while respecting cultural values is a growing priority in the region.

7. Globalization and Cultural Exchange: Globalization has brought increased exposure to ideas and cultures from around the world, influencing the Gulf ideological system. The dynamics of globalization, including the rise of global media, migration, and transnational connections, shape the cultural dimensions and contribute to ideological changes within the Gulf. The influx of expatriate communities and the integration of global knowledge have prompted Gulf societies to navigate the intersections of local values and global influences, leading to ongoing discussions and debates on cultural assimilation, identity, and national cohesion. The rise of multiculturalism and intercultural dialogue has presented both challenges and opportunities for Gulf countries as they aim to balance local traditions with global progress.

8. Cultural Diversity and Coexistence: The Gulf region is home to diverse populations, including both Gulf citizens and expatriate communities. This cultural di-

versity contributes to the Gulf ideological system, fostering discourses on multiculturalism, identity, and coexistence. Managing cultural diversity presents challenges and opportunities for Gulf societies. Striking a balance between preserving Gulf cultural identity and embracing the contributions of diverse communities is essential for promoting social harmony and stability. Initiatives promoting multiculturalism, tolerance, and understanding have gained traction, encouraging dialogue and collaboration among different cultural groups in the Gulf.

9. Aesthetic Expressions and Cultural Heritage: Cultural heritage and aesthetic expressions, such as traditional music, dance, architecture, and food, are integral to the Gulf cultural dimensions. These expressions reflect the shared histories and values of the Gulf countries, contributing to a sense of cohesive identity and cultural continuity within the Gulf. Traditional music, such as the Arabian Maqam and the Sawt genre, showcases the rich musical traditions of the Gulf. Architectural marvels like the historic mud-brick houses of Yemen, the fortified towers of Bahrain, and the modern skyscrapers that define cityscapes across the Gulf serve as testaments to the region's architectural heritage. Culinary traditions, like the popular dishes of Mansaf, Machboos, and Harees, embody the fusion of flavors and cultural influences that characterize Gulf cuisine. Preservation efforts, including the reno-

vation of historical sites and the revival of traditional arts, demonstrate the Gulf countries' commitment to safeguarding their cultural heritage while embracing modernization.

Understanding the cultural dimensions of the Gulf ideological system provides valuable insights into the intricacies of Gulf societies. By acknowledging and exploring these dimensions, policymakers, researchers, and individuals can gain a comprehensive understanding of the complexities that shape Gulf ideologies, ultimately fostering a more nuanced dialogue and approach to regional unity and discord.

F. Determinants and interplay of the Gulf ideological system

The Gulf ideological system is a complex web of interconnected factors that shape the political, economic, social, and cultural dynamics within the region. Understanding the determinants and interplay of this system is crucial in comprehending the nuances and complexities of Gulf societies and their interactions.

1. **Historical Context:** The historical context of the Gulf region has deep-rooted influences on its ideological system. Over the centuries, the region experienced a tumultuous past that included colonization, tribal traditions, and significant historical events like the Arab Spring. The struggle for independence, regional geopolitics, and post-colonial influences have all contributed to the diverse nature of the Gulf ideological

landscape.

- ○ Colonization and Decolonization: The Gulf region, particularly countries such as Bahrain, Kuwait, and Qatar, experienced colonial rule by European powers like Britain and Portugal. The impacts of colonization, including political and economic exploitation, have left a lasting impression on the region's ideological development. Decolonization movements and the subsequent establishment of independent states brought new challenges and opportunities for shaping ideologies.

  - The experience of colonization left behind deep-seated resentment, as it led to the imposition of foreign norms, values, and governance systems. Post-independence, the Gulf countries sought to assert their own identities and ideologies, striving for a balance between preserving indigenous traditions and embracing modernization.

- ○ Tribal Traditions: Tribal systems, with their distinct values, customs, and structures, have had a profound impact on the ideological system of the region. Despite the rapid modernization, many Gulf societies maintain connections to their tribal roots, shaping collective values such as honor, loyalty, and hospitality.

- Tribal traditions have influenced political structures, with tribal leaders and kinship networks playing a significant role in shaping ideologies. The concept of wasta (connections) and the importance of family ties continue to have an impact on social and economic dynamics, as well as political decision-making processes within the Gulf countries.

○ Arab Spring: The Arab Spring, a wave of uprisings in the Middle East in 2011, also played a role in influencing the Gulf ideological system. The protests, demands for political reforms, and aspirations for greater social justice had reverberations in the Gulf countries, albeit to differing degrees. The consequences of the Arab Spring have led to both fragmentation and evolvement of ideologies in the region.

- The Arab Spring brought to the forefront issues such as political participation, human rights, and accountability, triggering debates and calls for change within Gulf societies. While some countries responded with suppression, others initiated limited reforms to address public demands. These responses influenced the ideological climate, with segments of the Gulf population adopting or embracing new ideologies promoting democratic governance, social equality, and civil liberties.

2. **Political Complexities:** Political determinants of the Gulf ideological system encompass the forms of governance and the ideology of ruling elites. Gulf countries exhibit a spectrum of political structures, ranging from absolute monarchies to federal republics. These differing models contribute to the diversity and interplay of ideologies.

   ○ Balance of Power: The balance of power within Gulf politics influences the ideological landscape. Ruling elites contend for influence, often relying on ideological narratives to legitimize their positions. The dynamics between ruling regimes, political parties, and opposition groups shape the ideological discourse and affect governance.

      • The balance of power is often influenced by historical, tribal, or familial alliances, as well as economic considerations. The ruling elites seek to maintain stability and control while responding to the demands and aspirations of the population. Ideological narratives, such as those emphasizing tradition, religious values, or modernization, are strategically employed to navigate the challenges and competitions between various power centers.

   ○ Monarchies and Republics: The presence of both monarchies and republics in the region contributes to the diversity within the Gulf ideological system.

Monarchies, with their emphasis on traditional values and kinship ties, foster specific ideologies that endorse stability and continuity. Republics, on the other hand, promote ideologies grounded in democratic principles and popular sovereignty.

- Monarchies often employ ideologies centered on legitimacy, heritage, and national identity. The belief in the divine right to rule, as well as the custodianship of Islamic holy sites, has a profound influence on the ideological landscape of these countries. Conversely, in republics like Iraq and Yemen, ideologies revolve around concepts of nationalism, Arabism, and popular sovereignty.

○ Role of Political Institutions: The role and influence of political institutions, such as parliaments, councils, and judiciary, also impact the Gulf ideological system. The interplay between these institutions and the ruling elites shapes the overall ideological climate, directing policies and decision-making processes.

- The functioning of political institutions within Gulf countries varies significantly. Some countries have established representative bodies, such as advisory councils or elected parliaments, which allow for debate and interaction between ruling elites and citizens. In contrast, other countries have more centralized power structures, with institutions serving as extensions of the ruling elites. These distinctions influence the pluralistic or authoritarian nature of ideologies within the region.

3. **Socioeconomic Factors:** Economic determinants, such as resource wealth, labor markets, and economic policies, play a significant role in shaping Gulf ideologies. The distribution of wealth, socioeconomic disparities, and the influence of oil and gas industries impact societal values, priorities, and aspirations.

   ○ Resource Wealth: The abundance of natural resources, particularly oil and gas, has fueled economic prosperity in the Gulf region. The resulting wealth has shaped and influenced ideologies, including the reliance on rentier economies and the role of the state in providing welfare and services. Resource wealth can also create tensions between economic aspirations and environmental sustainability.

     • The oil and gas industry, which drives the economies of most Gulf countries, shapes ideologies by facilitating an emphasis on economic growth, modernization, and socio-political stability. The reliance on oil revenues can also lead to a sense of entitlement and dependence, affecting the aspirations and expectations of the population.

○ Labor Markets and Migration: The reliance on migrant labor in Gulf countries has socioeconomic implications that intersect with the ideological system. The presence of diverse expatriate communities, often working in low-wage sectors, can create social and cultural tensions that impact local and national ideologies.

  • Labor markets in the Gulf countries are shaped by both local and foreign influences, impacting ideologies in multiple ways. The influx of migrant workers has led to demographic changes and cultural diversification, which can challenge traditional notions of national identity and cultural homogeneity. Simultaneously, Gulf countries employ ideologies that promote stability and national identity to counterbalance potential social conflicts arising from labor market dynamics.

○ Economic Policies: Economic policies and strategies pursued by Gulf governments impact the ideological landscape. Development plans, diversification efforts, and initiatives promoting private sector growth can shape societal expectations, foster entrepreneurial ideals, and influence the overall direction of Gulf ideologies.

- Economic policies within the Gulf region often prioritize job creation, economic diversification, and social welfare. The adoption of market-oriented reforms, efforts to enhance innovation and knowledge-based economies, and the encouragement of entrepreneurship influence ideological narratives related to economic development, technological advancement, and social progress. These policies often aim to strike a balance between the preservation of cultural values and the embrace of global competitiveness.

4. **Social Dynamics**: The social determinants of the Gulf ideological system encompass a variety of factors, including religion, social norms, gender dynamics, and education. These factors contribute to the formation and evolution of ideologies within Gulf societies.

   ○ Religion: Religion, particularly Islam, plays a central role in shaping the Gulf ideological system. Islamic beliefs and values influence policies and regulations, as well as individual and collective behaviors. The interpretation and application of Islamic teachings vary across the Gulf countries, leading to diverse ideological outlooks.

     - Islamic religious institutions, such as mosques, madrasas, and religious scholars, contribute to the dissemination and shaping of ideologies.

Different Islamic sects and interpretations can also lead to ideological divisions within Gulf societies, as seen in the case of Sunni-Shia tensions.

○ Social Norms and Values: Social norms and values, rooted in cultural, tribal, and religious traditions, shape the Gulf ideological system. Concepts such as honor, modesty, and family cohesion influence societal expectations and the formation of individual and group identities. These norms and values can affect various aspects of Gulf societies, including gender roles, family structures, and social interactions.

• The interplay between traditional norms and modern influences, such as globalization and urbanization, creates tensions and challenges within the Gulf ideological system. The desire to embrace modernity and global trends while preserving cultural values can lead to ideological debates and clashes.

○ Gender Dynamics: Gender dynamics and women's rights are integral components of the Gulf ideological system. The status and role of women within Gulf societies can vary significantly, influenced by a combination of religious, cultural, and political factors. Women's empowerment movements, calls for gender equality, and efforts to combat gender-based violence and discrimination have emerged in recent years, challenging traditional gender norms and ideologies.

- The interplay between conservative and progressive ideologies shapes the discourse on women's rights. Gulf societies increasingly confront questions related to women's political participation, access to education and employment, and the balance between religious values and gender equality.

○ Education: Education systems and curricula play a significant role in shaping ideologies within Gulf countries. The content and emphasis of education can promote particular values, beliefs, and worldviews. Educational institutions, from primary schools to universities, contribute to the formation of national identities and the transmission of cultural norms.

- In recent years, Gulf countries have sought to reform their education systems, emphasizing quality, relevance, and the integration of technology. These reforms aim to nurture critical thinking skills, promote innovation, and prepare the younger generation for the challenges of a globalized world. However, questions of ideological bias, curriculum content, and the balance between national identity and global perspectives continue to be debated.

Understanding the complex interplay of determinants shaping the Gulf ideological system is a continuous and evolving process. The dynamic nature of Gulf societies, driven by historical, political, socioeconomic, and social factors, necessitates ongoing analysis to comprehend the nuances and changes in ideologies and their impacts within the region.

G. Landmarks

The Gulf region is not only a hub of economic and geopolitical power but also a center for diverse ideological movements that shape the sociopolitical landscape. Understanding the ideological dynamics at play is crucial for comprehending the complex dynamics in the region. This section explores some of the key ideological factors that have influenced the Gulf countries, including Islamism, nationalism, sectarianism, the role of oil, and the impact of globalization.

Islamism has been a significant ideological force in the Gulf countries, with varying degrees of influence across the region. Islamism represents a political ideology that seeks to establish Islamic law and governance, sometimes conflicting with the interests of the ruling regimes. Islamist movements, like the Muslim Brotherhood and its offshoots, have gained support among segments of the population by addressing social and economic grievances. However, Gulf governments have also utilized Islamism as a tool for consolidating their own rule, emphasizing their Islamic credentials while asserting control over religious institutions.

Nationalism has also played a crucial role in shaping the ideological landscape of the Gulf countries. While the Gulf states share common linguistic and cultural ties, each country has its distinct national identity. Nationalist sentiments were particularly pronounced during the period of decolonization when Gulf countries sought to assert their independence from colonial powers. Nationalism has been instrumental in forging social cohesion, promoting cultural heritage, and shaping domestic and foreign policy priorities. Gulf countries have created national narratives that emphasize the advent of modernity, economic progress, and geopolitical influence, further fueling nationalist sentiments.

Sectarianism is another ideological factor that has influenced the Gulf region, particularly evident in the divide between the Sunni and Shia denominations of Islam. Conflicts in the wider Middle East, such as those in Iraq, Syria, and Yemen, have heightened sectarian tensions and had a spill-over effect on the Gulf. Proxy battles between regional powers, often along sectarian lines, have exacerbated these divisions, leading to a climate where sectarian identities and affiliations become more salient, further complicating the region's ideological dynamics. Sectarianism in the Gulf is not only confined to religious differences but is also deeply intertwined with political, economic, and social factors.

Oil has also contributed significantly to shaping the ideologies of the Gulf countries. The discovery of vast oil reserves transformed the region and led to dramatic economic and social changes. The wealth generated by oil has enabled Gulf governments to implement ambitious development projects and welfare programs, thereby legitimizing their rule and ensuring social stability. However, oil dependency has also created challenges, such as rentierism and over-reliance on oil revenues, which have impacted the region's economic diversification efforts and fostered various social and political dynamics. Additionally, oil has given the Gulf countries significant international influence, shaping their foreign policies and strategic relationships.

The Gulf countries' ideological dynamics are no longer confined within their borders but are increasingly influenced by globalization. The rise of information technology and communications has connected the Gulf populations to the wider world, facilitating the spread of ideas, ideologies, and social movements. Global trends, such as the rise of populism and activism, as well as regional geopolitical shifts, have the potential to reshape the ideological dynamics in the Gulf countries. The politics of identity and the rise of social media have amplified ideological clashes and facilitated the formation of transnational networks that challenge the traditional structures of power within the region.

Understanding these complex and intersecting ideologies is crucial for comprehending and analyzing the sociopolitical landscape of the Gulf and its implications for the region and beyond. The ideological landscape of the Gulf is constantly evolving, influenced by both domestic and external factors. Policy decisions, reforms, and social movements all contribute to shaping the trajectory of these ideologies. Moreover, recognizing the interplay between ideology, governance, and socioeconomic factors is essential for formulating effective policies that address the diverse challenges and aspirations of the Gulf countries. By engaging with these ideological dynamics, regional and international actors can contribute to a more stable and prosperous future for the Gulf and its people.

CASE STUDY: THE QATAR CRISIS OF 2017-2020

Background and Context

The Qatar Crisis, one of the most significant events in Gulf regional dynamics, unfolded between 2017 and 2020, leaving lasting repercussions on the region. To gain a comprehensive understanding of the crisis, it is essential to delve into an in-depth analysis of its background and contextual factors, unearthing the intricacies that fueled its escalation.

At its core, the crisis emerged from long-standing rifts between Qatar and other Gulf Cooperation Council (GCC) member states, primarily Saudi Arabia, the United Arab Emirates (UAE), Bahrain, and Egypt. These tensions, dating back years before the crisis, were multifaceted, encompassing political disagreements, conflicting approaches towards Islamist movements, media influence, and Qatar's independent foreign policy. An exploration of these factors will illuminate the underpinnings of the crisis.

Analysis of Factors Contributing to the Crisis

The Qatar Crisis was fueled by a myriad of interrelated factors, each playing a unique role in exacerbating tensions and deepening fractures within the Gulf region. One significant aspect was the ideological differences among the Gulf states. Qatar's support for Islamist movements, particularly the Muslim Brotherhood, drew vehement criticism from its neighboring countries. Saudi Arabia and the UAE, in particular, viewed these movements as threats to their stability and security. This clash of ideologies, driven by differing interpretations of Islam, became a major point of contention.

Furthermore, regional influence emerged as a contentious issue, contributing to the crisis. Qatar's rise as a significant player, leveraging its immense wealth and ambition, aimed to shape regional dynamics beyond its borders. This raised concerns among other Gulf states, who saw Qatar's growing influence as a challenge to their regional standing. The competition for regional prominence, particularly in the context of the shifting power dynamics in the wake of the Arab Spring, further intensified the existing tensions.

Economic competition, predominantly centered around energy production, also played a role in exacerbating the crisis.

Qatar's emergence as a dominant force in liquefied natural gas (LNG) production threatened the market share and economic interests of other Gulf countries. This prompted economic concerns among Qatar's neighbors and fanned the flames of animosity. Moreover, control over media outlets added another layer of complexity to the crisis. Qatar's influential news network, Al Jazeera, became a point of contention as it offered unprecedented coverage and diverse perspectives, often seen as challenging the narratives promoted by other Gulf media outlets. This divergence in media influence created an information war that further fueled the crisis.

The Role of the Gulf Ideological System in Managing or Exacerbating the Crisis

The Gulf ideological system, deeply rooted in historical, cultural, and religious dynamics, played a central role in both managing and exacerbating the Qatar Crisis. Within the region, differing interpretations and practices of Islam gave rise to ideological rivalries and competing narratives. Qatar's support for Islamist movements, particularly the Muslim Brotherhood, was seen as threatening to the conservative bloc led by Saudi Arabia, which favored a more authoritarian and statist approach. This deep-seated ideological clash amplified tensions and hindered effective dialogue, entrenching positions on both sides and deepening the divisions within the Gulf.

Moreover, Gulf media outlets played a significant role in exacerbating the crisis. Each side, including Qatar and its opponents, utilized their respective media platforms to propagate narratives that favored their positions. Over the years, media outlets in the region have been vehicles for promoting national interests and ideologies. The media landscape became polarized, further entrenching positions and intensifying animosity. The Qatari-owned Al Jazeera, known for its independent and critical coverage, provided a platform for alternative voices and diverse perspectives, which directly challenged the hegemony of other Gulf media outlets. This media war further amplified the ideological divisions within the Gulf and hindered efforts towards resolution.

Impact of the Crisis on Gulf Regional Dynamics

The Qatar Crisis had profound and far-reaching implications for Gulf regional dynamics. The breakdown in diplomatic relations between Qatar and its neighboring countries led to a full-scale blockade imposed on Qatar, severing ties and imposing significant restrictions on trade, investment, and even familial relations. This blockade had immense economic consequences, impacting regional cooperation and stability. It disrupted the flow of goods, services, and people, further straining already fragile relations between the Gulf states.

The crisis also deeply affected regional security cooperation. Shared concerns over terrorism, Iran's regional influence, and the need for a united front were abruptly overshadowed by the conflict itself. Counterterrorism collaboration, which had previously been a cornerstone of Gulf cooperation, suffered as the divisions deepened. The crisis also highlighted the deep fractures within the GCC itself, undermining the organization's unity and collective efforts.

Furthermore, the Qatar Crisis caused a significant recalibration of relationships, with both Qatar and its opponents seeking new alliances and partnerships beyond the Gulf region. Qatar turned to Turkey and Iran for political and economic support, deepening Tehran's influence in the Gulf and exacerbating regional sectarian tensions. Meanwhile, countries such as Saudi Arabia and the UAE strengthened their strategic ties with the United States, amplifying their regional influence indirectly. These realignments reshaped the regional dynamics, leading to a fragmented Gulf region with shifting alliances and strained cooperation.

Lessons Learned and Implications for the Future of Gulf Unity

The Qatar Crisis offers valuable lessons that could guide the future of Gulf unity and cooperation. Firstly, it underscores the importance of dialogue, compromise, and mutual understanding in resolving regional disputes. The crisis vividly showcased the consequences of escalating tensions and the urgent need for a diplomatic approach. The adoption of a more conciliatory and inclusive approach by all parties could have averted the blockade and minimized the negative impact on regional stability and cooperation.

Secondly, the crisis highlighted the need for stronger institutional frameworks within the GCC. The absence of robust mechanisms to address and manage ideological differences hindered effective communication and resolution. Establishing well-defined institutional structures that promote dialogue, foster trust, and address divergent perspectives could help prevent future crises and enhance intra-Gulf cooperation.

Lastly, future efforts towards Gulf unity must prioritize a shared vision that respects and accommodates the diversity within the Gulf region. Embracing the diversity of ideologies, interests, and aspirations within the Gulf is crucial for sustainable unity and cooperation. Recognizing and acknowledging that each Gulf state has its unique approach and priorities will foster an environment of mutual respect, trust, and genuine collaboration.

In summary

The Qatar Crisis, a complex and multi-faceted event in Gulf regional dynamics, provided a compelling case study for understanding the intricate web of factors that contribute to the escalation of crises. Through a comprehensive analysis of its background, factors, and implications, a deeper understanding of the challenges and opportunities for future Gulf unity emerges. The crisis highlighted the complex interplay of ideology, politics, competition, and media influence within the Gulf ideological system. Drawing on the lessons learned from this crisis can guide the region towards a more cohesive and resilient future, where differences are respected, dialogue is prioritized, and cooperation is fostered for the greater good of the Gulf region.

A. Background and context of the crisis

Throughout history, the Gulf region has been characterized by complex socio-political dynamics influenced by a unique set of factors. In recent years, the Qatar Crisis of 2017-2020 emerged as a significant event that shaped these dynamics further, deepening existing fault lines and challenging the Gulf's quest for unity.

1.1 The Historical Context

To understand the Qatar Crisis fully, it is essential to examine the historical context of the Gulf region. The formation of the Gulf Cooperation Council (GCC) in 1981 aimed to promote economic cooperation and regional security among the member states, which included Bahrain, Kuwait, Oman, Qatar, Saudi Arabia, and the United Arab Emirates (UAE). This regional grouping was a response to the Iran-Iraq War and the need to establish a collective security framework.

However, underlying tensions and ideological differences persisted within the GCC. Qatar, from the early 1990s, pursued an independent foreign policy, deviating from the collective Gulf consensus on numerous occasions. While maintaining a strategic alliance with the United States, Qatar also sought to engage with a wide range of regional and global actors, including Iran, fostering greater independence and sovereignty in its decision-making.

1.2 Emergence of Tensions

Disagreements and tensions between Qatar and its Gulf neighbors had been simmering beneath the surface for years. However, these tensions reached a tipping point in June 2017 when Saudi Arabia, Bahrain, the UAE, and Egypt announced a diplomatic and economic blockade against Qatar. This marked the beginning of the Qatar Crisis.

The catalyst for the crisis lay in Qatar's alleged support for political movements that its neighbors considered to be extremist or destabilizing. Qatar's robust backing of the Muslim Brotherhood, for instance, generated concerns among Saudi Arabia and the UAE, who viewed the Brotherhood as a threat to their own domestic security and the stability of the region. Qatar's support for political Islam, combined with the platform provided by its controversial media outlet, Al Jazeera, exacerbated these tensions.

1.3 Economic and Security Concerns

The economic and security dimensions of the Qatar Crisis cannot be understated. Qatar, as a major exporter of liquefied natural gas (LNG), held a relatively strong economic position compared to its neighbors. This economic strength provided Qatar with some degree of independence in its decision-making, leading to resentment from other Gulf states. Qatar's ability to shape its foreign policy independently without consulting its neighbors was seen as a challenge to the Gulf's collective stability.

Furthermore, the perception of Qatar's relatively amicable relationship with Iran raised concerns about its commitment to the collective security architecture of the Gulf. Iran's geopolitical rivalry with Saudi Arabia, in particular, had deep-rooted historical and sectarian dimensions, causing apprehension among Qatar's neighbors. The fear of Iran's influence in the region added a layer of complexity to the crisis, straining diplomatic relations further.

1.4 Regional Ramifications and Geopolitical Realignment

The Qatar Crisis had wide-ranging implications for Gulf regional dynamics. It revealed the fragility of the GCC as a platform for regional cooperation and demonstrated the growing societal divisions within Gulf societies. The imposition of the blockade led to fractures not only at the governmental level but also within families and communities, heightening social tensions.

As Qatar faced the diplomatic and economic blockade, it sought support from other regional and global players. Turkey emerged as its key ally, providing logistical and economic aid. Moreover, Qatar strengthened its ties with Iran, with both countries deepening bilateral cooperation in various sectors. These realignments molded the regional dynamics of the Gulf and highlighted the vulnerability of small states within a system dominated by larger regional powers.

1.5 Lessons Learned and Way Forward

The Qatar Crisis serves as a crucial case study for understanding the challenges of maintaining Gulf unity and for shaping future policy approaches. It underscores the importance of open and constructive dialogue in resolving differences among

Gulf countries. The crisis also highlights the need to establish inclusive regional security frameworks that address common security concerns while accommodating diverse political ideologies.

Furthermore, the crisis emphasizes the significance of shared economic interests in fostering cooperation and stability in the Gulf region. Relying solely on political or ideological consensus may prove inadequate in the face of divergent interests and geopolitical rivalries. Gulf countries must strive to find common ground and pursue mutually beneficial economic partnerships to mitigate the risks of future crises.

Moreover, the Qatar Crisis prompted a reevaluation of the dynamics between small and large states in the Gulf region. Small states like Qatar, despite their economic strength, face challenges in influencing the policies and decisions of larger regional powers. This highlights the importance of small states utilizing strategic alliances and building strong diplomatic ties to safeguard their interests.

The crisis also revealed the extent to which media outlets can impact regional dynamics. Qatar's Al Jazeera, known for its independent reporting and coverage of controversial issues, played a significant role in shaping public opinion during the crisis. This highlighted the necessity for responsible and balanced media coverage that considers the broader consequences of inflammatory reporting.

In summary, by delving into the background and context of the Qatar Crisis, this chapter provides readers with an in-depth understanding of the events leading up to this major Gulf crisis. It highlights the historical, ideological, economic, security, and media factors that contributed to the eruption of the crisis. Moreover, it reveals the wider implications of the crisis on Gulf regional dynamics and the lessons learned for future regional cooperation and stability.

B. Analysis of factors contributing to the crisis

The Qatar crisis of 2017-2020 was a multifaceted event that shook the Gulf region and had far-reaching implications. To truly grasp the complexities of this crisis, an in-depth analysis of the contributing factors is necessary. By delving deeper into these elements, we gain valuable insights into the dynamics driving the conflict and the underlying causes that underpin it.

- **Political Factors:** The political dimension laid the foundation for the Qatar crisis, as longstanding rivalries and ideological differences among the Gulf states resurfaced. Qatar's independent foreign policy, its support for Islamist movements, and its critical stance towards other Arab governments posed a challenge to the established order. Saudi Arabia and the UAE, in particular, sought to protect their regional dominance and perceived Qatar's actions as a threat.

The decades-long enmity between Qatar and Saudi Arabia was intensified when Qatar emerged as a regional power player with its vast natural gas reserves and global investments. Saudi Arabia, as a dominant force within the Gulf Cooperation

Council (GCC), perceived Qatar's ascendancy as a direct challenge to its influence and sought to curtail its regional reach.

Additionally, political differences regarding the Muslim Brotherhood further widened the rift. While Qatar supported the organization as an instrument of political Islam, Saudi Arabia, the UAE, and Bahrain labeled it as a terrorist group and sought to suppress it regionally. The contrasting views on the Brotherhood intensified the tensions between Qatar and its neighbors.

- **Economic Factors**: Economic factors significantly contributed to the Qatar crisis, as diverging economic strategies and competition for economic dominance fueled the conflict. Qatar's economic success, driven largely by its liquefied natural gas (LNG) exports, enabled the country to assert itself on the global stage. This newfound economic prowess raised concerns among its Gulf neighbors who perceived Qatar's rising influence as a challenge to their own economic power.

Accusations of Qatar providing financial support to terrorist organizations became a focal point of the crisis. Its neighbors, particularly Saudi Arabia and the UAE, accused Qatar of funding extremist groups, thereby threatening regional stability. While there is little concrete evidence to support these allegations, they served as a catalyst for the economic boycott imposed on Qatar by its neighbors.

Furthermore, competition for global business partnerships and investments escalated the crisis. Qatar's efforts to diversify its economy and draw international corporations into the country unsettled its neighbors who sought similar ventures. This economic rivalry further deepened the divisions and fueled the tensions between Qatar and the blockading states.

- **Geopolitical Geographies**: The geopolitical geography of the Gulf region played a significant role in intensifying the Qatar crisis. The presence of external powers with interests in the region, such as the United States, Iran, and Turkey, complicated the dynamics and shaped the responses of Gulf states. These external actors sought to leverage their relationships with the Gulf states to assert influence, exacerbating the existing tensions.

The United States, which maintains strategic military bases in Qatar, found itself in a challenging position of balancing its alliances with both Qatar and its regional rivals. This further complicated the crisis, as the United States had to navigate its relationships in the Gulf while managing wider geopolitical concerns.

Iran, a regional rival of the Gulf Cooperation Council states, seized the opportunity to deepen its ties with Qatar amidst the crisis. Iran's support for Qatar, which included providing alternative trade routes and airspace access, further heightened concerns among Qatar's neighbors. The fear of increased Iranian influence in the region became a rallying point for the blockading states.

Additionally, Turkey's involvement in the crisis added another layer of complexity. Turkey's strong ties with Qatar and its military deployment to a Turkish military base in Qatar demonstrated the transnational nature of the crisis. Turkey's assertive stance in support of Qatar undermined the unity of the GCC and contributed to the escalating tensions.

- **Ideological and Religious Differences**: The Qatar crisis highlighted deep-seated ideological and religious differences within the Gulf region. Qatar's support for political Islam, particularly the Muslim Brotherhood and other Islamist movements like Hamas, placed it at odds with its neighbors. Qatar viewed these groups as legitimate political actors, while its neighbors considered them threats to their own stability.

The Muslim Brotherhood, considered a divisive organization by some Gulf countries, became a focal point of contention during the crisis. Qatar's support for the Brotherhood and the organization's presence in Doha through media outlets like Al Jazeera were major sources of disagreement. This ideological divide underscored the challenges of reconciling differing political and religious ideologies within the Gulf states and contributed to the growing Gulf rift.

- **Media and Propaganda**: The media played a substantial role in perpetuating and intensifying the Qatar crisis. State-controlled media outlets from all sides engaged in an information war, using propaganda to influence public opinion domestically and internationally. These media narratives reinforced pre-existing biases and solidified divisions among the feuding states.

Qatar's Al Jazeera, known for its independent reporting, was accused of promoting dissident voices and inciting unrest within the region. Conversely, Saudi Arabia, the UAE, and their allies utilized their media channels to portray Qatar negatively in order to shape public perception. Through biased reporting and distribution of misinformation, media outlets on all sides propagated narratives that heightened animosity and fueled public anger.

- **Historical Rivalries and Divisions**: Underlying historical rivalries and unresolved conflicts heavily contributed to the Qatar crisis. Gulf states, including Qatar, have long-standing border disputes and territorial disagreements that date back decades. These unresolved conflicts created longstanding tensions and a fragile foundation for the Gulf states to navigate already complex regional dynamics.

The Qatar crisis also had historical roots in past differences and divisions within the Gulf Cooperation Council. Disagreements over regional politics, alliances, and influence have shaped the dynamics of the GCC since its formation in 1981. These deep-seated divisions played a role in the escalation of the crisis, as they provided historical context and underpinned the prevailing animosities among the Gulf states.

In summary, a comprehensive analysis of the Qatar crisis reveals the intricate web of political, economic, geopolitical, ideological, media, and historical factors that contributed to its occurrence. Understanding these contributing elements provides valuable insights into the deep-rooted dynamics and complex challenges faced by the Gulf states. By acknowledging these factors, stakeholders can work towards addressing the underlying issues and fostering a more harmonious and stable Gulf region.

C. The role of the Gulf ideological system in managing or exacerbating the crisis

The Gulf ideological system plays a significant role in managing or exacerbating crises within the region. In times of tensions or conflicts, the ideological differences among Gulf states often come to the forefront, shaping the responses and actions taken by the involved parties.

One of the key aspects of the Gulf ideological system is the deep-rooted political and religious divide among the various Gulf states. The region comprises primarily two major ideological camps: the Sunni-led bloc, consisting of Saudi Arabia, the United Arab Emirates, Bahrain, and Egypt, and the Shiite-led bloc, with Iran prominently at the helm. This divide stems from differing political ideologies, governance structures, and national interests, which influence each state's foreign policies and regional strategies.

When a crisis arises, these ideological differences can either fuel the conflict or serve as a means for managing and resolving it. On one hand, the Gulf ideological system can exacerbate crises by amplifying existing divisions and promoting mistrust among the states. Each state may adhere to its distinct ideological framework, whether it be the promotion of political Islam, a strong monarchy, or a secular identity. These ideological positions often shape the states' decisions and actions, creating obstacles to finding common ground and reaching a resolution. This can lead to an escalation in tensions and a prolonged crisis, as each Gulf state seeks to advance its own interests and protect its ideological position.

For example, the Syrian conflict highlighted the ideological divisions within the Gulf region. While some states supported the Syrian government, others backed opposition groups, reflecting their divergent ideological stances. This ideological polarization impacted efforts to find a peaceful resolution, as the Gulf states' support for different factions intensified the conflict. Moreover, the rivalry between the Sunni-led bloc and the Shiite-led bloc further complicated the crisis, with Saudi Arabia and Iran vying for regional influence through proxies in Syria.

On the other hand, the Gulf ideological system can also serve as a platform for managing and resolving crises. In some instances, shared ideological values and aspirations can act as a basis for initiating dialogue and fostering cooperation among Gulf states. When common ground and mutual understanding are achieved, the ideological system can facilitate diplomatic negotiations and pave the way for conflict resolution.

For instance, the successful conclusion of the Joint Comprehensive Plan of Action (JCPOA) in 2015, also known as the Iran Nuclear Deal, exemplified how shared ideological concerns about nuclear proliferation drove Gulf states to coordinate their efforts. Saudi Arabia and Gulf Cooperation Council countries expressed their support for the deal, highlighting a common goal of regional stability and nuclear non-proliferation despite their ideological differences with Iran. This cooperative stance demonstrated the potential for the Gulf ideological system to contribute positively to crisis management.

However, it is crucial to recognize that the Gulf ideological system alone is not the sole determinant in managing or exacerbating a crisis. External factors, such as the involvement of external powers or regional dynamics, can influence the course and outcome of a crisis. Additionally, the willingness of Gulf states to prioritize unity and compromise over ideological differences also plays a crucial role in crisis management efforts.

In the case of the Qatar Crisis of 2017-2020, the role of the Gulf ideological system was apparent. The crisis erupted due to differing ideological positions and political disputes among Gulf states, particularly regarding Qatar's perceived support for terrorism and its ties with Iran. The ideological divisions within the Gulf region hindered initial efforts at finding a resolution, as each state fiercely defended its stance. Nonetheless, with the intervention of external mediators and diplomatic initiatives, a gradual rapprochement was achieved, showcasing the potential for the Gulf ideological system to contribute to crisis management.

Moreover, the Gulf ideological system also intertwines with historical, cultural, and socioeconomic factors that shape the political landscape of the region. These additional layers of complexity influence how crises are managed or exacerbated within the Gulf. Historical conflicts and rivalries, such as the centuries-old power struggle between Sunni and Shiite sects, heavily influence the Gulf ideological system's dynamics. This historical context feeds into the narratives and ideologies upheld by different Gulf states, further exacerbating divisions during times of crisis.

Furthermore, the cultural and socioeconomic disparities within the Gulf region can also contribute to the exacerbation or management of crises. For instance, the divide between the wealthier Gulf states and those facing economic challenges can be a source of tension and create ideological differences in the region. Economic disparities can fuel resentment and give rise to ideological grievances, making it more challenging to manage crises effectively. On the other hand, efforts to address these economic disparities and promote inclusive development can help mitigate tensions and foster cooperation, thereby positively impacting crisis management.

In conclusion, the Gulf ideological system has a multifaceted role in managing or exacerbating crises within the region. While ideological divisions can fuel tensions and prolong conflicts, shared values and aspirations can provide a platform for dialogue and negotiation. The interplay between historical, cultural, and socioeconomic factors further adds complexity to the dynamics of crises within the Gulf. It is essential for Gulf states to recognize the potential of the ideological system as a tool for crisis management, thus prioritizing unity, compromise, and mutual understanding to effectively address and resolve conflicts. By doing so, the Gulf region can move towards greater stability, cooperation, and prosperity.

D. Impact of the crisis on Gulf regional dynamics

The Qatar Crisis of 2017-2020 introduced a significant disruption in Gulf regional dynamics, leaving lasting impacts on various aspects of political, economic, social, and security dimensions. This chapter delves into the extensive and far-reaching consequences the crisis had on Gulf regional dynamics, unveiling the complexities and intricacies of the situation.

Politically, the Qatar Crisis shattered the sense of unity that once characterized the Gulf Cooperation Council (GCC). The blockade imposed on Qatar by Saudi Arabia, the United Arab Emirates (UAE), Bahrain, and Egypt not only strained their diplomatic relations but also created deep divisions within the organization. Traditional inter-Gulf alliances were shaken, and new alignments of interests emerged as some states, such as Kuwait and Oman, adopted a more neutral stance, while others supported the blockading nations. This fragmentation of Gulf political cohesion not only impacted regional decision-making processes but also undermined the GCC's ability to collectively address pressing regional challenges. Furthermore, the crisis exposed underlying political rivalries and power dynamics among the Gulf states, leading to a dampening of the prospects for genuine regional integration.

Economically, the Qatar Crisis had a mixed impact on Gulf regional dynamics. Initially heavily reliant on imports from its neighboring Gulf states, Qatar swiftly diversified its trading partners to mitigate the economic impact of the blockade. It forged new trade routes towards countries like Turkey, Iran, and India, leading to a reconfiguration of Qatar's economic interdependencies. This diversification strategy brought both benefits and challenges. On the one hand, Qatar's investments in key sectors such as agriculture, manufacturing, and tourism aimed to reduce its reliance on neighboring countries and bolster its self-sufficiency. On the other hand, the blockade inflicted economic strain on the blockading nations, disrupting trade flows, investment flows, and tourism activities. As a result, the once-promising vision of Gulf economic integration took a step back, with the crisis impeding progress and hindering collaboration in the regional economic arena.

Socially, the Qatar Crisis exacerbated existing tensions within Gulf societies, generating a profound impact on the lives of Gulf citizens. The blockade's implementation led to the separation of families, both emotionally and economically, as individuals found themselves stranded on opposite sides. Marriages between citizens of different Gulf states faced challenges, as restrictions on travel and communication were imposed. Cultural exchange programs that were once vibrant within the Gulf region suffered disruptions, hindering the shared understanding and exchange of ideas among Gulf citizens. Moreover, the Qatari population, particularly expatriates, encountered difficulties in accessing healthcare, education, and other essential services due to the restrictions imposed by the blockading nations. These social dynamics further fueled divisions and created rifts among Gulf citizens, exacerbating the overall sense of disunity within the Gulf region.

In terms of security, the Qatar Crisis had significant implications for Gulf regional dynamics, intensifying the underlying geopolitical rivalries and shifting the balance of power. The fracture within the region's security architecture was palpable, hindering the effective addressing of common security threats. The crisis also prompted Qatar to bolster its defense capabilities, deepening military ties with countries outside the Gulf region. It enhanced its security cooperation with Turkey, signing agreements for military training and defense equipment procurement. This shift in security alliances, coupled with the perceived threat perception among various Gulf states, further heightened insecurity and distrust within the region, impairing regional cooperation and stability.

Overall, the Qatar Crisis acted as a catalyst for a major shift in Gulf regional dynamics, unraveling deep-seated fault lines and complexities among the Gulf states. The impact of the crisis on political, economic, social, and security dimensions resulted in a divergence of interests, decreased trust, and hindered cooperation among Gulf nations. Navigating these complex interplays and finding avenues for reconciliation and unity poses a daunting challenge for the future of the Gulf region. Addressing the underlying issues that led to the crisis, fostering dialogue, and nurturing a renewed sense of shared purpose and mutual respect becomes imperative in rebuilding Gulf regional dynamics. Only then can the Gulf states embark on a path towards sustainable stability, prosperity, and genuine cooperation in the region.

E. Lessons learned and implications for the future of Gulf unity

The Qatar Crisis of 2017-2020 served as a pivotal moment in understanding the complexities of Gulf ideological dynamics and its implications for unity within the region. It highlighted the fragility of Gulf unity and the potential for ideological differences to escalate into full-blown crises. Examining the lessons learned from this crisis allows us to delve deeper into the challenges and opportunities for future Gulf unity.

One of the key lessons from the Qatar Crisis is the need for effective communication and dialogue among Gulf states. Miscommunication and misunderstandings can quickly escalate tensions and lead to significant rifts. Developing mechanisms for regular and meaningful dialogue can help address grievances, clarify positions, and prevent misunderstandings from spiraling out of control. Initiating structured diplomatic efforts and open channels of communication, such as high-level summits and diplomatic exchanges, can foster understanding and cooperation among Gulf nations. These efforts can also be complemented by track II diplomacy, which involves engaging non-governmental actors, scholars, and experts to facilitate discussions and bridge ideological gaps.

Additionally, the Qatar Crisis shed light on the influence of external actors on Gulf unity. The involvement of regional and global powers exacerbated the crisis and complicated the resolution efforts. Gulf states must assert their autonomy and minimize external interference in their internal affairs to safeguard unity. This can be achieved through strategic alliances, diversification of diplomatic partnerships, and assertive diplomacy. By balancing relationships with multiple global and regional powers, Gulf nations can mitigate external pressures and maintain their sovereignty.

The crisis also underscored the importance of building trust and mutual respect among Gulf states. Suspicions, accusations, and lack of trust can hinder cooperation and unity. Addressing historical grievances and promoting reconciliation efforts can contribute to rebuilding trust and strengthening relationships within the Gulf region. Formal apologies, reparations for damages, and truth and reconciliation commissions can be instrumental in acknowledging past wrongdoings and fostering a culture of forgiveness and understanding. Encouraging cultural exchanges, promoting common heritage, and facilitating people-to-people diplomacy can also play a significant role in bridging ideological gaps and nurturing a sense of shared identity among Gulf nationals.

Furthermore, the Qatar Crisis highlighted the need for greater inclusivity and engagement within Gulf societies. Acknowledging and addressing societal divisions, including political, social, and economic disparities, is crucial for building a unified Gulf. Enhancing citizen participation, empowering marginalized groups, and promoting inclusivity in decision-making processes can help foster a collective sense of ownership and commitment to Gulf unity. Gulf states should focus on promoting inclusive policies, ensuring fair distribution of resources, and providing equal opportunities for all citizens. The establishment of diversified economies that prioritize sustainable development, innovation, and job creation can reduce social and economic disparities, foster regional stability, and contribute to long-term unity.

Moving forward, Gulf states should prioritize the diversification of their economies and reduce dependency on oil. Economic diversification not only strengthens resilience to external shocks but also fosters greater interdependence and shared interests among Gulf countries. Collaborative economic initiatives, such as free trade agreements, investment partnerships, and joint ventures, can contribute to greater economic integration and, consequently, enhanced unity. Gulf nations can explore opportunities for diversification in sectors such as tourism, technology, renewable energy, manufacturing, and knowledge-based industries. Investing in education and research and development can also cultivate a skilled workforce and promote innovation, further boosting the region's economic diversification efforts.

In terms of security, the Qatar Crisis illustrated the importance of coordinated approaches to regional challenges. Gulf states must work together to address common security threats, including terrorism, extremism, and external aggression. Cooperation in intelligence-sharing, military capabilities, and joint defense mechanisms can help safeguard the region's security and promote unity. Establishing regional security frameworks, such as joint military drills, intelligence coordination centers, and collective defense pacts, can enhance trust, cooperation, and united responses to emerging security challenges. Gulf states can also collaborate in countering radical ideologies through educational initiatives, media campaigns, and religious dialogues to promote a shared understanding and rejection of extremism.

Moreover, the Qatar Crisis highlighted the urgency of capacity-building in conflict resolution within the Gulf region. By investing in the development of skilled diplomats and negotiators, Gulf states can enhance their ability to effectively manage future disputes and prevent them from escalating into full-scale crises. This can be achieved through the establishment of training programs, educational exchanges, and research centers focused on conflict resolution and diplomatic strategies. Equipping Gulf diplomats with the necessary skills, knowledge, and experiences in mediation, negotiation, and strategic communication can contribute to a more peaceful and united Gulf.

The lessons learned from the Qatar Crisis provide an opportunity for Gulf states to reassess their ideological dynamics and reshape their approach to unity. It requires a collective commitment to overcome divisions, prioritize dialogue and diplomacy, and embrace shared goals and values. While challenges remain, the potential benefits of a united Gulf outweigh the obstacles. By learning from past experiences, engaging in genuine dialogue, and prioritizing the interests of their people, Gulf nations can pave the way for a more stable, prosperous, and united future. The journey towards Gulf unity is a continuous process that demands the dedication and perseverance of all Gulf nations, their leaders, and their citizens.

F. Landmarks

The Gulf region has long been a hub of diverse ideologies that have shaped its political, social, and cultural landscape. This chapter delves deeper into the complexities and historical development of Gulf ideological dynamics, exploring the key ideologies and their impacts on the region.

1. The Rise of Islamic Fundamentalism in the Gulf

One of the most significant ideologies that emerged in the Gulf is Islamic fundamentalism. This ideology gained prominence during the aftermath of the Iranian Revolution in 1979, which led to a wave of political Islam across the region. Islamic fundamentalism, often associated with Salafism and Wahhabism, emphasizes a return to the Islamic principles as defined in the Holy Quran and the Hadiths (sayings and actions of the Prophet Muhammad). It advocates for the establishment of an Islamic state governed by Shari'a law.

Saudi Arabia, the birthplace of Wahhabism, has played a central role in promoting and exporting this ideology throughout the Gulf region. The Saudi state has supported the construction of mosques, madrasas (religious schools), and publishing houses that propagate Wahhabi teachings. The influence of Islamic fundamentalism is particularly evident in the Saudi education system, where a strict interpretation of Islam is taught. This approach, combined with the Saudi state's financial support, has furthered the spread of this ideology, contributing to a conservative and socially rigid environment in the Gulf. It has also resulted in the exportation of this ideology and the funding of extremist groups in other parts of the Muslim world, leading to regional and international security concerns.

2. Gulf Nationalism and Pan-Arabism

Gulf nationalism and pan-Arabism also hold significance in the region's ideological landscape. Gulf nationalism emerged in the early 20th century as a response to foreign domination and the desire for independence. These nationalist movements sought to promote a collective Gulf Arab identity, emphasizing common cultural, linguistic, and historical ties. Nationalism played a crucial role during the decolonization period, leading to the formation of independent Gulf states. However, Gulf nationalism has not developed into a strong pan-Gulf movement, and each Gulf state maintains its distinct national identity and interests.

Pan-Arabism, on the other hand, advocates for the unification of all Arab nations into a single Arab state. It gained momentum in the mid-20th century, inspired by leaders like Egypt's Gamal Abdel Nasser. Although Gulf Arab states did not fully embrace pan-Arabism, they maintained close relations with other Arab countries based on shared interests, cultural affinities, and the desire for regional unity. However, the failed attempts at achieving pan-Arabism and the subsequent rise of Gulf nationalism have diminished the influence of this ideology in the Gulf region.

3. Secularism and Western Influence

Secularism is another ideological force in the Gulf region, advocating for the separation of religion and state. While Gulf states have predominantly adopted Islamic principles as the basis of their legal systems, secularism has gained some traction among intellectual circles and liberal-minded individuals. The call for secularism often arises from a desire to balance religious tenets with modern governance principles, human rights, and individual freedoms. However, the broader Gulf society remains deeply rooted in religious traditions and cultures, posing challenges to the widespread acceptance and integration of secularist ideas.

Western influence has also played a significant role in shaping Gulf ideologies. The discovery of vast oil reserves in the region created economic ties with the West, leading to the importation of Western culture, education, and ideas. Western concepts of democracy, human rights, and individual freedoms have exerted a transformative influence, challenging traditional Gulf societal norms. This clash between Western and traditional values has resulted in a complex ideological landscape and ongoing tensions within the region. While Gulf states have adopted certain aspects of Western governance models, they have often done so selectively, aiming to preserve the dominance of ruling families and maintain socio-political stability.

4. Regional and Sectarian Tensions

The Gulf region is also marked by regional and sectarian tensions, which intersect with ideological dynamics. One of the most significant regional rivalries is between Saudi Arabia and Iran, often referred to as the "Cold War of the Middle East." Saudi Arabia, as the bastion of Sunni Islam, and Iran, as the leading Shi'a power, have engaged in proxy wars and ideological battles across the region. These tensions are rooted in both political and theological differences and are often fueled by competition for regional influence.

The sectarian dimension of Gulf ideological dynamics is significant. While the majority of the Gulf population adheres to Sunni Islam, there are sizeable Shi'a Muslim communities, particularly in Bahrain, Saudi Arabia's Eastern Province, and Kuwait. These sectarian divisions have historically been exploited by regional powers, exacerbating tensions and fueling ideological clashes. The Arab uprisings that swept the region in 2011 further highlighted these sectarian divisions, as Sunni-Shi'a conflicts emerged within and across Gulf states.

In addition to sectarianism, tribal affiliations and regional divisions within Gulf countries further complicate the ideological dynamics. Historical rivalries and power struggles between tribes and regions have influenced political and ideological alignments. For instance, in countries like Oman and the United Arab Emirates, tribal identities and their historic roles in shaping political structures have been instrumental in balancing power and maintaining stability. These dynamics shape the ideological landscape by influencing alliances, political decision-making, and social dynamics.

In summary

Gulf ideological dynamics are the product of a complex interplay of historical, political, religious, and societal factors. Islamic fundamentalism, Gulf nationalism, pan-Arabism, secularism, Western influence, regional tensions, sectarianism, and tribal affiliations all shape and redefine the ideological landscape across the Gulf region. Understanding these ideologies and their impacts is essential for comprehending the region's political developments, social dynamics, and cultural transformations. Through analyzing these ideological dynamics, one can gain insights into the challenges and opportunities that lie ahead for the Gulf region. The constant interaction and evolution of these ideologies will continue to shape the Gulf's future, as its societies grapple with the tensions and complexities of a rapidly changing globalized world.

HISTORICAL AND CULTURAL FACTORS SHAPING GULF IDENTITIES

Historical and cultural factors have played a pivotal role in shaping the identities of the Gulf region. The Gulf countries have a rich and diverse history that has shaped their present-day societies, values, and beliefs. Understanding these historical legacies is key to comprehending the complexities of Gulf identities and the factors influencing Gulf ideological dynamics.

The Gulf region's history can be traced back thousands of years and encompasses the rise and fall of various civilizations. Mesopotamia, known as the "Cradle of Civilization," left its mark on the region with its advanced agricultural practices, trade networks, and system of governance. The remnants of these ancient civilizations, such as archaeological sites and artifacts, continue to be a testament to Gulf's roots.

The arrival of Islam in the Gulf region during the 7th century brought profound changes to the societies and cultures of the region. Islam not only provided a new religious framework but also influenced all aspects of life, including governance, law, education, and social norms. The spread of Islamic civilization in the region led to the emergence of Arab-Islamic identity, as well as the development of Arabic as the predominant language and Islam as the primary religion.

Throughout history, the Gulf region has been a crossroads of trade and commerce. Its strategic location on major trade routes, such as the Silk Road, made it a melting pot of cultures and influenced the development of Gulf identities. Trade facilitated the exchange of goods, ideas, and traditions, leading to a vibrant cultural exchange between the Gulf countries and other regions. This continuous interaction with different cultures enriched the social fabric of the Gulf, contributing to its cultural diversity.

The region's history also witnessed the rise and fall of major empires that left an indelible mark on Gulf identities. The Persian Achaemenids, led by Cyrus the Great, established a vast empire that encompassed the Gulf region. Their influence can be seen in the ancient ruins of Persepolis, which demonstrate their architectural and artistic achievements. The Hellenistic Seleucids, who followed the Achaemenids, introduced Greek culture and language to the region.

The arrival of the Islamic caliphates and the rise of the Arab empire in the 7th century significantly impacted Gulf identities. The Umayyad and Abbasid caliphates, with their centers in Damascus and Baghdad, respectively, brought significant political, cultural, and scientific advancements to the Gulf region. Trade flourished under their rule, connecting the Gulf with the wider Islamic world and beyond.

In the 16th century, the region fell under the control of the powerful Ottoman Empire. The Ottomans ruled over the Gulf for several centuries, leaving a lasting impact on the cultural, social, and architectural aspects of the region. The Ottoman legacy can be seen in the traditional Gulf architecture, local dialects, customs, and food.

In the 19th and 20th centuries, the Gulf region underwent significant changes due to the increasing influence of Western powers. The British Empire, in particular, established a presence in the Gulf region to protect its interests in trade and oil. The establishment of British protectorates in the region ensured stability and provided opportunities for economic development. The British influence led to the emergence of modern transportation networks, the introduction of Western education systems, and the establishment of political structures under British supervision.

The discovery of oil in the Gulf region in the early 20th century transformed the region's societies and identities. The newfound wealth from oil revenues allowed the Gulf countries to invest in infrastructure, education, healthcare, and social welfare programs. This economic boom led to rapid modernization, urbanization, and a shift from traditional lifestyles to a more cosmopolitan way of living. These changes sparked debates about maintaining cultural heritage while embracing progress and modernity.

Cultural diversity is a fundamental aspect of Gulf identities. In addition to the Arab population, the Gulf region is home to various ethnic groups and immigrant communities that have contributed to the cultural tapestry of the region. The influence of Persian, Indian, Pakistani, and East African communities, among others, can be seen in the Gulf's culinary traditions, language variations, and festivals. These intercultural exchanges have enriched the Gulf's social and cultural landscape.

In recent decades, Gulf societies have undergone significant transformations regarding gender roles and women's empowerment. Traditional gender norms, deeply rooted in cultural and religious traditions, have shaped Gulf societies for centuries. However, there has been an increasing push for gender equality and the inclusion of women in various aspects of public life. Efforts to enhance women's education, provide equal job opportunities, and promote women's rights have been made, leading to a gradual shift in gender dynamics and challenging traditional norms.

Moreover, identity formation in the Gulf region does not solely rest on historical and cultural factors but also extends to geopolitical events of the contemporary era. The Gulf has emerged as a vital player in regional and global affairs due to its strategic location, energy resources, and economic influence. The formation of the Gulf Cooperation Council (GCC) in 1981 brought together the Gulf countries to promote unity, collaboration, and economic integration. The GCC has served as a platform for fostering a collective identity reflective of the shared interests and aspirations among its member states.

The influx of migrant workers from various parts of the world has also shaped Gulf identities. These workers play significant roles in the region's economies, contributing to the construction, service, healthcare, and domestic sectors. Their presence has added another layer of diversity, with cultural exchanges occurring between the local population and expatriate communities. The interactions and experiences between locals and expatriates have given rise to hybrid identities, influenced by both the home cultures of the expatriates and the host culture of the Gulf region.

In summary, historical, geopolitical, and cultural factors have played intertwined roles in shaping the identities of the Gulf region. From ancient civilizations and empires to the influence of Islam and the advent of oil wealth, the Gulf's history is a complex tapestry of influences. The ongoing quest for unity, identity, and cultural preservation in the Gulf is a reflection of the region's rich historical legacy and its ability to embrace change while retaining its core values and traditions.

A. Historical legacies influencing Gulf identities

Throughout history, the Gulf region has been shaped by numerous historical events and influences that have left a lasting impact on the identities of its people. These historical legacies have played a crucial role in shaping the social, cultural, and political dynamics of Gulf societies. Understanding these influences is therefore essential in comprehending the complexities of Gulf identities.

One significant historical legacy in the Gulf region is the establishment and growth of trade routes. Stretching back thousands of years, the Gulf has been a hub for trade and commerce, attracting various civilizations and cultures. The ancient city of Dilmun, located in present-day Bahrain, was a key trading center, connecting Mesopotamia and the Indus Valley. The trade networks that flourished in the Gulf connected Asia, Africa, and Europe, facilitating the exchange of goods, ideas, and technologies. Luxuries such as spices, silk, and precious metals were transported through the Gulf, transforming it into a center of economic exchange and cultural interaction. This legacy of trade has not only brought economic prosperity but has also contributed to the cultural diversity of the Gulf.

Another pivotal historical legacy is the arrival of Islam in the region. With the advent of Islam in the 7th century, the Arabian Peninsula witnessed a unifying force that transcended tribal and ethnic boundaries. The spread of Islamic values and the establishment of Islamic empires, such as the Abbasids and the Umayyads, left an indelible mark on Gulf societies, shaping their religious and cultural identities. Islam provided a shared framework that influenced various aspects of Gulf life, including language, customs, and legal systems. The pilgrimage to Mecca, an essential pillar of Islam, has also been a unifying factor, forging connections among Muslims from different Gulf countries and reinforcing a collective Gulf identity grounded in their shared religious beliefs and practices.

Colonialism has also played a significant role in shaping Gulf identities. During the 19th and 20th centuries, European powers, particularly the British, exerted their influence across the

Gulf, establishing protectorates and exploiting the region's resources. This colonial experience left a lasting impact on the political, social, and economic structures of Gulf countries, as well as on their relationships with the outside world. The establishment of protectorates oversaw significant changes in governance structures and introduced elements of modern education, technology, and infrastructure. However, colonialism also resulted in the loss of authority for traditional rulers and the weakening of indigenous institutions. This legacy of colonialism fostered a complex relationship between Gulf societies and their colonial past, resulting in both resentment and the adoption of certain aspects of Western culture.

The discovery of oil in the Gulf region in the 20th century brought about a transformative legacy. As oil revenues surged, Gulf countries experienced rapid modernization and urbanization, leading to immense socio-cultural changes. The influx of wealth brought about by the oil industry enabled Gulf countries to invest heavily in infrastructure, education, healthcare, and social welfare services, significantly improving the quality of life for their citizens. The development of modern cities, such as Dubai and Doha, with their iconic towering skylines and luxurious amenities, became symbols of Gulf wealth and ambition. However, this newfound wealth also brought about economic dependencies and power dynamics, influencing the relationships between Gulf states and external actors. The quest for economic diversification and sustainability remains a central challenge for Gulf nations, as they seek to reduce their reliance on oil and create more resilient and diversified economies. Moreover, the development of oil-dependent economies has shaped the socio-economic dynamics within Gulf societies, creating disparities and challenges of resource management, as well as issues of wealth inequality and social cohesion.

Additionally, the Iran-Iraq War (1980-1988) and the Gulf War (1990-1991) have had a profound impact on Gulf identities. These conflicts, fueled by territorial disputes and political rivalries, highlighted the fragility of regional security and sparked a sense of unity and solidarity among the Gulf states. The experiences of these wars and external threats further entrenched the sense of collective identity and a shared desire for stability and security. The Gulf Cooperation Council (GCC) was established in 1981 as a political and economic alliance, aimed at fostering cooperation and ensuring regional security. The GCC has contributed to the strengthening of Gulf identities by providing a platform for shared decision-making and collective action, emphasizing the notion of Gulf unity in the face of external challenges.

Furthermore, the historical legacies in the Gulf region have also influenced the social fabric and cultural practices of its societies. Traditional Bedouin values of hospitality, honor, and kinship continue to shape Gulf social interactions, even as urbanization and modernization bring about new social dynamics. Family and community remain central to Gulf identities, with strong ties to kinship networks and a sense of collective responsibility. Indigenous arts, such as calligraphy, poetry, and storytelling, have been preserved through generations and are valued as expressions of cultural heritage. Festivals, such as the Qatari Spring Festival and the Emirati Al Dhafra Festival, provide opportunities for people to gather and celebrate their shared traditions, fostering a sense of collective identity.

In conclusion, historical legacies have played a pivotal role in shaping Gulf identities. The trade routes, the advent of Islam, colonialism, the discovery of oil, and regional conflicts have all contributed to the rich tapestry of Gulf identities. The Gulf's history is a complex interplay of economic, cultural, religious, and political factors. Understanding the deep-rooted historical influences enables us to appreciate the forces that have shaped the Gulf region and continue to impact its societies. By delving into these legacies, we gain a deeper understanding of the complexities and dynamics of Gulf societies today, allowing us to approach the topic of Gulf identities with greater depth and nuance.

B. Cultural diversity and its impact on Gulf unity

Cultural diversity in the Gulf region is a vast tapestry woven with intricate threads of history, heritage, and human connections. To truly appreciate the depth of this diversity, one must delve into the myriad of influences that have shaped the Gulf's mosaic of cultures.

From the earliest civilizations, the Gulf region has been a crossroads of trade, connecting Asia, Africa, and Europe. The ancient civilizations of Mesopotamia, Dilmun, and Magan flourished along the coastal regions of present-day Kuwait, Bahrain, and Oman respectively, acting as cultural conduits with far-reaching impacts. These early interactions left an indelible mark on the region, with archaeological sites and artifacts unveiling a rich tapestry of customs, religious beliefs, and artistic expressions that have endured through the ages.

As time progressed, the Gulf continued to be a magnet for various waves of migration, fostering cultural syntheses and exchanges. The arrival of Arab tribes expanded the region's linguistic and cultural landscape, contributing to the spread and dominance of Arabic as the primary language. Meanwhile, Persian influences through the Sassanian Empire and later the Safavid dynasty infused the region with Persian language, literature, and artistic traditions, particularly in Bahrain, Qatar, and the eastern shores of Saudi Arabia.

It is impossible to ignore the profound impact of Islam on cultural diversity in the Gulf. The advent of Islam in the 7th century brought with it a unifying force, establishing Arabic as the language of the Quran and nurturing a shared religious identity. However, within the framework of Islam, various sects and schools of thought emerged, leading to further diversity in religious practices and interpretations across the Gulf. The Sunni-Shia divide, while often highlighted for the tensions it has engendered, has also enriched the region's cultural fabric, resulting in distinctive rituals, customs, and ways of life.

Gulf societies have also been shaped by the African diaspora, which dates back to the era of the Indian Ocean slave trade. Africans, primarily from East Africa, were brought to the Gulf as traders, laborers, and servants, leaving an indelible mark on the cultural heritage of the region. Music, dance, spirituality, and cuisine in coastal areas of Oman, the United Arab Emirates, and Qatar bear echoes of African influence, celebrated through traditional performances, unique rhythms, and flavorsome dishes.

The trail of cultural diversity in the Gulf extends further with the arrival of migrant communities from South Asia, Southeast Asia, and beyond. Indian, Pakistani, Bangladeshi, Filipino, Indonesian, and other nationalities have brought their languages, religions, customs, and traditions, enriching the region's culinary delights, festivals, and religious observances. This convergence of cultures can be witnessed in the bustling streets of Dubai or Doha, where the sights, sounds, and flavors reflect a tapestry woven from different corners of the globe.

Furthermore, the Gulf's indigenous communities, particularly the Bedouin tribes, contribute significantly to the region's cultural diversity. The Bedouin way of life, rooted in the harsh desert environment, shaped a unique set of customs, values, and skills that have endured over generations. Their intimate knowledge of survival and navigation in the desert, their hospitality rituals, and the craftsmanship evident in their traditional attire, such as the intricately embroidered thobes and the striking headgear, showcase the preserved heritage of these indigenous communities.

It is essential to recognize that the cultural diversity in the Gulf is not solely shaped by external influences; it is also nurtured and safeguarded by Gulf societies themselves. Families, communities, and institutions play a vital role in transmitting cultural practices and values from one generation to the next. Traditional art forms, such as calligraphy, music, dance, and storytelling, thrive through the tireless efforts of dedicated practitioners and institutions that ensure their preservation and promotion.

However, as with any multicultural society, challenges and tensions do exist. Economic disparities, social divisions, and sometimes deep-rooted prejudices can hinder the full realization of embracing cultural diversity. Nationality-based systems, differing labor rights, and unequal access to opportunities can create gaps that impede the unity and inclusivity that cultural diversity can foster.

To bridge these divides, Gulf nations have begun to undertake initiatives aimed at promoting social cohesion and equal rights. Educational reforms that emphasize multicultural education and fostering intercultural understanding can play a crucial role in fostering greater acceptance and empathy among diverse communities. Encouraging the preservation and dissemination of local languages and cultural practices, alongside supporting migrant integration and providing equal opportunities, can help reconstruct the bridges between different communities.

Moreover, cultural diplomacy, exchange programs, and festivals that celebrate the region's diversity can foster mutual understanding and appreciation among Gulf societies. The establishment of cultural institutions, museums, and community centers that serve as spaces for dialogue and engagement can further bridge the gap between diverse cultural backgrounds and promote a sense of belonging for all residents.

In conclusion, the Gulf region's cultural diversity is an intricate tapestry woven with historical legacies, transnational connections, and indigenous practices. From ancient civilizations to present-day migrations, the exchange of ideas and traditions has shaped the region's cultural mosaic. While challenges persist, recognizing and embracing this diversity can contribute to a more inclusive, harmonious, and culturally vibrant Gulf. By fostering social integration, promoting equal opportunities, and celebrating shared heritages, the Gulf can transform its cultural diversity into a powerful force that strengthens the unity and resilience of its societies.

C. Role of religion in shaping Gulf identities

Religion plays a crucial and multifaceted role in shaping the identities of individuals and communities in the Gulf region. With Islam being the dominant religion in the Gulf countries, its influence extends across social, political, and cultural domains. This extended chapter will delve deeper into the significant role religion plays in shaping Gulf identities, exploring various dimensions and contexts.

- Islam as the Dominant Religion:

Islam permeates every aspect of life in the Gulf, providing a shared religious foundation and shaping the collective identity of Gulf societies. The overwhelming majority of Gulf nationals are Muslims, and their adherence to Islamic principles creates a strong sense of unity and shared values. The centrality of Islam in everyday life manifests in various forms, from daily prayers to religious festivals, and from social attitudes to political ideologies.

Within Islam, there are different schools of thought and interpretations, which can influence the religious identity of individuals. For example, the Sunni and Shia branches of Islam have distinct practices and beliefs, and these differences can shape the religious identity and sense of belonging of individuals within the Gulf region.

- Islamic Law and Governance:

Sharia law, derived from Islamic principles, has a profound impact on governance systems in the Gulf countries. Islamic teachings influence legal frameworks, social policies, and even economic practices. While the degree of implementation may vary across countries, the integration of religious laws into governance reflects the deep-rooted connection between religion and identity in the Gulf. This influence is evident in family law, criminal justice, and societal norms that are often shaped by Islamic principles.

The Gulf countries have different approaches to the implementation of Sharia law. Some countries, like Saudi Arabia and Iran, strictly implement Sharia as the basis for their legal systems, while others incorporate Islamic principles to varying degrees. These variations in the application of Islamic law contribute to nuanced differences in the religious identities and cultural practices within the Gulf countries.

- Influence on Gender Roles and Relations:

Religion, particularly Islam, has a significant influence on gender roles and relations within Gulf societies. Traditional interpretations of Islamic teachings often define societal expectations, with distinct roles assigned to men and women. These expectations can be seen in areas such as family structure, education, employment opportunities, and dress codes.

However, it is important to note that gender roles and relations in the Gulf are not solely shaped by religion. There are diverse perspectives and ongoing discussions within Gulf societies about gender equality and the reinterpretation of religious texts to promote more equitable gender dynamics. The influence of religion on gender identity and relations, therefore, is subject to both traditional interpretations and evolving understandings of gender equality within the context of Islamic teachings.

- Religious Education and Institutions:

Religious education plays a crucial role in shaping Gulf identities, as it instills religious values, rituals, and traditions from an early age. Islamic institutes, schools, and religious scholars contribute to the preservation and promotion of religious teachings, fostering a deep understanding of Islamic beliefs and practices. Religious institutions serve as a platform for transmitting religious knowledge, fostering a sense of belonging, and shaping individual and communal identities.

In addition to formal religious education, there is also a proliferation of religious programming and content through various media channels, including television, radio, and the internet. This exposure to religious teachings outside of formal education further contributes to the shaping of religious identities in the Gulf region.

- Religious Practices and Rituals:

Religious practices and rituals play a central role in shaping Gulf identities, as they provide a framework for worship, connection, and community cohesion. From daily prayers to fasting during Ramadan, Islamic practices are deeply ingrained in the lives of Gulf Muslims. The observance of religious rituals strengthens the religious identity of individuals and reinforces the shared cultural and communal aspects of Gulf societies.

Religious practices in the Gulf region are not limited to individual acts of worship but also include collective rituals such as Friday prayers at mosques and the annual Islamic Hajj pilgrimage to Mecca. These communal practices provide opportunities for religious reflection, strengthening the sense of religious identity and the connection between individuals and their communities.

- Interfaith Relations and Religious Pluralism:

While Islam is the dominant religion in the Gulf, there are also diverse expatriate communities representing various faiths. Interfaith dialogue and relations among different religious communities contribute to a broader understanding of religious diversity. The coexistence of multiple religions in the Gulf fosters discussions on religious pluralism, tolerance, and acceptance, shaping the identities of both locals and expatriates in the region.

Religious pluralism in the Gulf has gained attention and recognition in recent years, with efforts aimed at promoting dialogue and understanding between different religious communities. Various initiatives, such as interfaith conferences, forums, and cultural events, are organized to encourage dialogue and foster a sense of religious coexistence and mutual respect.

- Challenges and Debates:

Religion in the Gulf region is not without its challenges and debates. The interpretation, application, and role of religion in society often spark discussions and disagreements. These debates contribute to ongoing conversations on identity formation, modernization, and social change within Gulf societies. Issues such as religious conservatism, the rise of extremism, and the balance between religious values and global influences continue to shape the religious dynamics and subsequent identities in the Gulf.

The influence of religious ideologies and conservative interpretations can sometimes lead to tensions within the Gulf societies, particularly in the face of globalization and the increasing exposure to diverse cultural and religious influences. These tensions give rise to debates about the intersection of religion, identity, and individual freedoms, highlighting the complexities and ongoing negotiations surrounding religious identity in the Gulf.

In conclusion, religion, particularly Islam, plays a multifaceted role in shaping Gulf identities. It influences various aspects of social, political, and cultural life, providing a shared foundation and a strong sense of belonging among Gulf nationals. Understanding the intricate interplay of religion and identity formation is essential for comprehending the complexities of the Gulf region and its ongoing ideological dynamics.

D. Social norms and values in Gulf societies

Understanding the social norms and values prevalent in Gulf societies is crucial to gaining insights into the unique dynamics of the region. These norms and values are deeply ingrained in the social fabric and significantly influence the behavior and perceptions of individuals in Gulf countries. In this section, we will explore the key social norms and values that shape Gulf societies, shedding light on their significance and impact.

- **Importance of Social Norms**: Social norms are an integral part of Gulf societies as they provide a framework for behavior and interactions. These norms are often rooted in religious and cultural beliefs, serving as guidelines for moral conduct and interpersonal relationships. They are seen as essential in maintaining social order, preserving cultural traditions, and upholding moral and ethical values. Adhering to social norms helps create a harmonious society where individuals understand and respect each other, facilitating smoother interactions and stronger social cohesion.

- **Family and Community Bonds:** The importance placed on family and community ties in Gulf societies cannot be overstated. Family is regarded as the nucleus of society, and maintaining strong relationships with family members is highly valued. Respect, loyalty, and support towards one's family are deeply ingrained values. Extended families often live in close proximity to each other, fostering a sense of unity and collective responsibility. Regular family gatherings and celebrations, such as weddings and Eid holidays, serve as opportunities to strengthen familial bonds and highlight the significance of kinship. Similarly, community values are highly cherished in Gulf societies. The concept of community extends beyond family to include neighbors, friends, and colleagues. Social gatherings, such as diwaniyas, majlis, and iftars, are commonplace events where people come together to discuss various topics, strengthen relationships, and contribute to community welfare. The support and involvement of community members in both joyful and challenging times demonstrate the strong sense of solidarity and interdependence.

- **Gender Roles and Social Hierarchy:** Gulf societies have traditionally been patriarchal, with distinct gender roles and expectations. Men have historically been considered the primary providers and decision-makers, while women have played crucial roles as caregivers and homemakers. However, there has been a significant shift in recent years, particularly in urban areas, with women entering the workforce and gaining more agency in decision-making processes. Efforts have been made to enhance women's empowerment through educational opportunities, employment rights, and legislation promoting gender equality. Despite progress, certain traditional gender roles and expectations persist, especially in more conservative and rural communities. Social hierarchy is another aspect that shapes Gulf societies. Social position is often determined by

factors such as age, tribal affiliations, and social status. Respect for authority, particularly towards older
individuals and those in positions of power, is highly
valued. The concept of "wasta," which refers to the
use of personal connections and influential contacts,
is also deeply entrenched in Gulf societies. It plays a
role in various aspects of life, including business trans-
actions, employment opportunities, and bureaucratic
processes. While the use of wasta can sometimes be
controversial, it is regarded as a means of navigating social hierarchies and establishing connections that can
benefit individuals and their communities.

- **Hospitality and Generosity:** Hospitality is a revered
  value deeply embedded in Gulf societies. It is regarded
  as a cultural and religious obligation to welcome guests
  with warmth and generosity. The concept of "shee-
  lah" encapsulates this exemplary hospitality. Guests are
  treated with utmost respect and care, often provided with accommodations, meals, and entertainment.
  It is not uncommon for hosts to go above and beyond to make visitors feel comfortable and valued.
  This tradition reflects the values of kindness, generosity, and the importance placed on social connectedness.
  Beyond personal hospitality, community-wide acts of
  generosity and charity are prominent facets of Gulf
  societies. Philanthropy and charitable giving, often associated with the concept of "zakat" (giving alms), are
  heavily emphasized and practiced. Wealthy individu-

als and organizations regularly contribute towards social welfare initiatives, educational development, and healthcare advancements, promoting the principles of compassion, solidarity, and taking care of those in need. These acts of generosity strengthen community bonds, uplift disadvantaged segments of society, and provide opportunities for societal progress.

- **Modesty and Conservatism**: Gulf societies, while evolving, often maintain a strong emphasis on modesty and conservatism, particularly regarding dress and behavior. The cultural attire of Gulf nationals, such as the abaya for women and dishdasha for men, symbolizes cultural identity and adherence to religious beliefs. However, it is important to note that dress codes and levels of conservativeness may vary across Gulf countries and communities. In public settings, individuals are expected to dress modestly, avoiding clothing that may be perceived as provocative or overly revealing. PDA (public displays of affection) and behavior deemed as inappropriate are generally frowned upon, as they are seen as contradicting the values of modesty and conservativeness. Similarly, the consumption of alcohol, particularly in public spaces, is restricted due to religious and cultural beliefs. The adherence to modesty and conservative norms is seen as promoting moral integrity and upholding societal values.

- **Religiosity and Islamic Influence:** Religion, particularly Islam, has a profound influence on the social norms and values in Gulf societies. Islamic principles guide various aspects of daily life, including ethical conduct, family life, decision-making processes, and governance. Mosques and religious institutions are central to the fabric of Gulf societies, acting as spiritual and community centers where individuals come together to pray, seek guidance, and connect with their faith. Islamic festivals and rituals hold immense significance in Gulf societies. Celebrations such as Ramadan, the holy month of fasting, and Eid al-Fitr, marking the end of Ramadan, are observed with great enthusiasm and unity. These occasions foster a sense of spirituality, self-reflection, and community bonding. Additionally, the Hajj pilgrimage, one of the Five Pillars of Islam, is considered a pinnacle of devotion and a transformative experience for those who undertake it. The religious teachings and practices of Islam, including acts of charity, kindness, and compassion, permeate daily life, reinforcing the values of righteousness and building a strong moral foundation.

Understanding the social norms and values in Gulf societies provides valuable insights into the cultural foundations of the region. While there is diversity across Gulf countries, these shared norms and values contribute to the sense of identity and cohesion among Gulf nationals. Recognizing and navigating these dynamics is essential for fostering dialogue, understanding, and unity among Gulf societies and beyond.

E. Landmarks

The Gulf States, encompassing Bahrain, Kuwait, Oman, Qatar, Saudi Arabia, and the United Arab Emirates (UAE), are renowned for their distinctive blend of tradition and modernity. In addition to their economic prowess and political influence, these states exhibit intricate ideological dynamics that significantly shape their domestic and foreign policies. This section delves deeper into the nuanced ideological landscape within the Gulf region and explores the complex interplay between religion, nationalism, sectarianism, and political Islam.

- *Historical Context*

To gain a comprehensive understanding of the ideological dynamics of the Gulf States, it is crucial to delve into their historical context. The formation of these states was greatly influenced by factors such as tribal affiliations, regional identity, and religious sects. For instance, in Saudi Arabia, the rise of the House of Saud, a conservative Wahhabi dynasty, transformed Saudi society into a stronghold of Sunni Islam. This close association between the Saudi monarchy and ultraconservative Wahhabi interpretations of Islam shaped not only domestic policies but also the kingdom's global religious influence. Similarly, Bahrain and Kuwait have historically experienced tensions between their Sunni ruling elites and marginalized Shia populations, with the latter often facing discrimination and political marginalization.

- *Religious Charisma and Sunni Extremism*

Religion, particularly Sunni Islam, plays a central role in shaping the ideological landscape of the Gulf. Saudi Arabia, as the custodian of Islam's two holiest sites, Mecca and Medina, wields religious authority that extends beyond its borders. The religious legitimacy of the Saudi monarchy, intertwined with ultraconservative Wahhabi interpretations of Islam, has contributed to the emergence and spread of Salafist ideology. This ideology ranges from forms that advocate for a strict adherence to Islam's early practices to more extreme variations that promote violence and terrorism. The spread of these extremist interpretations, especially through education systems and religious networks, has posed both domestic and international challenges, with certain Salafist groups becoming sources of radicalization and terrorist recruitment.

- *Political Islam and the Muslim Brotherhood*

Another noteworthy dimension of ideological dynamics in the Gulf revolves around political Islam, particularly the influence of the Muslim Brotherhood. Across the Gulf States, different branches of the Muslim Brotherhood have sought to challenge the legitimacy of ruling regimes by advocating for political reform, social justice, and the application of Islamic principles in governance. The level of acceptance or repression towards the Muslim Brotherhood varies among the Gulf States, with some governments accommodating limited participation while others outrightly suppress their activities. This ideological competition has had a significant impact on the political environment within the region, with governments attempting to navigate competing Islamist and secular ideologies while retaining control.

- *Sectarianism and Regional Rivalries*

Sectarianism, particularly the Shia-Sunni divide, represents a critical factor influencing the ideological dynamics of the Gulf States. Bahrain, with its Shia-majority population ruled by a Sunni monarchy, has experienced persistent sectarian tensions, occasionally resulting in protests and violence. The security dilemma between Saudi Arabia, as the leader of the Sunni bloc, and Iran, as a champion of Shia causes, has amplified sectarian fault lines in the region. Iran's revolutionary ideology, rooted in Shia Islam, has heightened sectarian rivalries, leading to proxy conflicts in countries such as Syria, Yemen, and Lebanon. As a result, sectarianism has become a significant factor that shapes the ideological landscape and influences regional geopolitics.

- *Nationalism and Identity Politics*

Ideological dynamics in the Gulf are also influenced by nationalism and identity politics. While the ruling families emphasize Arab and Islamic identity to maintain legitimacy and regional influence, subnational identities based on tribal, regional, and ethnic affiliations persist. In Oman, the notion of Omanism, which emphasizes Omani identity and historical traditions, coexists with broader Gulf Arab nationalism. The United Arab Emirates, composed of seven distinct Emirates with varying historical backgrounds, has aimed to foster a shared Emirati national identity through state-led initiatives. Similarly, Qatar has cultivated a strong national identity, projecting its influence globally through its media outlets and proactive diplomacy. These multiple identities within the Gulf States contribute to a nuanced and complex ideological landscape.

• *Social Movements and Civil Society*

Despite the generally autocratic rule in the Gulf States, social movements and civil society organizations have emerged as spaces for ideological contestation. From labor movements demanding better working conditions and protection of worker's rights to youth-led movements calling for political reforms and societal change, these grassroots initiatives challenge the status quo and advocate for diverse ideological perspectives. However, the ruling regimes often respond with varying degrees of repression, aiming to maintain control over the ideological narrative and prevent challenges to their authority.

Conclusion

Understanding the deep-rooted ideological dynamics of the Gulf States is integral to comprehending their domestic affairs, foreign policies, and regional dynamics. The interplay between religion, nationalism, sectarianism, and political Islam shapes the region's political discourse and influences its complex relationship with both internal and external actors. The Gulf States must navigate these ideologies' intricacies and challenges as they strive to balance domestic stability, regional rivalries, and their positioning in the global order.

GEOPOLITICAL RIVALRIES AND ALLIANCES IN THE GULF REGION

Geopolitical rivalries and alliances have played a significant role in shaping the dynamics of the Gulf region. The Gulf states have experienced various tensions and conflicts throughout history due to their positioning between major global powers. Understanding the complexity of these rivalries and alliances is crucial in comprehending the ideological landscape of the Gulf.

Historical Context of Geopolitical Rivalries:

The history of rivalries in the Gulf region can be traced back centuries. From the early days of Islamic empires to the Ottoman Empire's expansion, external powers sought to control the strategic waterways and resources of the Gulf. These ambitions often clashed with the interests of local rulers, leading to conflicts and tensions.

During the 19th century, the British Empire's influence in the Gulf became particularly significant. Driven by geostrategic and economic motives, the British established protectorates and influence over Gulf territories, ensuring control over the vital maritime routes. This presence influenced the Gulf's development course and set the stage for future geopolitical rivalries and alliances.

B. Gulf States' Alliance

The Gulf states have formed various alliances throughout history in response to external pressures and internal challenges. These alliances primarily aim to counter perceived threats, protect shared interests, and promote regional stability. The most notable alliance is the Gulf Cooperation Council (GCC), formed in 1981, which includes Bahrain, Kuwait, Oman, Qatar, Saudi Arabia, and the United Arab Emirates (UAE).

The GCC is a platform for economic cooperation, security coordination, and collective decision-making among its member states. It has played a significant role in fostering unity and addressing common challenges in the Gulf. Additionally, Gulf states have engaged in bilateral alliances with external powers like the United States, often focusing on security cooperation or economic partnerships.

C. Impact of Alliances on Gulf Unity

While alliances have been established to enhance security co-operation and bolster the region's collective strength, they have also created divisions and fractures among the Gulf states. Diverse geopolitical alignments, varying priorities, and capacity building have made it challenging to achieve unified positions on ideological fronts.

For instance, differences in political systems, religious sects, and regional objectives have sometimes strained intra-Gulf relations. The ongoing Qatar blockade, primarily led by Saudi Arabia, Bahrain, and the UAE, showcases the fragility of Gulf unity. While the embargo was motivated by concerns related to Qatar's foreign policies and alleged support for certain groups, it highlighted the divisions within the Gulf and the limitations of regional alliances.

Moreover, historical rivalries and disputes, such as the long-standing Iran-Saudi Arabia rivalry, have further complicated Gulf unity. The ideological and sectarian differences between Shia-majority Iran and Sunni-majority Gulf states have fueled tensions, proxy conflicts, and geopolitical rivalries. These rivalries often spill over into regional conflicts, exacerbating divisions and hindering efforts to achieve a cohesive Gulf ideological landscape.

D. Role of External Powers in Shaping Gulf Dynamics

External powers have historically exercised influence in the Gulf region for economic, security, and geopolitical reasons. The United States, in particular, has been a significant player, aiming to protect its strategic interests, including access to oil and countering rival powers' influence, such as Iran. The US military presence in the Gulf, with bases in Qatar, Bahrain, and the UAE, has significantly shaped regional dynamics.

Russia, too, has sought to expand its influence in the Gulf region through diplomatic, economic, and military means. Moscow has cultivated relationships with various Gulf states, including Saudi Arabia and Iran, positioning itself as a key player in the region. Russia's involvement in the Syrian conflict and its military partnerships in the Gulf have further complicated the geopolitical landscape.

China's rise as a global power has also impacted Gulf dynamics. With its growing energy needs, Beijing has intensified its economic relations with Gulf states and invested heavily in infrastructure projects. This economic engagement has implications for the Gulf's geopolitical alignments and the balance of power among external actors. China's Belt and Road Initiative, which aims to enhance connectivity and trade links, has brought China closer to the Gulf, creating potential opportunities and challenges for regional powers.

The geopolitical maneuvers of external powers have ramifications for Gulf alliances and rivalries. As these external actors pursue their interests and seek favorable outcomes, Gulf states navigate a complex network of alliances and rivalries to protect their sovereignty and secure their national interests.

E. Implications of Rivalries and Alliances for Gulf Ideological Unity:

The existence of rivalries and alliances has had both positive and negative implications for Gulf ideological unity. Rivalries have often led to divisions, competition, and attempts at dominance, hindering the development of a fully unified Gulf ideological system.

On the other hand, alliances and cooperation on specific issues, such as security or economic development, have fostered limited convergence of ideologies among Gulf states. The GCC, despite its challenges, has facilitated dialogue and coordination on regional affairs, reinforcing common identities and fostering a sense of Gulf unity.

However, achieving a comprehensive and enduring Gulf ideological unity remains a complex task. The divergent interests of external powers, inconsistent regional priorities, and historical and cultural differences continue to shape the Gulf's ideological landscape.

Furthermore, the Gulf's geopolitical landscape is constantly evolving. Emerging challenges, such as climate change, economic diversification, and shifting global power dynamics, present new opportunities for Gulf states to redefine their alliances and foster a more cohesive ideological unity.

In conclusion, geopolitical rivalries and alliances have greatly influenced the Gulf region's ideological dynamics. The historical context of these rivalries, Gulf states' alliances, external power interference, and the impact on Gulf unity all contribute to the complex and delicate nature of ideological relationships in the region.

Understanding these dynamics is crucial for comprehending the prospects and challenges of achieving greater Gulf ideological unity. The interconnectedness of regional and global geopolitical interests highlights the importance of constructive dialogue, mutual understanding, and concerted efforts to forge a more cohesive ideological landscape in the Gulf.

A. Historical context of geopolitical rivalries

The Gulf region has a long and complex history of geopolitical rivalries that have shaped its dynamics and influenced the ideologies of the countries within it. A thorough understanding of the historical context is imperative to grasp the intricate nature of the current rivalries and their impact. This section will delve deeper into the historical factors that have molded the geopolitical landscape of the Gulf.

The roots of rivalries in the Gulf can be traced back to the 7th century when Islam emerged as a dominant religion in the region. The division between Sunni and Shia Islam, stemming from a dispute over the rightful successor to the Prophet Muhammad, became an enduring schism. This religious divide not only shaped the religious and social fabric of the Gulf but also influenced the political establishment in the region. Different branches of Islam aligned with different political entities, giving rise to competing ideologies and power struggles that continue to influence the Gulf today.

The Sunni-Shia divide took on a political dimension during the Umayyad and Abbasid caliphates. The Umayyads, who were seen as representing the political establishment, favored the Sunni interpretation of Islam while marginalizing the Shia community. Conversely, the Abbasids, who managed to over-

throw the Umayyads, sought support from the Shia population to solidify their political authority. This cycle of shifting
alliances and rivalries during the caliphate era laid the groundwork for the deep-rooted Sunni-Shia divide that persists in the
Gulf to this day.

Moving forward in history, the discovery of vast oil reserves
in the Gulf region in the early 20th century brought the international spotlight upon these small nations. These newfound resources made the Gulf countries crucial players in the
global energy market and attracted significant strategic interest
from major global powers. This heightened attention laid the
groundwork for geopolitical rivalries to take root in the region.

The Gulf's strategic location further magnified its importance. It became a gateway between Europe, Asia, and Africa,
making it a vital trade route. Global powers, including the
British, Portuguese, and Ottoman empires have historically
coveted the control and influence over this maritime passage.
The power dynamics among these imperial forces during the
19th and early 20th centuries contributed to the geopolitical
tensions in the region. The establishment of British protectorates and the division of territories among these powers further fueled rivalries and frictions in the Gulf region.

During the Cold War era, the Gulf region became a battleground for proxy conflicts between the United States and the
Soviet Union. As the United States aimed to secure its interests
and contain Soviet influence in the region, it aligned with various Gulf countries, particularly those aligned with Sunni Islam.
This alliance system deepened existing rivalries, as countries vied
for the support and protection of their respective patrons. It

effectively turned the Gulf into a geostrategic chessboard, where the rivalries between nations were played out under different ideological banners. These rivalries' consequences continue reverberating today, shaping the Gulf's ideological frictions.

The Iran-Iraq War (1980-1988) holds tremendous significance in understanding the contemporary geopolitical rivalries in the Gulf. This brutal conflict not only exacerbated the already existing Sunni-Shia divide but also intensified the competition for regional dominance between Iraq and Iran. Both countries sought to expand their spheres of influence, leading to heightened tensions and rivalries that persist to this day. The consequences of this war can be observed in countries like Bahrain, where the rivalry between Sunni Saudi Arabia and Shia Iran has had a substantial impact on the local dynamics.

More recently, the Arab Spring uprisings that swept across the region in 2011 brought about further shifts in the Gulf's geopolitical landscape. The uprisings, which resulted in the overthrow of several authoritarian regimes, challenged the existing power structures in the region. Gulf countries, particularly Saudi Arabia and Iran, perceived these events as opportunities to enhance their influence and protect their interests. This led to increased rivalry and proxy conflicts in countries like Syria and Yemen, deepening the already established regional divides.

The historical context of these geopolitical rivalries forms the backdrop against which the ideologies of the Gulf countries have emerged. The competition for power, influence, and resources has shaped the way these nations perceive and interact with one another. The historical legacy of rivalries has created a complex web of alliances, enmities, and conflicting ideologies that continue to impact regional stability, security, and development.

Throughout history, the Gulf countries have also experienced colonization and foreign domination. The presence of European powers, be it the Portuguese in Oman, the British in Bahrain, or the Dutch in Indonesia, influenced the political and economic landscapes of the region. Colonialism fostered rivalries among the local tribes and political entities as they sought to resist or accommodate the foreign powers. The struggle for independence and the subsequent establishment of nation-states further shaped geopolitical rivalries as different groups vied for power and control.

Moreover, the formation of organizations like the Gulf Cooperation Council (GCC) in 1981 added another layer to the regional rivalries. The GCC, comprising Bahrain, Kuwait, Oman, Qatar, Saudi Arabia, and the United Arab Emirates, sought to enhance cooperation and address common challenges the Gulf countries face. However, underlying power dynamics and divergent national interests have at times weakened the effectiveness and unity of the GCC, reinforcing existing rivalries and limiting coordinated efforts for a shared Gulf vision.

Another key element in understanding Gulf rivalries is the influence of non-state actors, including extremist and terrorist groups. The rise of organizations such as Al-Qaeda and the Islamic State (ISIS) has deeply impacted the region, exacerbating existing rivalries and creating further instability. These groups exploit local grievances, religious tensions, and power struggles, thereby deepening the divide along sectarian lines and challenging the stability and security of the Gulf countries.

In conclusion, the historical context of Gulf rivalries is a complex tapestry woven by centuries of religious schisms, geopolitical ambitions, colonialism, and the influence of non-state actors. The competition for power, influence, and resources has shaped the ideologies and interactions of the Gulf countries, leading to enduring rivalries that continue to impact regional dynamics. In the subsequent chapters, we will explore the specific rivalries in greater detail, analyzing their multifaceted nature and implications for Gulf ideological dynamics. We will also delve into potential pathways for unity amidst these rivalries, while also addressing the challenges that need to be overcome to achieve a more harmonious and cooperative future for the Gulf region.

B. Gulf states' alliances and their impact on unity

In the Gulf region, alliances between states have played a significant role in shaping the dynamics of unity among the Gulf countries. These alliances, although at times driven by shared interests and objectives, have also contributed to discord and fragmentation among the states.

Historically, alliances in the Gulf have been formed based on various factors such as security concerns, regional power struggles, ideological affinities, and economic partnerships. The most prominent alliances in the Gulf include the Gulf Cooperation Council (GCC), the Arab League, and the Organization of Islamic Cooperation (OIC).

The Gulf Cooperation Council (GCC), established in 1981, initially aimed to foster unity, cooperation, and stability among its member states - Saudi Arabia, Kuwait, Bahrain, Oman, Qatar, and the United Arab Emirates (UAE). The organization has been instrumental in promoting economic integration, joint defense initiatives, and diplomatic coordination among its members. It has facilitated the establishment of common policies in areas such as education, health, finance, trade, and infrastructure development. For instance, the GCC has implemented a common customs union, created a common market, and facilitated the free movement of goods and citizens within its member states. Countries within the GCC have also seen the benefit of pooling their resources for joint infrastructure projects, such as the development of transportation networks, energy grids, and industrial zones.

However, diverging interests and regional rivalries have occasionally strained the unity within the GCC. This was evident during the diplomatic dispute between Qatar and several other GCC countries in 2017. Saudi Arabia, Bahrain, the UAE, and Egypt severed diplomatic ties with Qatar, accusing it of supporting terrorism and interfering in their internal affairs. The incident highlighted the challenge of maintaining cohesion within the GCC, as conflicting interests and differing approaches to regional issues can create tensions among member states.

Similarly, the Arab League and the Organization of Islamic Cooperation (OIC) have also sought to unite the Gulf states under the broader banner of Arab and Islamic unity, respectively. These alliances have provided platforms for dialogue, cooperation, and collective decision-making on regional issues. While the Arab League includes countries beyond the Gulf region and faces challenges in achieving consensus due to the diversity of member states, it has played a role in coordinating positions on issues such as the Israeli-Palestinian conflict, regional stability, and Arab political developments. The OIC, on the other hand, focuses on promoting Islamic solidarity and cooperation among member states, including those in the Gulf. It has been instrumental in addressing issues concerning Muslim communities worldwide and providing a forum for multilateral engagement and collaboration.

Nevertheless, differences in political ideologies, national interests, and historical conflicts have sometimes hindered the overall unity and effectiveness of these alliances. Within the Arab League, for example, differences between member states on approaches to regional unrest, government transitions, and the role of foreign powers have led to divisions and strained cooperation. Similarly, the OIC faces challenges in dealing with diverging perspectives on issues such as religious and sectarian tensions, conflicts in the Middle East, and the role of Islam in contemporary societies.

One of the critical impacts of Gulf states' alliances on unity has been the polarizing effect of external powers' involvement in the region. The Gulf has become a battleground for proxy conflicts between regional and international powers. These interventions have often exploited existing divisions within alliances, exacerbating tensions and hindering progress towards unity. The presence of global powers such as the United States, Russia, and China in the Gulf region has further complicated matters.

These powers often seek alliances with individual Gulf states to advance their own strategic interests, which can contribute to fragmentation and a lack of coherence within the region.

Furthermore, alliances have also influenced the regional balance of power and geopolitical rivalries. The Gulf states have sought alliances with global powers to enhance their security and economic interests. For example, Saudi Arabia has maintained a longstanding alliance with the United States, which provides security guarantees and military support. The UAE has also sought closer ties with various global powers, aiming to diversify its alliances and strengthen its position as a regional power player. While these alliances serve the purpose of protecting national interests, they can lead to further fragmentation and discord within the Gulf region.

The impact of alliances on unity is also evident in the different approaches taken by Gulf states towards key regional challenges. For example, the ongoing conflicts in Yemen, Syria, and Iraq have witnessed Gulf states aligning with different factions and supporting opposing sides. Saudi Arabia and the UAE have been involved in the Yemeni conflict, supporting the internationally recognized government, while Qatar has taken a more neutral stance, advocating for dialogue and a political settlement. These differences in alliances have not only deepened divisions among Gulf countries but also complicated efforts for regional cooperation and resolution.

In recent years, the Gulf region has experienced shifts in alliances as new actors emerge and geopolitical dynamics change. The blockade against Qatar by Saudi Arabia, Bahrain, the UAE, and Egypt in 2017 highlighted the fragility of Gulf alliances and the potential for disunity. This crisis demonstrated the intricacies of internal and external factors that influence Gulf unity and the role alliances play in shaping regional dynamics.

Overall, Gulf states' alliances have both positive and negative impacts on unity in the region. While they can foster cooperation, security, and economic development, alliances can also exacerbate divisions, fuel rivalries, and hinder progress towards a unified Gulf ideological system. Understanding the complexities of alliance dynamics is crucial for comprehending the challenges and opportunities for achieving greater unity among the Gulf states. Ultimately, a delicate balance between national interests and collective regional objectives needs to be struck in order to navigate the intricate web of alliances in the Gulf and foster a more cohesive and united region.

C. The role of external powers in shaping Gulf dynamics

The Gulf region has always been of strategic importance to external powers due to its vast oil reserves, geopolitical location, and the potential for economic and political influence. This section explores the multifaceted role of these external powers in shaping Gulf dynamics, both historically and in the present day. By delving into the motivations, actions, and implications, we gain a deeper understanding of the complexities of the Gulf ideological system.

- *Historical Context:*

The involvement of external powers in Gulf affairs can be traced back to colonial times when European empires sought to secure their interests in the region. During the late 19th and early 20th centuries, British imperialism was dominant, establishing British protectorates and subsequent influence over the Gulf states. This colonial legacy has left a lasting impact on the political, economic, and legal systems of the Gulf, shaping external powers' involvement in the region.

The presence of external powers in the Gulf further intensified during the Cold War era as the United States and the Soviet Union competed for global influence. In the Gulf, this rivalry took the form of geopolitics, with the United States largely aligning with pro-Western Gulf states to counter Soviet influence. The Soviet Union, on the other hand, provided support to left-leaning governments, fostering ideological divisions within the Gulf region. This Cold War rivalry continued to shape the geopolitical dynamics of the Gulf and influenced regional security alliances.

- *Current Geopolitical Dynamics:*

In the present day, several major powers continue to play a significant role in shaping Gulf dynamics. The United States, Russia, China, and various European nations vie for influence and seek to assert their interests in the region. The United States, driven by its strategic goal of protecting its energy security and countering regional threats, has maintained a strong military presence in the Gulf for decades. The naval base in Bahrain and military cooperation agreements with Gulf states exemplify this presence.

In recent years, Russia has sought to enhance its presence in the Gulf as part of its broader strategy to expand its influence in the Middle East. It has deepened ties with traditional partners such as Iran and expanded its influence through military cooperation, energy investments, and arms sales. Russia's involvement in the Syrian conflict has also shaped its role in the region, aligning its interests with various actors involved in the conflict.

As a major consumer of Gulf energy resources, China has also strengthened economic ties with the region. Through its Belt and Road Initiative, China aims to deepen infrastructure and connectivity networks in the Gulf, enhancing its economic influence. Chinese state-owned enterprises have invested in various industries in the Gulf, including energy, construction, and telecommunications, fostering closer economic partnerships with Gulf states.

European powers, including the United Kingdom, France, and Germany, maintain longstanding historical and economic ties with the Gulf region. These countries have significant investments in the Gulf, particularly in the areas of energy, defense, and infrastructure. Moreover, European powers often advocate for human rights, democracy, and stability in the region, occasionally emphasizing these values in their relationships with Gulf nations.

The evolving dynamics of external power involvement in the Gulf demand that Gulf states adeptly navigate a complex web of relationships and interests, balancing their own priorities with those of external powers.

- *Economic Interests:*

The Gulf's vast oil and gas reserves make it a focal point for countries heavily dependent on these resources. External powers, especially major energy consumers, often seek to secure their access to these resources, influence production and pricing, and ensure stability in the energy market. Investment opportunities in Gulf economies further incentivize external powers to maintain a stake in the region. Gulf states, recognizing their economic leverage, have actively sought to diversify their economies to reduce dependence on oil revenues. This diversification effort has attracted the attention of foreign investors and further amplified the role of external powers in shaping economic policies and development strategies.

With their influence in Gulf economies, external powers can contribute to economic growth through technology transfer, knowledge sharing, and market access. Yet, the involvement of external powers raises concerns regarding the sustainability of Gulf economies, their reliance on foreign investment, and potential challenges to domestic interests and sovereignty.

- *Security Concerns:*

The Gulf region's strategic location near major global shipping routes and its proximity to conflict-prone areas, such as Iran and Iraq, make it an area of interest for external powers concerned with regional security. The presence of major powers, such as the United States and its allies, plays a crucial role in deterring potential threats and maintaining stability. These external powers often provide security guarantees, military assistance, and defense cooperation agreements, bolstering the defense capabilities of Gulf states.

However, the pursuit of security interests can sometimes lead to increased tensions and rivalries among external powers, exacerbating Gulf dynamics. The nuclear ambitions of Iran, coupled with ongoing conflicts in Syria, Yemen, and Iraq, have heightened security concerns for both Gulf states and external powers. The presence and involvement of external powers in Gulf security affairs have been felt through diplomatic efforts, arms sales, and military interventions aimed at managing regional conflicts. Nevertheless, these interventions also carry the risk of escalating tensions and perpetuating proxy wars, potentially further destabilizing the region.

The interplay between regional and global security concerns adds another layer of complexity to Gulf dynamics, necessitating careful management and collaboration between Gulf states and external powers.

- ***Soft Power and Ideological Influence:***

External powers often employ soft power strategies to shape Gulf dynamics. Through cultural exchanges, educational programs, media influence, and ideological promotion, these powers seek to shape perceptions, values, and political alignments within Gulf societies. Ideas and ideologies imported from abroad can have profound effects on the internal dynamics of Gulf states, potentially influencing their ideological systems.

Gulf states actively engage with external powers' soft power strategies to further their own interests. They leverage cultural diplomacy, tourism, and educational partnerships to showcase their cultural heritage, promote regional stability, and project their vision for the Gulf. However, the influence of external powers cannot be underestimated, as their cultural and ideological narratives can introduce both transformative and divisive elements into the Gulf's social fabric.

The challenge for Gulf states lies in balancing their engagement with external powers' soft power strategies while preserving their cultural heritage, national identity, and long-term stability. Careful scrutiny and proactive measures ensure Gulf states maintain agency and control over their own ideological systems.

- *Implications and Challenges:*

The involvement of external powers in shaping Gulf dynamics presents both opportunities and challenges for the region. On one hand, external powers can contribute to stability, economic development, and security cooperation. Their investments, technologies, and expertise can fuel diversified economic growth and enhance regional security capabilities. Close partnerships with external powers enable Gulf states to benefit from global networks and mitigate security risks. Furthermore, external powers can act as mediators in regional conflicts, enabling diplomatic solutions and de-escalation.

On the other hand, external power involvement may exacerbate rivalries, perpetuate conflicts, and impede regional initiatives for unity. Geopolitical competition among external powers can intensify tensions and proxy wars within the Gulf, further complicating the path to stability. Gulf states must navigate this complex terrain with diplomacy, pragmatism, and an acute awareness of their own long-term interests.

To summarize:

External powers' persistent engagement and influence in Gulf affairs have left an indelible mark on the region's ideological dynamics. Understanding the motivations, strategies, and implications of external powers is essential for comprehending the complexities of Gulf dynamics. The historical context of colonialism and the Cold War has shaped the current geopolitical landscape, with major powers like the United States, Russia, China, and European nations vying for influence.

Economic interests, particularly the Gulf's vast oil and gas reserves, drive external powers' involvement in the region. Energy security, investment opportunities, and economic partnerships incentivize external powers to maintain a stake in Gulf economies. However, concerns arise regarding the dependency of Gulf economies on foreign investment and potential challenges to domestic interests and sovereignty.

Security concerns also play a significant role in shaping Gulf dynamics, with the Gulf region's strategic location and proximity to conflict-prone areas attracting the attention of external powers. These powers contribute to regional security through defense cooperation agreements, military assistance, and security guarantees. However, pursuing security interests can lead to increased tensions and rivalries among external powers, potentially escalating conflicts and destabilizing the region.

Soft power and ideological influence are also employed by external powers to shape Gulf dynamics. Cultural exchanges, educational programs, media influence, and ideological promotion profoundly affect the internal dynamics of Gulf states.

Gulf states engage with external powers' soft power strategies but must carefully balance their engagement with preserving their cultural heritage, national identity, and long-term stability.

The implications and challenges of external power involvement in Gulf dynamics are both opportunities and risks. Close partnerships with external powers can contribute to stability, economic growth, and security cooperation. However, geopolitical competition among external powers can exacerbate tensions and perpetuate conflicts within the Gulf.

Gulf states must navigate this complex web of relationships and interests with diplomacy, pragmatism, and a keen awareness of their own long-term interests. They should carefully manage their economic dependencies, security partnerships, and soft power engagements to ensure their agency, sovereignty, and stability in the face of external power involvement. By understanding the multifaceted role of external powers, Gulf states can effectively shape their own future and engage with external powers in a way that serves their interests and aspirations.

D. Implications of rivalries and alliances for Gulf Ideological Unity

Rivalries and alliances play a profound and complex role in shaping the Gulf ideological landscape, impacting the region's unity in various ways. Understanding these implications is critical for comprehending the Gulf countries' dynamics and challenges. In this section, we will explore the multifaceted ways rivalries and alliances affect Gulf ideological unity.

1. Fragmentation and Divisions: Rivalries and alliances

have the potential to significantly deepen existing divisions among Gulf countries, leading to fragmentation within the region. Disputes over political ideologies, territorial claims, or differing national interests can create deep-rooted rifts that undermine efforts towards Gulf unity. One such example is the Saudi-Iranian rivalry, fueled by ideological and geopolitical differences, exacerbating divisions within the Gulf Cooperation Council (GCC) and hindering progress towards shared goals. This fragmentation weakens the collective bargaining power of Gulf countries and impedes their ability to address shared challenges and foster regional integration.

2. Threats to Regional Security: Rivalries and alliances can intensify security concerns in the Gulf region. Competing ideological visions and interests may lead to proxy conflicts or even direct confrontations, which can destabilize the entire region. The escalation of tensions and militarization fueled by rivalries, such as the Saudi-led coalition's intervention in Yemen against the Houthi rebels supported by Iran, pose significant challenges to the fragile security architecture of the Gulf. This not only puts the safety and stability of Gulf countries at risk but also increases the vulnerability of critical energy and maritime infrastructure. Such threats to regional security reinforce the urgency of finding dialogue and conflict resolution avenues.

3. Economic Implications: Rivalries and alliances have

substantial economic implications for the Gulf region. Trade and investment patterns may be disrupted or redirected due to political disputes or the formation of exclusive economic alliances. Gulf countries competing for economic dominance, like Saudi Arabia and the United Arab Emirates, may resort to economically coercive measures against each other, such as trade embargoes or restrictions. This disrupts economic cooperation and hampers the potential for shared prosperity among Gulf countries. Furthermore, economic alliances formed on ideological grounds may lead to the exclusion of certain countries based on differing political or ideological orientations, hindering the economic integration and diversification efforts desired for sustainable development.

4. Strains on Diplomatic Relations: Rivalries and alliances can strain diplomatic relations among Gulf countries and impede effective communication and cooperation. Pursuing conflicting ideological or political agendas can strain diplomatic channels, making resolving disputes or finding common ground challenging. The Qatar crisis in 2017 exemplified the breakdown of diplomatic ties between Qatar and its fellow GCC member states, primarily Saudi Arabia, the UAE, and Bahrain, due to their differing ideological and strategic orientations. This strained diplomacy not only impedes efforts to address common challenges but also hampers finding solutions to region-

al issues, such as the ongoing conflicts in Syria and Yemen. Engaging in meaningful diplomatic dialogue is crucial to overcoming such strains and promoting regional stability.

5. Cultural and Social Polarization: Rivalries and alliances contribute to the Gulf region's polarization of cultural and social identities. Different ideological affiliations may fuel animosity and increase societal tensions, leading to social fragmentation and divisions. Gulf countries, such as Saudi Arabia and Iran, with divergent interpretations of Islam and differing visions for regional influence, play significant roles in reinforcing the broader sectarian fault lines dividing Sunni and Shia communities. This polarization hampers efforts to foster a shared cultural identity, undermines social cohesion, and diminishes prospects for Gulf unity. Encouraging inclusive dialogue and promoting intercultural understanding can counter these trends and foster greater regional harmony.

6. Limitations on Regional Cooperation: Rivalries and alliances can impede regional cooperation and hinder the development of shared policies and initiatives. Disagreements and competing interests may lead to a lack of consensus on key regional issues, hampering collaboration on security, economic integration, and social development. The standoff between Saudi Arabia and Iran, for instance, has hindered the prospects of a unified regional approach to resolving conflicts in

Yemen, Syria, and Iraq. This limited regional cooperation reduces the effectiveness of coordinated efforts to address common challenges and hampers the realization of a cohesive Gulf approach. Overcoming these limitations requires fostering a culture of compromise, promoting trust-building measures, and de-escalating the ideological rivalries that hinder regional progress.

7. Opportunity for Cooperation: Despite the challenges posed by rivalries and alliances, there are also opportunities for cooperation and collaboration within the Gulf region. Rivalries and ideological differences can spur Gulf countries to seek alliances and partnerships with other nations, opening avenues for broader diplomatic engagement and new economic opportunities. Gulf states have sought strategic partnerships with global powers, including the United States, China, and India, to bolster their regional positions and safeguard their interests. Based on cooperation and shared goals, these alliances may help build bridges and foster greater understanding among Gulf states, thereby reducing tensions and facilitating dialogue towards a more cohesive regional framework. Recognizing and capitalizing on these opportunities is essential for building a more integrated and resilient Gulf region.

In conclusion, the implications of rivalries and alliances for Gulf ideological unity are complex and multifaceted. While they can exacerbate divisions and undermine regional stability, they also present opportunities for cooperation and resilience. Recognizing and navigating these challenges and opportunities is crucial for Gulf countries as they strive for sustainable security, economic prosperity, and social cohesion amidst evolving geopolitical realities. By understanding the implications and actively working towards mitigating the negative effects of rivalries and alliances, Gulf countries can foster a more inclusive and harmonious future for the region.

E. Landmarks

The Gulf States, encompassing Bahrain, Kuwait, Oman, Qatar, Saudi Arabia, and the United Arab Emirates (UAE), are renowned for their distinctive blend of tradition and modernity. In addition to their economic prowess and political influence, these states exhibit intricate ideological dynamics that significantly shape their domestic and foreign policies. This section delves deeper into the nuanced ideological landscape within the Gulf region and explores the complex interplay between religion, nationalism, sectarianism, and political Islam.

- ***Historical Context***

To gain a comprehensive understanding of the ideological dynamics of the Gulf States, it is crucial to delve into their historical context. The formation of these states was greatly influenced by factors such as tribal affiliations, regional identity, and religious sects. For instance, in Saudi Arabia, the rise of the House of Saud, a conservative Wahhabi dynasty, transformed Saudi society into a stronghold of Sunni Islam. This close association between the Saudi monarchy and ultraconservative Wahhabi interpretations of Islam shaped not only domestic policies but also the kingdom's global religious influence. Similarly, Bahrain and Kuwait have historically experienced tensions between their Sunni ruling elites and marginalized Shia populations, with the latter often facing discrimination and political marginalization.

- ### *Religious Charisma and Sunni Extremism*

Religion, particularly Sunni Islam, plays a central role in shaping the ideological landscape of the Gulf. Saudi Arabia, as the custodian of Islam's two holiest sites, Mecca and Medina, wields religious authority that extends beyond its borders. The religious legitimacy of the Saudi monarchy, intertwined with ultraconservative Wahhabi interpretations of Islam, has contributed to the emergence and spread of Salafist ideology. This ideology ranges from forms that advocate for strict adherence to Islam's early practices to more extreme variations that promote violence and terrorism. The spread of these extremist interpretations, especially through education systems and religious networks, has posed both domestic and international challenges, with certain Salafist groups becoming sources of radicalization and terrorist recruitment.

- ### *Political Islam and the Muslim Brotherhood*

Another noteworthy dimension of ideological dynamics in the Gulf revolves around political Islam, particularly the influence of the Muslim Brotherhood. Across the Gulf States, different branches of the Muslim Brotherhood have sought to challenge the legitimacy of ruling regimes by advocating for political reform, social justice, and applying Islamic principles in governance. The level of acceptance or repression towards the Muslim Brotherhood varies among the Gulf States, with some governments accommodating limited participation while others outrightly suppress their activities. This ideological competition has had a significant impact on the political environment within the region, with governments attempting to navigate competing Islamist and secular ideologies while retaining control.

- ### *Sectarianism and Regional Rivalries*

Sectarianism, particularly the Shia-Sunni divide, represents a critical factor influencing the ideological dynamics of the Gulf States. Bahrain, with its Shia-majority population ruled by a Sunni monarchy, has experienced persistent sectarian tensions, occasionally resulting in protests and violence. The security dilemma between Saudi Arabia, as the leader of the Sunni bloc, and Iran, as a champion of Shia causes, has amplified sectarian fault lines in the region. Iran's revolutionary ideology, rooted in Shia Islam, has heightened sectarian rivalries, leading to proxy conflicts in countries such as Syria, Yemen, and Lebanon. As a result, sectarianism has become a significant factor that shapes the ideological landscape and influences regional geopolitics.

- ### *Nationalism and Identity Politics*

Ideological dynamics in the Gulf are also influenced by nationalism and identity politics. While the ruling families emphasize Arab and Islamic identity to maintain legitimacy and regional influence, subnational identities based on tribal, regional, and ethnic affiliations persist. In Oman, the notion of Omanism, which emphasizes Omani identity and historical traditions, coexists with broader Gulf Arab nationalism. The United Arab Emirates, composed of seven distinct Emirates with varying historical backgrounds, has aimed to foster a shared Emirati national identity through state-led initiatives. Similarly, Qatar has cultivated a strong national identity, projecting its influence globally through its media outlets and proactive diplomacy. These multiple identities within the Gulf States contribute to a nuanced and complex ideological landscape.

- ### *Social Movements and Civil Society*

Despite the generally autocratic rule in the Gulf States, social movements and civil society organizations have emerged as spaces for ideological contestation. From labor movements demanding better working conditions and protection of workers' rights to youth-led movements calling for political reforms and societal change, these grassroots initiatives challenge the status quo and advocate for diverse ideological perspectives. However, the ruling regimes often respond with varying degrees of repression, aiming to maintain control over the ideological narrative and prevent challenges to their authority.

Conclusion

Understanding the deep-rooted ideological dynamics of the Gulf States is integral to comprehending their domestic affairs, foreign policies, and regional dynamics. The interplay between religion, nationalism, sectarianism, and political Islam shapes the region's political discourse and influences its complex relationship with both internal and external actors. The Gulf States must navigate these ideologies' intricacies and challenges as they strive to balance domestic stability, regional rivalries, and their positioning in the global order.

EXTERNAL INFLUENCES AND GLOBAL DYNAMICS IN THE GULF

The Gulf region has never been isolated from global dynamics. It has always been intertwined with the rest of the world through extensive trade routes, cultural exchanges, and geopolitical interactions. In this chapter, we will explore the role of external influences and global dynamics in shaping the ideological landscape of the Gulf.

A significant aspect of external influence in the Gulf stems from global economic forces. The Gulf countries have been major players in the global energy market with their vast oil and gas reserves. The rise and fall of oil prices, influenced by global demand and supply dynamics, profoundly impact the economic policies and development strategies of the Gulf states. The reliance on oil revenues, coupled with market fluctuations, has led to an increased focus on regional economic diversification.

The interconnectedness of the Gulf economies with global markets has led to a variety of ideological responses. Some Gulf states have embraced neoliberal economic policies, promoting free markets, privatization, and foreign investment. The pursuit of economic diversification and reducing dependency on oil revenues has been a priority for many Gulf governments, leading to the adoption of market-oriented ideologies that prioritize liberalization and business-friendly environments. The Gulf countries have recently launched significant economic reforms to attract foreign investment, develop non-oil sectors, and promote entrepreneurship and innovation.

Furthermore, international relations play a crucial role in shaping Gulf ideological dynamics. The Gulf states have actively participated in regional and international organizations, such as the Arab League, the Organization of Islamic Cooperation, and the United Nations. Their involvement in these forums reflects their desire for regional cooperation, addressing common challenges, and finding mutually beneficial solutions. It also exposes them to global norms, values, and conflicts, thereby influencing their ideological choices.

The Gulf's engagement with international organizations has been a catalyst for ideological transformations. Gulf states have tried aligning their policies with human rights standards, governance practices, and sustainable development goals set by these organizations. This has led to the adoption of ideologies that emphasize development, modernization, and inclusivity. However, tensions can arise between global norms and local ideologies, especially regarding issues such as women's rights, religious freedom, and democratic governance. Striking a balance between the demands of international organizations and their own cultural, religious, and social norms remains challenging for the Gulf states.

The Gulf region has also witnessed the presence and interference of external powers in its dynamics. Global powers, including the United States, European countries, and emerging powers like China, have vested interests in the Gulf due to its strategic location, energy resources, security concerns, and economic opportunities. These external powers may seek to influence Gulf ideologies and politics to safeguard their interests, leading to both collaboration and contention within the region.

External powers can exert influence through various means, such as military presence, economic aid, and diplomatic engagement. Gulf states may align themselves with certain external powers based on perceived benefits, shared ideologies, or strategic considerations. This can lead to adopting and promoting ideologies that resonate with those of the external power, which can either facilitate cooperation or amplify regional divisions. The Gulf states often navigate complex relationships with external powers, trying to balance their own interests, regional stability, and the demands of their allies and partners.

International organizations also have a role to play in shaping Gulf ideologies. Organizations like the World Trade Organization, International Monetary Fund, and World Bank provide frameworks and guidelines for economic policies, development strategies, and governance practices. Gulf states' engagement with these organizations can lead to the adoption of certain ideologies or policy preferences to align with global standards and meet international obligations. However, adherence to global norms can sometimes clash with local customs and traditions, leading to a delicate balancing act between external pressures and cultural preservation.

Additionally, global security challenges have a significant impact on Gulf ideological dynamics. The Gulf region is situated at the crossroads of major conflicts and power struggles, such as the Israeli-Palestinian conflict, the Iran-Saudi Arabia rivalry, and the ongoing fight against terrorism. These security challenges necessitate coordinated approaches among Gulf states as they navigate a complex regional landscape.

Gulf states' responses to security challenges are rooted in their ideological positions and alliances. Some Gulf states prioritize stability and security above all else, which can lead to the consolidation of power and the suppression of dissent. Others emphasize diplomacy, dialogue, and mediation, which can foster collaboration and de-escalation. The ideologies adopted by Gulf states in response to these security challenges can either foster unity or deepen divisions, depending on the perceived threats and the proposed solutions.

Furthermore, Gulf states' security arrangements with external powers significantly impact ideological dynamics. The presence of foreign militaries in the region, such as the US military, plays a significant role in shaping political and security ideologies. It can influence the balance of power among Gulf states and determine their regional allegiances. The security arrangements with external powers have long-lasting implications on regional stability and the ideological choices made by Gulf states.

In conclusion, external influences and global dynamics are crucial in shaping Gulf ideological dynamics. Economic forces, international relations, external powers, international organizations, and security challenges all significantly impact the ideological choices of Gulf states. They form the backdrop against which Gulf governments shape their policies, navigate alliances, and grapple with the complexities of preserving their cultural identities while adapting to the demands of the globalized world. Understanding and analyzing these external influences is fundamental to comprehending the complexities and potentials of Gulf unity and discord. By recognizing and navigating these influences, Gulf states can better position themselves in the global arena while also preserving their unique identities and aspirations for the future.

A. The influence of global economic forces on Gulf ideologies

In today's interconnected world, the influence of global economic forces on the Gulf region cannot be ignored. Economic factors have played a significant role in shaping Gulf ideologies, impacting both individual countries and the region as a whole. This section aims to provide a comprehensive analysis of how global economic forces have shaped Gulf ideologies by delving deeper into the various mechanisms through which they exert their influence.

One of the primary ways global economic forces impact Gulf ideologies is through trade and investment. The Gulf region, rich in oil and natural resources, has become a key player in the global economy. The discovery and extraction of oil resources in the early 20th century transformed the Gulf states, propelling them into positions of economic significance. The immense wealth generated by oil exports has influenced economic policies and shaped ideologies related to resource management, national development strategies, and self-identity. Gulf ideologies have been deeply shaped by the fluctuating fortunes of the global oil market, prompting discussions on diversification strategies, sustainable development models, and the need for post-oil visions to ensure long-term economic stability and prosperity.

Global economic forces also shape Gulf ideologies through the flow of capital, foreign direct investment (FDI), and the establishment of multinational corporations. The presence of international companies in the Gulf not only brings economic opportunities but also introduces foreign ideologies and cultural values. These influences can be seen in incorporating Western business practices, management styles, and consumerist values. As a result, Gulf societies have witnessed shifts in their ideologies regarding entrepreneurship, competitiveness, and market-driven economic systems. Moreover, the desire to attract FDI has driven Gulf countries to adopt economic liberalization policies, privatization of state-owned enterprises, and diversified investment regimes. These ideas and practices have influenced Gulf ideologies, which now place greater emphasis on market-oriented economic policies and increased integration into the global economy.

Furthermore, Gulf economies are increasingly integrating into the global financial system. The financialization of the Gulf economies, marked by the establishment of robust banking and finance sectors, has led to greater exposure to global economic trends. The 2008 global financial crisis served as a wake-up call for Gulf countries, prompting them to reassess their economic policies and ideologies. They recognized the need for stronger regulatory frameworks, improved risk management practices, and enhanced cooperation with international financial institutions. As a result, there has been a noticeable shift in Gulf ideologies towards more cautious and sustainable financial practices. Additionally, the rise of Islamic finance, driven by Gulf countries' desire to align their financial systems with Islamic principles, has influenced ideologies related to ethical and alternative forms of banking and investment, promoting a distinct perspective within the global financial landscape.

The Gulf region's economic dependency on foreign labor also profoundly influences its ideologies. The vast influx of foreign workers, mainly from South and Southeast Asia, brings with it cultural and social dynamics that challenge traditional Gulf norms and practices. This interplay between global economic forces and labor migration contributes to the evolution of Gulf ideologies regarding multiculturalism, diversity, and the role of foreign communities within their societies. The presence of diverse expatriate communities has led to discussions and policy debates on issues like labor rights, social integration, and the preservation of local identity in the face of demographic shifts. Politicians, policymakers, and society at large have had to confront questions of social cohesion, cultural sustainability, and the rights of expatriate workers, which have shaped Gulf ideologies on issues of immigration, demographic diversity, and equality.

Global economic forces also shape the Gulf's stance on international cooperation and global governance. The growing economic power of Gulf countries has enabled them to play a more assertive role in global economic affairs. As economic powerhouses, Gulf countries increasingly engage in international organizations such as the World Trade Organization (WTO), the International Monetary Fund (IMF), and forums like the G20. Through these platforms, they influence global economic policies and advocate for their interests, shaping the agendas of international economic governance. This participation not only reflects Gulf economic ideologies but also impacts their domestic socio-political ideologies. Gulf countries often leverage their economic power to pursue geopolitical objectives, shape regional alliances, and project soft power, contributing to the formation of ideologies based on regional hegemony and interdependence.

Nevertheless, the influence of global economic forces on Gulf ideologies is not unidirectional. With their substantial financial resources, Gulf countries also play an influential role in shaping global economic dynamics. Their investment strategies, sovereign wealth funds (SWFs), and partnerships with international financial institutions position them as significant players in shaping economic ideologies beyond their own borders. Gulf countries' SWFs, for example, have become key sources of capital for investment in international markets, enabling them to exercise significant influence over global investment trends and policies. Their involvement in development projects and infrastructure financing in both emerging and developed economies further strengthens the Gulf's role in shaping global economic patterns and policies while aligning with their own interests and ideological objectives.

The intricate interplay between global economic forces and Gulf ideologies unveils a complex web of regional interactions and power dynamics. Recognizing the influence of global economic forces is crucial to understanding the broader dynamics of the Gulf region and its role in the global economy. Moreover, understanding how Gulf ideologies are shaped and redefined in response to economic trends provides valuable insights into the future trajectories of the region and its evolving role within an increasingly interconnected world.

B. International relations and their impact on Gulf unity

Throughout history, various external powers and interactions have influenced and shaped the Gulf region. The dynamics of international relations have played a significant role in the quest for Gulf unity. This section explores the impact of external influences on the Gulf ideological system and the challenges and opportunities they present.

The Gulf region has long been a focal point of regional and global powers due to its strategic geographical location and abundant natural resources. Over the years, external powers have sought to assert their interests in the region through political, economic, and military means. These interactions have had both positive and negative repercussions for Gulf unity.

One of the key aspects is the role of major powers such as the United States, Russia, and China in shaping Gulf dynamics.

The United States, for instance, has been a primary player in the region since the end of World War II, primarily due to its oil interests. Its relationship with Gulf states has been complex, with periods of strong alliance and occasional tensions. The U.S. has provided military support to Gulf states, sold arms, and established military bases, all in an effort to ensure stability and protect its interests. However, this close relationship has often challenged Gulf unity, as some states have felt overly dependent on or influenced by the United States, triggering skepticism and division among Gulf states.

In recent years, the United States has also shifted its focus towards energy independence, reducing its reliance on Gulf oil. This shift has altered the dynamics of U.S.-Gulf relations, prompting Gulf states to diversify their foreign policy priorities and seek alternative partnerships. These changes present both challenges and opportunities for Gulf unity. On the one hand, the reduced U.S. presence may lead to a power vacuum, potentially increasing regional rivalries and conflicts. On the other hand, it provides an opportunity for Gulf states to strengthen their own cooperation and take a more proactive role in shaping regional dynamics.

Russia's engagement in the Gulf has been shaped by its own geopolitical interests. The Soviet Union's historical rivalry with the United States and its aspirations for a stronger presence in the Middle East during the Cold War influenced its relations with Gulf states. Today, Russia continues to seek economic opportunities and military partnerships in the Gulf, enhancing its regional strategic presence. While Russia's involvement has provided some Gulf states with an alternative to Western powers, it has also triggered concerns about maintaining Gulf unity, as competing interests and alliances can undermine regional cohesion.

China, as a rising global power, has also become a relevant player in the Gulf. With its growing energy needs and economic expansion, China has increasingly engaged with Gulf states, establishing trade, investment, and infrastructure projects. China's focus on economic cooperation, rather than political interference, has been well-received by many Gulf states, especially those seeking to diversify their partnerships. Moreover, China's involvement in Gulf economies raises questions about potential dependency and its long-term impact on the region's stability and unity.

In addition to major powers, the Gulf region has also been entangled in wider geopolitical rivalries that often impact Gulf unity. The Iran-Saudi Arabia rivalry, driven by sectarian, political, and regional considerations, has had a significant impact on Gulf ideological systems. Both countries have sought to expand their influence by supporting different factions within the region, often fueling conflicts and dividing Gulf states along sectarian lines. The ongoing conflicts in Yemen, Syria, and Iraq have exacerbated regional tensions, and external powers have taken advantage of these conflicts to advance their own interests, further challenging the unity of the Gulf.

Gulf states have sought to establish and enhance regional organizations and multilateral institutions to navigate these challenges. The Arab League and the Gulf Cooperation Council (GCC) serve as platforms for dialogue, cooperation, and coordination among Gulf states. These institutions aim to foster unity and address common challenges. However, internal disagreements, varying priorities, and the pursuit of national interests occasionally undermine the effectiveness of these organizations, highlighting the complexities of maintaining Gulf unity.

Furthermore, the global security landscape significantly affects Gulf unity. The Gulf region faces various security challenges, including terrorism, maritime security threats, and cyber warfare. Addressing these shared concerns requires cooperation and coordination not only among Gulf states but also with external powers. For instance, the fight against terrorism has led to increased collaboration between Gulf states and the United States, as well as other international actors. Such collaborations can enhance Gulf unity by fostering trust and shared objectives. However, security challenges can also expose existing divisions and conflicting interests, calling into question the prospects of unity within the Gulf ideological system.

The economic dimension of international relations is equally significant in shaping Gulf ideological dynamics. The region's reliance on oil revenues and its interactions with global energy markets make it susceptible to international economic factors. Fluctuations in oil prices, global economic crises, and trade policies of major powers can substantially impact the Gulf states' economic stability. Economic disruptions can further complicate unity efforts, as states might prioritize individual economic interests over regional solidarity.

Gulf states have recognized the need to diversify their economies and reduce their dependency on oil. This economic diversification strategy involves various sectors such as tourism, finance, logistics, and technology. Gulf states are actively seeking foreign investment and partnerships to support these initiatives and spur economic growth. This approach opens doors for increased collaboration and interdependence with external parties, providing opportunities for knowledge transfer, economic integration, and potentially furthering Gulf unity.

Nonetheless, economic diversification also presents challenges to Gulf unity. Competing interests and differing priorities among Gulf states can hinder collective efforts to diversify and transform their economies. Additionally, external powers that engage in economic partnerships with Gulf states may seek to exploit divisions and influence regional dynamics to their advantage, potentially undermining unity.

In conclusion, international relations profoundly influence Gulf unity and the stability of the Gulf ideological system. The actions and interests of external powers, geopolitical rivalries, the roles of international organizations, and economic factors all contribute to the challenges and opportunities Gulf states face in their pursuit of unity. Recognizing and understanding these influences are crucial for the future of Gulf ideological dynamics and the region's overall stability and development. Balancing national interests with the collective goals of the Gulf states will be essential in navigating complex international relations while forging a path towards greater unity and cooperation.

C. The role of international organizations in shaping Gulf ideologies

International organizations play a significant and multifaceted role in shaping Gulf ideologies, exerting influence through a range of activities and initiatives that contribute to the region's ideological discourse, unity, and development. These organizations provide a platform for dialogue, cooperation, and knowledge exchange, allowing Gulf countries to learn from one another and adopt new ideas, norms, and values that shape their ideological landscape.

One prominent international organization in the Gulf region is the Gulf Cooperation Council (GCC). Established in 1981, the GCC serves as a regional forum for cooperation and integration among Saudi Arabia, Qatar, Kuwait, Bahrain, Oman, and the United Arab Emirates. The organization's objectives include enhancing solidarity, strengthening economic ties, fostering political coordination, and promoting cultural exchange. Through its various committees and working groups, the GCC plays an instrumental role in shaping Gulf ideologies by encouraging cooperation and unity among its member countries. It facilitates dialogue and consensus building, helping establish common priorities and approaches to regional challenges, thereby influencing the Gulf's ideological landscape.

Furthermore, the United Nations (UN) plays a critical role in shaping Gulf ideologies through its broad engagement with the region. The UN serves as a platform for Gulf countries to discuss and address regional challenges, collaborate on sustainable development initiatives, and promote peace and security. Its various agencies and programs provide technical assistance, expertise, and funding for projects that align with the Gulf's ideological priorities, such as human rights, gender equality, and environmental sustainability. The UN's involvement in the Gulf helps shape Gulf ideologies by advocating norms and values central to international relations and development, fostering the integration of these principles into local policies and practices.

Similarly, organizations like the Organization of Islamic Cooperation (OIC) and the Arab League contribute to shaping Gulf ideologies by emphasizing shared religious and cultural identity. The OIC, comprising Muslim-majority countries, including several Gulf states, promotes Islamic solidarity, fosters peace, and supports socioeconomic development. Its various initiatives and programs highlight the importance of Islamic values and principles in governance, thereby influencing the ideological perspectives of Gulf countries. The Arab League, on the other hand, aims to strengthen political cooperation and integration among Arab countries, including those in the Gulf. Its activities and resolutions contribute to the ideological discourse and priorities of Gulf states, particularly regarding regional conflicts, Arab identity, and the pursuit of collective interests.

In addition to political and cultural organizations, international financial institutions also shape Gulf ideologies. Organizations such as the World Bank and the International Monetary Fund (IMF) play a vital role in supporting economic development and governance in the Gulf region. These institutions provide financial assistance, technical expertise, and policy advice to Gulf countries, influencing their economic ideologies and priorities. By encouraging fiscal reforms, advocating for sustainable development practices, and promoting transparency and accountability, international financial institutions shape the Gulf's ideological landscape regarding economic governance, sustainability, and international financial norms.

Moreover, global governance initiatives have a considerable impact on Gulf ideologies. The Sustainable Development Goals (SDGs) set by the UN, for instance, have become a guiding framework for Gulf countries in their pursuit of economic, social, and environmental development. These goals influence the ideological perspectives and priorities regarding poverty reduction, education, health, gender equality, climate action, and more. International organisations contribute to shaping Gulf ideologies through initiatives, partnerships, and global platforms associated with the SDGs by providing guidance, resources, and best practices.

While international organizations have a substantive impact on shaping Gulf ideologies, it is important to recognize that their influence is not absolute. Their effectiveness often depends on the Gulf states' political will and cooperation, the region's existing ideological makeup, and the power dynamics within international organizations. Ideological differences among member countries and geopolitical tensions can also shape the extent to which international organizations can influence Gulf ideologies.

In conclusion, international organizations play a transformative role in shaping the ideologies of Gulf countries. Through their activities, initiatives, and influence, these organizations facilitate dialogue, encourage cooperation, and promote the exchange of ideas, norms, and values. From the GCC's regional cooperation to the UN's promotion of international norms, from the OIC's emphasis on Islamic solidarity to the Arab League's focus on Arab identity, from the World Bank and IMF's economic governance guidance to the nurturing of sustainability practices through the SDGs, international organizations leave an indelible mark on the ideological landscape of the Gulf region.

D. Global security challenges and their effects on Gulf ideological dynamics

In the dynamic and interconnected world we live in, global security challenges have far-reaching implications for countries and regions, including the Gulf. The Gulf region, with its unique characteristics and geopolitical importance, faces a variety of security challenges that impact its ideological dynamics. This section delves into the global security challenges and their effects on Gulf ideological dynamics in greater depth.

1. Terrorism and Extremism:

One of the most pressing global security challenges in the Gulf region is the threat of terrorism. Extremist ideologies and radical groups have emerged and gained traction within the region, posing a significant threat to stability and societal harmony. The complex factors contributing to the rise of these ideologies, such as socio-economic grievances, political alienation, and regional conflicts, have forced governments in the Gulf to implement comprehensive strategies to counter and combat terrorism.

The effects of terrorism on the Gulf ideological dynamics are multifaceted. On the one hand, Gulf states have ramped up efforts to modernize and promote moderate interpretations of Islam, countering the extremist narratives that fuel terrorism. This has led to the strengthening of institutional frameworks, educational reforms, and interfaith dialogue initiatives to foster a more inclusive and tolerant society.

Efforts to counter terrorism have also resulted in increased international cooperation. Gulf states have sought partnerships with countries worldwide, sharing intelligence, conducting joint military operations, and participating in counter-terrorism initiatives. This collaboration has reinforced regional security and influenced Gulf ideological dynamics by promoting dialogue, understanding, and the exchange of ideas with international partners.

On the other hand, the fight against terrorism has prompted states in the Gulf region to enhance security measures, surveillance capabilities, and collaborations with international partners. This sometimes results in a delicate balance between security imperatives and potential encroachments on civil liberties and freedom of expression. These ideological challenges highlight the need to create a conducive environment that safeguards both security and individual rights.

2. Foreign Military Presence:

The Gulf region has long been a strategic focal point for global powers due to its abundant energy resources and strategic location. Consequently, foreign military forces in the region have significantly shaped the Gulf ideological dynamics. Foreign military bases, interventions, and security cooperation agreements have impacted regional alliances, power dynamics, and the perception of national sovereignty.

While some Gulf states see the presence of foreign military forces as a security guarantee to deter potential threats, others perceive it as a violation of their sovereignty and a potential threat to stability. These divergent perspectives contribute to ideological fault lines, with some advocating for closer ties with global powers and others emphasizing the need for self-reliance and regional partnerships.

The presence of foreign military forces in the Gulf has also influenced the regional arms race. The influx of advanced weaponry and military technology has led to increased defense spending and the acquisition of sophisticated weapons systems by Gulf states. This, in turn, has impacted Gulf ideological dynamics, with some states prioritizing security cooperation and alignment with global powers, while others focus on building indigenous defense capabilities and forging regional alliances based on shared ideologies and interests.

3. Weapons of Mass Destruction (WMD) Proliferation:

The proliferation of weapons of mass destruction in the Gulf presents a grave security challenge that affects the ideological dynamics in the region. Concerns about nuclear programs, chemical weapons, and ballistic missile capabilities have escalated tensions among Gulf states and highlighted the imperative for regional security mechanisms.

Gulf states have had to navigate the complexities of the international non-proliferation regime, balancing their regional security interests with global obligations. The pursuit of nuclear energy for peaceful purposes, denuclearization efforts, and strengthening non-proliferation regimes have become central to the Gulf ideological agenda.

The effects of WMD proliferation on Gulf ideological dynamics extend beyond the traditional security realm. It has prompted Gulf states to prioritize scientific research and technological advancements to ensure their defense capabilities are up to par. Additionally, the pursuit of nuclear energy for peaceful purposes has led to an ideological shift towards promoting clean and sustainable energy sources, aligning with global efforts to combat climate change.

4. Cybersecurity Challenges:

With societies becoming increasingly reliant on technology, Gulf states face vulnerabilities in the digital domain, making cybersecurity a critical security challenge. Cyber attacks, whether originating from state-sponsored actors or non-state hackers, pose significant threats to critical infrastructures and national security. Gulf states are enhancing their cybersecurity capabilities and investing in infrastructure protection, incident response, and international cooperation to mitigate these risks.

The ideological dynamics in the Gulf are impacted by the need to address emerging cybersecurity challenges. Governments are promoting public-private partnerships, fostering cybersecurity awareness, and investing in research and development to stay ahead of evolving cyber threats. The inclusion of cybersecurity resilience and capabilities into the Gulf ideological system is essential to ensure the protection of national interests and bolster regional stability.

Cybersecurity challenges also raise questions about privacy, freedom of expression, and the balance between national security and individual rights. The ideological dynamics in the Gulf are shaped by ongoing discussions and debates on how to strike this delicate balance while effectively countering cyber threats.

5. Regional Conflicts and Proxy Wars:

The Gulf region has been deeply affected by ongoing conflicts in countries such as Syria, Yemen, and Iraq, which have contributed to the ideological fault lines and exacerbated existing divisions. These conflicts have fostered sectarian tensions, drawn Gulf states into broader regional power struggles, and deepened ideological rifts among states, thereby shaping the Gulf ideological dynamics.

The effects of regional conflicts on Gulf ideological dynamics are evident in the divergent approaches Gulf states adopt in supporting different factions within these conflicts. Complex webs of alliances, ideological divisions, and interests have emerged, leading to shifting alliances and creating challenges for regional unity. Addressing these ideological rifts and working towards conflict resolution is vital to restore stability and create a more cohesive Gulf region.

Moreover, regional conflicts have fueled the rise of non-state actors, militias, and extremist ideologies, thereby contributing to both the security challenges and ideological fault lines in the Gulf. The effects of these conflicts transcend borders, with Gulf states feeling compelled to intervene to protect their interests and stabilize the wider region.

6. Technological Advancements:

The rapid advancement of technology has presented both opportunities and challenges to Gulf security. As artificial intelligence, unmanned systems, and new forms of warfare continue to evolve, Gulf states must continuously adapt and invest in developing their defense capabilities. Technological advancements reshape the global security landscape, and the Gulf ideological system needs to incorporate these changes effectively.

Gulf states are investing in emerging technologies to enhance their military capabilities, develop cybersecurity frameworks, and foster economic diversification. However, the rapid pace of technological change also poses challenges in terms of adapting regulations, addressing ethical considerations, and safeguarding against potential vulnerabilities.

Technological advancements have also influenced the ideological dynamics in the Gulf by facilitating the spread of information, expanding communication channels, and empowering individuals and non-state actors. The democratization of information through social media, for example, has created a platform for diverse voices and ideologies, further shaping the Gulf ideological landscape.

In summary, global security challenges have significant effects on Gulf ideological dynamics, impacting areas such as terrorism, foreign military presence, WMD proliferation, cybersecurity threats, regional conflicts, and technological advancements. Understanding and effectively responding to these challenges is crucial for the Gulf region to navigate an increasingly complex security environment while fostering unity and harmony among its member states. The Gulf ideological system must continue adapting and balancing security imperatives and the pursuit of tolerance and individual rights. This requires a comprehensive approach that addresses the underlying causes of these security challenges and seeks collaborative solutions at the regional and international levels.

To effectively counter terrorism and extremism, Gulf states must continue to invest in education and social reform, promoting moderate interpretations of Islam, and fostering interfaith dialogue. Addressing socio-economic grievances and political alienation are also crucial factors in reducing the appeal of extremist ideologies. Furthermore, regional cooperation and international partnerships in intelligence sharing, law enforcement, and counter-terrorism efforts are essential in combating this global threat.

Regarding foreign military presence, Gulf states should strive for a balanced approach that maintains security partnerships with global powers while safeguarding their own sovereignty. Engaging in open dialogue and negotiations with foreign actors can help bridge ideological differences and enhance regional stability. At the same time, investing in indigenous defense capabilities and fostering regional alliances can promote self-reliance while maintaining a sense of autonomy.

To address the issue of WMD proliferation, Gulf states should continue their efforts to adhere to international non-proliferation agreements and strengthen regional security mechanisms. Investing in scientific research, technological advancements, and clean energy sources can address security concerns and align with global efforts to combat climate change and promote sustainable development. Regional initiatives that encourage dialogue, transparency, and confidence-building measures can further contribute to a more secure and stable Gulf region.

The growing realm of cybersecurity requires Gulf states to prioritize the development of comprehensive cybersecurity strategies and capabilities. Enhancing collaboration with international partners, promoting cybersecurity awareness among the public, and investing in research and development are necessary steps to mitigate cyber risks effectively. Striking a balance between national security and individual rights is crucial, with ongoing discussions and debates shaping the Gulf ideological system in this regard.

Addressing regional conflicts and proxy wars demands a commitment to diplomatic solutions and conflict resolution mechanisms. Engaging in dialogue, supporting, and mediating peace efforts in conflict-affected countries can help alleviate sectarian tensions and bridge ideological divides in the Gulf. Gulf states should prioritize the restoration of stability and work towards achieving a more cohesive regional framework to address shared challenges and promote long-term peace and security.

Finally, technological advancements require Gulf states to continuously adapt and invest in developing their defense capabilities and cybersecurity frameworks. This includes keeping up with emerging technologies, adapting regulations to account for new forms of warfare, and addressing ethical considerations. Embracing these advancements also means leveraging technology to foster communication, empower individuals, and strengthen the democratization of information.

In conclusion, global security challenges have far-reaching implications for Gulf ideological dynamics. To navigate an increasingly complex security environment, the Gulf region must adopt a comprehensive and adaptable approach. This includes countering terrorism and extremism through education and social reform, striking a balance between foreign military presence and national sovereignty, addressing WMD proliferation concerns while aligning with global initiatives, enhancing cybersecurity capabilities, resolving regional conflicts, and effectively leveraging technological advancements. By addressing these challenges, the Gulf region can foster unity, stability, and resilience while promoting inclusive and tolerant societies.

E. Landmarks

The Gulf States, encompassing Bahrain, Kuwait, Oman, Qatar, Saudi Arabia, and the United Arab Emirates (UAE), are renowned for their distinctive blend of tradition and modernity. In addition to their economic prowess and political influence, these states exhibit intricate ideological dynamics that significantly shape their domestic and foreign policies. This section delves deeper into the nuanced ideological landscape within the Gulf region and explores the complex interplay between religion, nationalism, sectarianism, and political Islam.

1. Historical Context

To gain a comprehensive understanding of the ideological dynamics of the Gulf States, it is crucial to delve into their historical context. The formation of these states was greatly influenced by factors such as tribal affiliations, regional identity, and religious sects. For instance, in Saudi Arabia, the rise of the House of Saud, a conservative Wahhabi dynasty, transformed Saudi society into a stronghold of Sunni Islam. This close association between the Saudi monarchy and ultraconservative Wahhabi interpretations of Islam shaped not only domestic policies but also the kingdom's global religious influence. Similarly, Bahrain and Kuwait have historically experienced tensions between their Sunni ruling elites and marginalized Shia populations, with the latter often facing discrimination and political marginalization.

2. Religious Charisma and Sunni Extremism

Religion, particularly Sunni Islam, plays a central role in shaping the ideological landscape of the Gulf. Saudi Arabia, as the custodian of Islam's two holiest sites, Mecca and Medina, wields religious authority that extends beyond its borders. The religious legitimacy of the Saudi monarchy, intertwined with ultraconservative Wahhabi interpretations of Islam, has contributed to the emergence and spread of Salafist ideology. This ideology ranges from forms that advocate for strict adherence to Islam's early practices to more extreme variations that promote violence and terrorism. The spread of these extremist interpretations, especially through education systems and religious networks, has posed both domestic and international challenges, with certain Salafist groups becoming sources of radicalization and terrorist recruitment.

3. Political Islam and the Muslim Brotherhood

Another noteworthy dimension of ideological dynamics in the Gulf revolves around political Islam, particularly the influence of the Muslim Brotherhood. Across the Gulf States, different branches of the Muslim Brotherhood have sought to challenge the legitimacy of ruling regimes by advocating for political reform, social justice, and the application of Islamic principles in governance. The level of acceptance or repression towards the Muslim Brotherhood varies among the Gulf States, with some governments accommodating limited participation while others outrightly suppress their activities. This ideological competition has had a significant impact on the political environment within the region, with governments attempting to navigate competing Islamist and secular ideologies while retaining control.

4. Sectarianism and Regional Rivalries

Sectarianism, particularly the Shia-Sunni divide, represents a critical factor influencing the ideological dynamics of the Gulf

States. Bahrain, with its Shia-majority population ruled by a Sunni monarchy, has experienced persistent sectarian tensions, occasionally resulting in protests and violence. The security dilemma between Saudi Arabia, as the leader of the Sunni bloc, and Iran, as a champion of Shia causes, has amplified sectarian fault lines in the region. Iran's revolutionary ideology, rooted in Shia Islam, has heightened sectarian rivalries, leading to proxy conflicts in countries such as Syria, Yemen, and Lebanon. As a result, sectarianism has become a significant factor that shapes the ideological landscape and influences regional geopolitics.

5. Nationalism and Identity Politics

Ideological dynamics in the Gulf are also influenced by nationalism and identity politics. While the ruling families emphasize Arab and Islamic identity to maintain legitimacy and regional influence, subnational identities based on tribal, regional, and ethnic affiliations persist. In Oman, the notion of Omanism, which emphasizes Omani identity and historical traditions, co-exists with broader Gulf Arab nationalism. The United Arab Emirates, composed of seven distinct Emirates with varying historical backgrounds, has aimed to foster a shared Emirati national identity through state-led initiatives. Similarly, Qatar has cultivated a strong national identity, projecting its influence globally through its media outlets and proactive diplomacy. These multiple identities within the Gulf States contribute to a nuanced and complex ideological landscape.

6. Social Movements and Civil Society

Despite the generally autocratic rule in the Gulf States, social movements and civil society organizations have emerged as spaces for ideological contestation. From labour movements demanding better working conditions and protection of workers' rights to youth-led movements calling for political reforms and societal change, these grassroots initiatives challenge the status quo and advocate for diverse ideological perspectives. However, the ruling regimes often respond with varying degrees of repression, aiming to maintain control over the ideological narrative and prevent challenges to their authority.

Conclusion

Understanding the deep-rooted ideological dynamics of the Gulf States is integral to comprehending their domestic affairs, foreign policies, and regional dynamics. The interplay between religion, nationalism, sectarianism, and political Islam shapes the region's political discourse and influences its complex relationship with both internal and external actors. The Gulf States must navigate these ideologies' intricacies and challenges as they strive to balance domestic stability, regional rivalries, and their positioning in the global order.

INTERNAL CHALLENGES AND CONTRADICTIONS WITHIN GULF SOCIETIES

Socioeconomic disparities, political divisions, youth, identity and the quest for change, and women empowerment are the topics that we will explore in this chapter:

A. Socioeconomic disparities within Gulf countries

The Gulf region is known for its immense wealth and abundant natural resources, contributing to its rapid economic development. However, despite these achievements, Gulf countries continue to face significant socioeconomic disparities within their societies. These disparities are characterized by differences in income distribution, access to basic services, and opportunities for upward mobility.

One of the key factors contributing to these disparities is the uneven distribution of natural resources, particularly oil and gas reserves. Countries with substantial oil reserves, such as Saudi Arabia, Qatar, and Kuwait, have experienced significant economic growth and prosperity. However, nations with limited natural resources, such as Bahrain and Oman, have faced greater challenges in achieving economic diversification and reducing dependency on these finite resources.

Furthermore, the economic structure of Gulf countries has been another contributing factor. The reliance on oil revenues has greatly emphasized the hydrocarbon sector, resulting in limited job opportunities in other sectors. This has created a disparity between the highly-paid jobs in the oil and gas industry and lower-paying jobs in non-energy industries, exacerbating income inequality and social disparities.

Additionally, there are significant disparities in access to quality education and healthcare within Gulf societies. While some countries have made significant investments in education and healthcare infrastructure, providing their citizens with world-class facilities, others have struggled to provide adequate services, particularly in remote and rural areas. This disparity in access to quality education and healthcare can further perpetuate socioeconomic inequalities and hinder social mobility.

Addressing these socioeconomic disparities requires a multi-faceted approach focusing on economic diversification, investment in human capital, and social protection measures. Gulf countries need to diversify their economies by investing in sectors beyond oil and gas, such as tourism, finance, and technology. This will create new job opportunities and reduce dependency on finite resources. Moreover, investing in education and vocational training programs will equip individuals with the skills necessary to succeed in a diversified economy, contributing to greater social mobility. Additionally, implementing social safety nets and strengthening social protection programs will ensure no one is left behind, promoting a more equitable distribution of wealth and opportunities.

B. Political divisions and their impact on Gulf unity

The Gulf region is characterized by diverse political systems and alliances, contributing to political divisions and occasional tensions between Gulf states. While some countries have embraced constitutional monarchies or parliamentary systems, others have maintained absolute monarchies. These differences in governance structures can result in varying policy priorities and conflicting interests and hinder efforts towards establishing a cohesive and unified Gulf ideological system.

One of the significant political divisions within the Gulf is the ongoing rift between Qatar and a coalition of countries led by Saudi Arabia and the United Arab Emirates. This division originated from disagreements over foreign policy, particularly Qatar's alleged support for Islamist movements. The rift has led to political, economic, and social consequences, impacting the unity of the Gulf region.

Furthermore, the influence of external actors, particularly Iran, has contributed to political divisions within the Gulf. The geopolitical rivalry between Saudi Arabia and Iran has further exacerbated sectarian tensions and hindered efforts towards a unified Gulf ideological framework.

It is essential to promote dialogue and diplomacy among Gulf political actors to foster a sense of unity and address political divisions within the Gulf. Engaging in open and respectful discussions, pursuing mutual understanding, and respecting the sovereignty of each nation can help bridge political divides and strengthen Gulf unity.

Establishing mechanisms for regular consultations and joint decision-making on issues of common interest, such as security, economic cooperation, and regional integration, is vital to building trust and promoting a unified Gulf identity. Moreover, fostering a culture of tolerance, respect for diversity, and embracing diverse perspectives can contribute to overcoming political divisions and establishing a more harmonious and cohesive Gulf society.

C. Youth, identity, and the quest for change in Gulf societies

The Gulf region is experiencing a significant demographic shift, with a large portion of its population comprised of young people. This demographic dividend presents both opportunities and challenges for Gulf societies. The youth's desire for change, personal growth, and aspiration to redefine Gulf identities can sometimes clash with traditional norms and conservative social values, leading to tensions and contradictions within Gulf societies.

The younger generation in the Gulf is increasingly connected to the global world through technology and social media. This exposure to diverse perspectives and ideas has fueled a desire for greater individual freedoms, social justice, and a more inclusive society. Many young Gulf citizens seek opportunities for personal expression, challenging traditional norms, and advocating for social change.

However, adapting to societal transformations while maintaining cultural heritage and traditional values is a delicate balancing act. The influence of conservative social norms, societal and religious institutions, and a generational gap in perspectives can restrict young people's aspirations for change, causing friction and a sense of dissonance within Gulf societies.

Fostering an environment that promotes dialogue, inclusivity, and active youth participation is crucial to address these challenges. Investing in quality education, emphasizing critical thinking, creativity, and innovation, will equip young minds with the necessary skills to navigate societal changes and positively contribute to their societies. Encouraging open and respectful debate that embraces diverse perspectives and allowing young people to voice their aspirations can foster a sense of belonging and ownership in shaping Gulf ideologies.

Engaging young people in community programs, civil society initiatives, and entrepreneurship can harness the energy and ideas of Gulf youth, empowering them to become change agents within their societies. Moreover, promoting cultural integration and understanding, where traditional values are combined with tolerance and respect for diversity, can help bridge generational divides and foster a more harmonious and cohesive Gulf society.

D. Women's roles and empowerment in Gulf societies

The Gulf region has witnessed significant progress in women's roles and their empowerment over the past few decades. Efforts to improve access to education and healthcare and increase women's participation in the workforce and decision-making positions have been noteworthy. However, gender equality remains an ongoing issue in Gulf societies.

Women in the Gulf often face gender-based discrimination, limited representation in political and economic spheres, and societal expectations that can hinder their full participation and contribution to Gulf ideological unity. Cultural norms, traditional gender roles, and legal frameworks that may perpetuate inequality pose challenges to achieving gender parity.

To address these challenges, it is crucial to strengthen legal frameworks and ensure their effective implementation to protect women's rights and promote gender equality. Enacting laws that prohibit discrimination, promote equal pay, and provide access to appropriate healthcare are essential steps towards achieving gender parity. Additionally, empowering women through targeted educational and training programs, mentorship initiatives, and providing opportunities for leadership roles can contribute to a more inclusive and empowered female workforce within Gulf societies.

Promoting women's participation in decision-making processes at various levels, including politics, business, and community organizations, is pivotal for ensuring that women's voices are heard and their perspectives are incorporated in developing and implementing Gulf ideologies. The active involvement of women in shaping the Gulf's future demonstrates a commitment to equality and social justice and strengthens its unity.

In conclusion, addressing internal challenges and contradictions within Gulf societies is crucial for establishing a cohesive and unified Gulf ideological system. Addressing socioeconomic disparities, bridging political divisions, empowering the youth, and promoting women's roles and empowerment are key areas that require attention and proactive measures. By tackling these challenges head-on, Gulf societies can build a more inclusive, equitable, and prosperous future for the region.

******

A. Socioeconomic disparities within Gulf countries

Throughout the Gulf region, socioeconomic disparities exist within and between countries. These disparities encompass various aspects such as wealth distribution, employment opportunities, education access, and living standards. This section delves deeper into the factors contributing to these disparities and their implications for Gulf societies.

Wealth Distribution:

1. The concentration of wealth among a small elite in

some Gulf countries In several Gulf countries, wealth is highly concentrated among a small elite, often composed of members of the ruling families or influential business tycoons. This concentration has resulted in significant disparities between the wealthy and the rest of the population, exacerbating income inequality.

2. Widening income gaps between the wealthy and the working class, The income gaps within Gulf countries have been widening over the years, primarily due to factors such as a lack of progressive taxation policies, limited social safety nets, and an overreliance on oil revenue. The growing disparities between the wealthy and the working class have raised concerns about social cohesion and perceptions of fairness.

3. Impact on Social Cohesion and Perceptions of Fairness The stark disparities in wealth distribution have tangible impacts on society. They foster feelings of marginalization, discontent, and disillusionment among those who feel excluded from economic opportunities. Such disparities can undermine social cohesion, erode trust in institutions, and increase social tensions within Gulf countries.

Employment Opportunities:

1. Dependence on expatriate labor in certain sectors Gulf economies heavily rely on expatriate labor, particularly

in sectors such as construction, hospitality, and domestic work. While this has facilitated rapid development and economic growth, it has also limited employment opportunities for national citizens in these sectors, creating an imbalance in the labor market.

2. Limited opportunities for nationals in specific industries The dependence on expatriate labor has contributed to limited job opportunities for national citizens in certain industries, including those requiring specialized skills or higher education levels. The lack of diversification in the job market often results in over-reliance on public-sector employment, leading to imbalances in the workforce.

3. Challenges of creating a diverse and sustainable job market Gulf countries face challenges in transitioning from oil-based economies to more diverse and sustainable job markets. This requires policies and investments aimed at fostering entrepreneurship, innovation, and the development of industries beyond the traditional sectors. Overcoming these challenges is crucial for creating employment opportunities for nationals and reducing disparities.

Education Access:

1. Disparities in the quality of education between urban and rural areas Disparities in education quali-

ty are often observed between urban and rural areas within Gulf countries. Urban areas tend to have better-equipped schools with access to advanced educational resources, while rural areas face significant challenges such as limited infrastructure and inadequate teaching staff.

2. Inequality in educational resources and facilities Inequality in educational resources is prevalent within Gulf countries, with some schools benefiting from state-of-the-art facilities while others struggle with outdated infrastructure and limited technological advancements. Such disparities hinder equal access to quality education and can perpetuate socioeconomic disparities.

3. Limited access to higher education for certain social groups Despite significant progress in expanding educational opportunities, certain social groups in Gulf countries continue to face barriers to higher education. This is influenced by factors such as gender inequality, income disparities, and regional disparities, preventing full access to educational opportunities and perpetuating socioeconomic disparities.

Living Standards:

1. Disparities in access to healthcare services Disparities exist in access to healthcare services within Gulf coun-

tries. While urban areas have well-equipped hospitals and advanced healthcare facilities, rural and remote regions face challenges such as inadequate healthcare infrastructure, limited medical professionals, and unequal distribution of healthcare resources, resulting in disparities in healthcare outcomes.

2. Housing affordability and availability challenges Affordable housing remains a significant challenge within Gulf countries, particularly for low-income individuals and families. Rapid urbanization, population growth, and a limited supply of affordable housing have led to soaring property prices, making it difficult for many citizens to access decent and affordable housing, further contributing to socioeconomic disparities.

3. Psychological impact on individuals and communities Socioeconomic disparities can have a profound psychological impact on individuals and communities. The stress, anxiety, and feelings of injustice associated with limited economic opportunities, educational disparities, and inadequate living conditions can negatively affect mental health and erode overall well-being, hampering social progress.

Societal Implications:

1. Social unrest and discontent from socioeconomic

disparities can contribute to social unrest and discontent as marginalized individuals and communities voice their grievances. Protests and demonstrations demanding greater economic opportunities, income redistribution, and social justice have occasionally emerged, reflecting the frustrations resulting from perceived inequalities.

2. Challenges to Social Cohesion and National Unity Persistent socioeconomic disparities challenge Gulf countries' social cohesion and national unity. When a significant section of society feels excluded or disadvantaged by economic systems, sectarian or ethnic tensions can emerge, potentially threatening the stability and unity of the nation.

3. Potential Impact on the Stability and Development of Gulf Countries Addressing socioeconomic disparities is crucial for fostering stability and promoting sustainable development in Gulf countries. Persistent disparities can hinder overall economic growth, perpetuate social inequalities, and impede efforts to diversify economies. Furthermore, they may deter foreign investments and impede progress toward a knowledge-based, inclusive society.

Government Initiatives:

1. Measures taken to tackle socioeconomic disparities

Governments in the Gulf region have embarked on various initiatives to address socioeconomic disparities. These include diversification plans to reduce dependence on oil, implementation of social protection programs, education reforms, and policies promoting youth employment. Efforts are being made to create a more inclusive and equal society.

2. Efforts to diversify economies and create job opportunities Recognizing the need to reduce dependency on oil and expand their economic base, governments have launched ambitious diversification plans. These initiatives aim to create opportunities in sectors such as technology, renewable energy, tourism, and finance, fostering economic growth and generating employment for nationals.

3. Social Welfare Programs and initiatives to Address Inequality Governments have introduced social welfare programs to support low-income citizens financially, improve healthcare access, and enhance educational opportunities for marginalized groups. Such programs aim to reduce disparities, promote social mobility, and alleviate poverty by ensuring basic needs are met, and access to essential services is more equitable.

Regional Cooperation:

1. Cross-country collaboration to address common so-

cioeconomic challenges Gulf countries recognize the importance of regional cooperation to address common socioeconomic challenges. Collaborative efforts such as sharing best practices, knowledge exchange, and joint initiatives can promote more equitable development across the region, reducing disparities and fostering sustainable growth.

2. Initiatives promoting equal opportunities and inclusivity Regional initiatives are being undertaken to promote equal opportunities and inclusivity. These encompass efforts to enhance the rights and integration of migrant workers, advance gender equality, and support initiatives that empower marginalized groups. Gulf nations can create a more inclusive and fair society by working together.

3. Regional organizations and their role in facilitating socioeconomic development Regional organizations such as the Gulf Cooperation Council (GCC) play a crucial role in facilitating socioeconomic development. Through collaboration, these organizations can coordinate efforts to address disparities, share resources, and implement policies that lead to fairer, more prosperous societies in the Gulf region.

Addressing socioeconomic disparities within Gulf countries requires a holistic approach involving governments, civil society organizations, and regional cooperation.8. Conclusion:

Addressing socioeconomic disparities within Gulf countries is a complex and multifaceted challenge. It requires concerted efforts from governments, civil society organizations, and regional cooperation to create a more equitable and inclusive society. While progress has been made in certain areas, much work remains to be done.

To tackle these disparities effectively, governments must implement policies that promote equitable wealth distribution, diversify the job market, improve access to quality education and healthcare, and ensure affordable housing for all citizens. These policies should also aim to empower marginalized groups, such as women, youth, and migrant workers, by providing them with equal opportunities and protections.

At the same time, regional cooperation is essential in addressing common challenges and sharing best practices. Gulf countries can collaborate on initiatives to promote equal opportunities, inclusivity, and sustainable development. They can leverage their collective resources and expertise to create a more equitable and prosperous region by working together.

Furthermore, civil society organizations are vital in advocating for change, raising awareness of socioeconomic disparities, and holding governments accountable. They can work on grassroots initiatives that provide support and resources to marginalized communities and promote social mobility and empowerment.

In conclusion, addressing socioeconomic disparities within Gulf countries is crucial for the stability, development, and inclusivity of these nations. By implementing comprehensive policies, promoting regional cooperation, and empowering marginalized groups, Gulf countries can work towards creating a more equal and prosperous future for all their citizens.

B. Political divisions and their impact on Gulf unity

Political divisions within the Gulf region have had a profound impact on the quest for unity and harmony in the region. These divisions are deeply rooted in historical, cultural, and geopolitical influences, and understanding their complexities is crucial in navigating the path towards a more cohesive Gulf identity.

At the heart of the political divisions in the Gulf lies the divergence in political systems and governance models adopted by the various Gulf states. The Kingdom of Saudi Arabia and the United Arab Emirates both have monarchical systems, where power is concentrated in the hands of the ruling families. These systems have historical roots and are often seen as guarantors of stability and continuity. However, they also give rise to concerns about political inclusivity and the concentration of power. In contrast, countries like Kuwait and Qatar have embraced constitutional monarchies, allowing for varying political participation. Such political structures have created different dynamics within each nation, shaping their respective political landscapes and contributing to the fragmentation of the Gulf region as a whole.

This divergence in political systems has led to significant geopolitical alignments and alliances among the Gulf states. The Gulf Cooperation Council (GCC), established in 1981, has been the most prominent attempt at fostering regional cooperation and unity. Led by Saudi Arabia and the UAE, the GCC aims to maintain stability and security in the Gulf by consolidating economic, political, and military cooperation. However, even within the GCC, divergent political ambitions and priorities among member states have caused strains. Qatar's independent foreign policy, for instance, has at times clashed with the collective objectives of the other member states, leading to diplomatic and political rifts.

Moreover, ideological divisions within Gulf societies have played a pivotal role in perpetuating political fragmentation. These divisions are influenced by a variety of factors, including socioeconomic disparities, differing religious interpretations, and conflicting visions for governance. Socioeconomic disparities, in particular, have contributed to tensions between citizens of Gulf states. While countries like Saudi Arabia and the UAE have experienced rapid economic growth and development, others such as Oman and Bahrain have faced challenges in diversifying their economies and addressing income inequality. These disparities have led to varying levels of political dissent and social discontent, further exacerbating ideological divisions.

Religious differences also contribute to political divisions within the Gulf. The predominantly Sunni Muslim states, led by Saudi Arabia, often find themselves at odds with the Shia-majority Iran, which seeks to exert its influence in the region. This longstanding rivalry between Saudi Arabia and Iran, born out of both geopolitical and ideological differences, perpetuates a cycle of instability and enmity. The conflicts in Yemen and Syria, for example, have been increasingly characterized as proxy battles between Saudi Arabia and Iran, heightening political tensions and deepening divisions in the region.

Importantly, these political divisions have implications for regional cooperation and decision-making. The Gulf states often struggle to find common ground on important matters such as regional conflicts, relations with international actors, and economic strategies. Disagreements over these key issues undermine collective efforts to address shared challenges and allow external powers to exploit these divisions for their own interests. For example, Iran has been known to exploit the divisions in the Gulf to exert its influence and expand its regional footprint, posing a significant challenge to regional stability.

Furthermore, political divisions profoundly affect other aspects of Gulf unity, including economic integration, social cohesion, and cultural exchanges. The lack of a unified political front has hindered further integration and cooperation among Gulf economies. While initiatives like the Gulf Common Market and the Gulf Monetary Union were established to promote economic integration, divergent political ambitions and interests have proven to be obstacles to their full realization. Economic rivalries between Gulf states, such as the competition for financial services dominance between Dubai and Qatar, have also impeded efforts to foster economic unity and diversification.

Likewise, social divisions based on political loyalties, sectarian differences, and national identities hinder the establishment of a shared Gulf identity. Gulf societies are diverse and multicultural, with expatriate populations composing a significant portion of the workforce in many Gulf states. Yet, cultural exchanges and integration often operate within specific national frameworks rather than embracing a broader Gulf perspective. The lack of a shared cultural narrative and the prominence of national identities contribute to suspicion and limited cooperation, inhibiting the realization of a united Gulf identity.

However, in recent years, the Gulf region has witnessed notable diplomatic initiatives to bridge the gaps and heal the wounds caused by political divisions. For example, the Qatar crisis of 2017-2020, which saw Saudi Arabia, the UAE, Bahrain, and Egypt impose a diplomatic and economic blockade on Qatar, was ultimately resolved through mediation efforts led by Kuwait and the United States. The resolution of the crisis and the restoration of diplomatic ties between the Gulf states serve as a testament to the potential for political divisions to be overcome through dialogue, compromise, and a shared commitment to regional stability.

In conclusion, the political divisions within the Gulf region have had a far-reaching impact on the pursuit of unity and cohesion. Divergent political systems, geopolitical rivalries, ideological differences, and competing interests have compounded the challenges facing establishing a cohesive Gulf identity. Nonetheless, the recent diplomatic initiatives and mediation efforts provide hope for resolving these divisions and nurturing a stronger sense of unity in the Gulf. It is through understanding and addressing these divisions while embracing the shared aspirations and interests of the Gulf states that a more inclusive and cohesive Gulf identity can be fostered.

C. Youth, identity, and the quest for change in Gulf societies

Introduction:

The Gulf region is undergoing profound transformations, and its youth are at the forefront of societal change. This chapter explores the complex interplay between youth identity, aspirations, and the quest for change in Gulf societies. By delving deeper into the societal, cultural, political, economic, and educational factors shaping youth experiences, we understand their motivations and the broader implications for Gulf societies.

- *Sociocultural Factors Shaping Youth Identity:*

A myriad of sociocultural factors influence youth identity formation in Gulf societies. Religion plays a significant role in providing a moral framework and influencing values, ethics, and social interactions. However, within the diverse tapestry of Gulf societies, religious interpretations vary, and youth navigate their identities accordingly. Furthermore, the traditional family structure maintains close-knit relationships, emphasizing respect for elders and reinforcing societal norms. This familial influence shapes the youth's perception of their societal roles, responsibilities, and expectations. Education, often rooted in traditional pedagogical methods, shapes youth perceptions of their role in society, opportunities, and the importance of conformity. Local customs and cultural traditions come into play, informing their sense of belonging and identity. However, exposure to global media and connectivity has led to cultural fusion and the emergence of hybrid identities among Gulf youth.

- *Youth Mobilization and Activism:*

The rise of social media and increased connectivity has revolutionized how Gulf youth engage in mobilization and activism. Online platforms and digital spaces have empowered young people to amplify their voices and coordinate efforts across borders. Hashtags, viral campaigns, and digital advocacy have allowed them to speak out against social injustices, express political dissent, and demand changes. However, undertaking street protests and direct action within a conservative sociopolitical context presents challenges. Limited spaces for dissent and restrictions on freedom of expression persist, requiring innovative approaches to activism that effectively navigate the cultural and political landscape.

- *Economic Challenges and the Youth Population:*

Gulf youth face a range of economic challenges, including high unemployment rates and a lack of diversified job opportunities. While oil wealth has provided economic stability for the region, it has also engendered dependence on a single resource and created job market imbalances. As the region transitions towards post-oil economies, youth seek meaningful employment that aligns with their aspirations and skills. Entrepreneurship, innovation, and technology-driven industries hold promise, but traditional expectations and structural barriers hinder their realization. Effective economic diversification, coupled with targeted youth-focused policies, mentorship programs, and skill development initiatives, are crucial for addressing these challenges and ensuring youth empowerment and economic stability in the region.

- *Political Participation and Youth Empowerment:*

Gulf youth increasingly desire active participation in decision-making processes and seek avenues for political engagement. While some Gulf countries have implemented initiatives to include youth in policymaking, substantial barriers persist. Political reforms that enhance youth representation and address generational gaps in political systems are necessary for fostering meaningful participation. Youth empowerment programs, political training, and mentorship opportunities can further contribute to civic engagement, bridge the generational gap, and lead to more inclusive governance structures. Strengthening democratic institutions, promoting transparency, and nurturing political awareness among youth will enable them to shape the future of their societies.

- *Educational Reforms and Skill Development:*

The education sector in the Gulf is undergoing significant reforms to equip youth with the necessary skills for a rapidly evolving job market. Curriculums are being revised to include critical thinking, problem-solving, creativity, and entrepreneurship. Emphasis is placed on lifelong learning, adaptability, and fostering a culture of innovation. Additionally, vocational and technical training programs are being expanded to address the mismatch between educational qualifications and market demands. Collaborative efforts between academia, industry, and government are essential for ensuring the relevance and effectiveness of educational reforms. Enhancing the quality of education, promoting research and development, and encouraging entrepreneurship will prepare Gulf youth for the opportunities and challenges of the future.

- *Gender Dynamics and Youth Identity:*

Gender norms and expectations shape the experiences and aspirations of Gulf youth, impacting their identity formation and choices. While progress towards gender equality has been made, numerous challenges persist within societal structures and attitudes. Young women face societal pressures, limited access to resources, and gender-based discrimination, which hinder their abilities to participate and lead fully. Efforts to promote gender equality, empower young women, and dismantle patriarchal norms are crucial for realizing the full potential of Gulf youth. Engaging young men and boys in discussions on gender equality and challenging traditional gender roles is also essential for fostering a more inclusive society.

- *Cross-Cultural Exchanges and the Globalized Youth:*

Identity Globalization and increased connectivity have exposed Gulf youth to a myriad of cultures, ideas, and perspectives. Cross-cultural exchanges offer opportunities for critical reflection on traditional norms and values, enabling Gulf youth to develop a more nuanced understanding of their identity. They engage in dialogues that explore the complexities of their cultural heritage and global influences. However, the impact of globalization is not without challenges, as it can lead to cultural conflicts, identity crises, and erosion of traditional values. Striking a balance between preserving cultural heritage and embracing global influences is key for cultivating a dynamic and inclusive youth identity. Encouraging intercultural exchange programs, fostering dialogue, and creating platforms for cultural expression can help youth navigate this complex terrain.

• *Youth Empowerment for Sustainable Development:*

Youth represent the future of Gulf societies and are crucial drivers of sustainable development. Encouraging their active involvement in decision-making processes, creating platforms for dialogue, and providing mentorship opportunities will foster their leadership skills, creativity, and innovation. Youth-led initiatives focusing on environmental conservation, social entrepreneurship, and community development exemplify their commitment to creating a better future for the Gulf region. Creating supportive ecosystems for youth-led initiatives and strengthening collaboration between youth and governmental organizations will pave the way for sustainable development in the Gulf.

• *Conclusion:*

Understanding youth identity and their quest for change is essential for fostering inclusive and progressive societies in the Gulf region. By addressing the challenges faced by Gulf youth, including economic opportunities, political participation, educational reforms, and gender dynamics, policymakers and stakeholders can collectively create an environment that harnesses the potential of young people for sustainable change. Embracing the aspirations, perspectives, and initiatives of youth will ensure a prosperous and dynamic future for Gulf societies.

D. Women's roles and empowerment in Gulf societies

In Gulf societies, traditional gender roles and societal norms have significantly shaped women's roles and opportunities. However, in recent years, there has been a growing recognition of the importance of women's empowerment and gender equality in both public and private spheres. This section delves deeper into the complex dynamics surrounding women's roles and the ongoing efforts towards their empowerment in Gulf societies.

Historically, Gulf societies have been predominantly patriarchal, with women's roles primarily focused on the home and family. Traditional gender roles prescribed women to be caretakers, responsible for raising children, managing household affairs, and maintaining family harmony. These roles were reinforced by cultural practices, religious interpretations, and social expectations, limiting women's access to formal education, economic opportunities, and participation in public life.

However, societal shifts, economic developments, and international influences have gradually brought about changes in perceptions and opportunities for women in the Gulf. The exploration of women's roles and empowerment begins with education, a key factor driving change. Gulf countries have made commendable progress in improving educational opportunities for girls and women. Policies and investments have been directed towards ensuring equal access to education, enabling girls to thrive academically and pursue higher education and professional careers.

Significant efforts have been made to challenge gender stereotypes and provide inclusive educational spaces that promote critical thinking, independence, and gender equality. Schools and universities have implemented programs to empower girls and young women, encouraging them to pursue their academic interests and develop their potential. Government initiatives have also prioritized STEM education for girls, recognizing the importance of their participation in science, technology, engineering, and mathematics fields.

However, the impact of traditional gender norms continues to linger, with some cultural beliefs reinforcing the idea that certain fields or professions are more suited for men. These stereotypes can discourage women from pursuing careers in non-traditional sectors such as engineering, IT, or construction. It is important to address these persistent stereotypes and support and guide young women pursuing non-traditional academic or career paths, highlighting successful female role models and showcasing the benefits of diversity in these industries.

In terms of political participation, Gulf countries have recognized the need for women's voices to be heard and their perspectives to shape public policies. Some countries have implemented quotas or reserved seats for women in legislative bodies, such as parliaments or advisory councils. These measures aim to bridge the gender gap in politics, increase women's representation, and ensure that decisions impacting society as a whole are made with gender-inclusive perspectives. By having women in positions of power and influence, societal and legislative changes can be made holistically, considering the needs and aspirations of all citizens.

While such advancements are commendable, it is crucial to go beyond mere representation and address the underlying barriers hindering women's meaningful participation in politics. Women still face obstacles in terms of financing campaigns, accessing political networks, and dismantling patriarchal norms that often marginalize their political ambitions. Furthermore, it is essential to build a culture that tolerates and encourages women's political leadership and fosters a safe environment where women can voice their opinions and contribute to decision-making processes.

Economic empowerment has emerged as a significant aspect of women's empowerment in the Gulf. Women increasingly join the workforce in various sectors, including finance, technology, healthcare, and education. These women contribute to economic growth, innovation, and social development. Legal and policy reforms have been enacted in some countries to ensure equal pay, protection against workplace discrimination, and maternity leave provisions, supporting women's economic participation.

In addition to working in traditional employment settings, entrepreneurship among women is also on the rise. Women-owned enterprises contribute to job creation, economic diversity, and entrepreneurial innovation. Government initiatives, such as providing access to funding and business support networks, have encouraged women to start their own businesses and pursue entrepreneurial endeavors. However, challenges persist in terms of accessing capital, navigating legal frameworks, and overcoming societal expectations regarding women's roles in the business world.

Notably, the COVID-19 pandemic has exposed and exacerbated some of the existing gender inequalities in the Gulf. The pandemic and related lockdowns have disproportionally affected women, as they often bear the brunt of increased domestic responsibilities, reduced access to childcare, and job losses in sectors heavily impacted by the pandemic. The crisis has highlighted the necessity of comprehensive social policies that support women's economic empowerment, address gendered barriers in the workplace, and provide social protection in times of crisis.

Furthermore, societal attitudes and cultural norms persist as significant obstacles in the journey towards women's empowerment. Deeply ingrained traditional gender roles and patriarchal expectations continue to shape perceptions of women's roles and limit their opportunities. Cultural norms around marriage, family, and societal expectations often act as barriers, dissuading women from pursuing education or professional careers. Addressing these norms requires a multi-faceted approach, including raising awareness, challenging stereotypes, and promoting critical dialogue within families, schools, and communities.

Efforts towards women's empowerment in the Gulf are not solely confined to governmental initiatives. Civil society organizations and grassroots movements have emerged, working towards fostering gender equality and promoting women's rights. These organizations provide platforms for advocacy, awareness-raising, and support networks for women, contributing to a more inclusive and empowering environment. These initiatives play a vital role in challenging societal norms, providing resources and support systems, and amplifying women's voices and achievements.

Overall, the topic of women's roles and empowerment in Gulf societies is multi-faceted, involving various dimensions such as education, politics, economics, and cultural change. While significant progress has been made in recent years, there are still barriers to be overcome, and a continued commitment to women's empowerment is crucial for achieving true gender equality in the Gulf. By challenging stereotypes, promoting women's education and economic opportunities, dismantling societal and cultural barriers, and fostering inclusive social environments, Gulf societies can create a more equitable and empowering future for all.

E. Landmarks

The Gulf States, encompassing Bahrain, Kuwait, Oman, Qatar, Saudi Arabia, and the United Arab Emirates (UAE), are renowned for their distinctive blend of tradition and modernity. In addition to their economic prowess and political influence, these states exhibit intricate ideological dynamics that significantly shape their domestic and foreign policies. This section delves deeper into the nuanced ideological landscape within the Gulf region and explores the complex interplay between religion, nationalism, sectarianism, and political Islam.

- *Historical Context*

To gain a comprehensive understanding of the ideological dynamics of the Gulf States, it is crucial to delve into their historical context. The formation of these states was greatly influenced by factors such as tribal affiliations, regional identity, and religious sects. For instance, in Saudi Arabia, the rise of the House of Saud, a conservative Wahhabi dynasty, transformed Saudi society into a stronghold of Sunni Islam. This close association between the Saudi monarchy and ultraconservative Wahhabi interpretations of Islam shaped not only domestic policies but also the kingdom's global religious influence. Similarly, Bahrain and Kuwait have historically experienced tensions between their Sunni ruling elites and marginalized Shia populations, with the latter often facing discrimination and political marginalization.

- *Religious Charisma and Sunni Extremism*

Religion, particularly Sunni Islam, plays a central role in shaping the ideological landscape of the Gulf. Saudi Arabia, as the custodian of Islam's two holiest sites, Mecca and Medina, wields religious authority that extends beyond its borders. The religious legitimacy of the Saudi monarchy, intertwined with ultraconservative Wahhabi interpretations of Islam, has contributed to the emergence and spread of Salafist ideology. This ideology ranges from forms that advocate for strict adherence to Islam's early practices to more extreme variations that promote violence and terrorism. The spread of these extremist interpretations, especially through education systems and religious networks, has posed both domestic and international challenges, with certain Salafist groups becoming sources of radicalization and terrorist recruitment.

- *Political Islam and the Muslim Brotherhood*

Another noteworthy dimension of ideological dynamics in the Gulf revolves around political Islam, particularly the influence of the Muslim Brotherhood. Across the Gulf States, different branches of the Muslim Brotherhood have sought to challenge the legitimacy of ruling regimes by advocating for political reform and social justice and applying Islamic principles in governance. The level of acceptance or repression towards the Muslim Brotherhood varies among the Gulf States, with some governments accommodating limited participation while others outrightly suppress their activities. This ideological competition has had a significant impact on the political environment within the region, with governments attempting to navigate competing Islamist and secular ideologies while retaining control.

- *Sectarianism and Regional Rivalries*

Sectarianism, particularly the Shia-Sunni divide, represents a critical factor influencing the ideological dynamics of the Gulf States. Bahrain, with its Shia-majority population ruled by a Sunni monarchy, has experienced persistent sectarian tensions, occasionally resulting in protests and violence. The security dilemma between Saudi Arabia, as the leader of the Sunni bloc, and Iran, as a champion of Shia causes, has amplified sectarian fault lines in the region. Iran's revolutionary ideology, rooted in Shia Islam, has heightened sectarian rivalries, leading to proxy conflicts in countries such as Syria, Yemen, and Lebanon. As a result, sectarianism has become a significant factor that shapes the ideological landscape and influences regional geopolitics.

- Nationalism and Identity Politics

Ideological dynamics in the Gulf are also influenced by nationalism and identity politics. While the ruling families emphasize Arab and Islamic identity to maintain legitimacy and regional influence, subnational identities based on tribal, regional, and ethnic affiliations persist. In Oman, the notion of Omanism, which emphasizes Omani identity and historical traditions, coexists with broader Gulf Arab nationalism. The United Arab Emirates, composed of seven distinct Emirates with varying historical backgrounds, has aimed to foster a shared Emirati national identity through state-led initiatives. Similarly, Qatar has cultivated a strong national identity, projecting its influence globally through its media outlets and proactive diplomacy. These multiple identities within the Gulf States contribute to a nuanced and complex ideological landscape.

- *Social Movements and Civil Society*

Despite the generally autocratic rule in the Gulf States, social movements and civil society organizations have emerged as spaces for ideological contestation. From labor movements demanding better working conditions and protection of workers' rights to youth-led movements calling for political reforms and societal change, these grassroots initiatives challenge the status quo and advocate for diverse ideological perspectives. However, the ruling regimes often respond with varying degrees of repression to maintain control over the ideological narrative and prevent challenges to their authority.

Conclusion

Understanding the deep-rooted ideological dynamics of the Gulf States is integral to comprehending their domestic affairs, foreign policies, and regional dynamics. The interplay between religion, nationalism, sectarianism, and political Islam shapes the region's political discourse and influences its complex relationship with both internal and external actors. The Gulf States must navigate these ideologies' intricacies and challenges as they strive to balance domestic stability, regional rivalries, and their positioning in the global order.

ASSESSING THE NEED FOR AND FEASIBILITY OF A UNIFIED GULF IDEOLOGICAL SYSTEM

Benefits and challenges of a unified Gulf ideological system

A unified Gulf ideological system has the potential to bring numerous benefits to the region. Firstly, it could foster a sense of unity and collective identity among Gulf states, leading to greater cooperation and collaboration in various spheres such as politics, economy, and social development. Gulf countries have historically faced challenges in aligning their values and interests, often leading to strained relationships. However, by establishing a unified ideological system, these differences can be bridged, enabling the region to work towards shared goals and common interests. The result would be increased trust and cooperation among Gulf states, ultimately enhancing regional stability and security.

Moreover, a unified Gulf ideological system could stream-line decision-making processes and simplify governance struc-tures. Currently, each Gulf country operates under its own set of policies and regulations, which can create complexities and bureaucratic hurdles for regional cooperation. By aligning their ideologies, Gulf states can harmonize their policies and regulations, facilitating smoother collaboration in trade, invest-ment, and other areas. This streamlined approach would attract foreign investments and contribute to economic growth and development, leading to greater prosperity for the region as a whole.

In addition, a unified Gulf ideological system can facilitate the integration of regional resources and capabilities, leading to enhanced cooperation in areas such as defense, education, and healthcare. Gulf states possess diverse resources and ex-pertise that if effectively harnessed and shared, can uplift the region collectively. By pooling their resources, sharing expertise, and jointly addressing common challenges, the Gulf states can strengthen their collective strength and influence on the global stage. This unified approach would also enable the region to tackle shared issues like climate change, water scarcity, and pub-lic health pandemics more effectively.

However, embarking on the path towards a unified Gulf ideological system poses significant challenges. Firstly, histori-cal and cultural differences among Gulf states may impede the process. Each Gulf country has its own unique traditions, his-tory, and social structures, which have shaped their individual identities. Reconciling these diverging ideologies and creating a consensus may require extensive dialogue and compromise. Respect for the distinct cultural heritage and traditions of each Gulf state will be crucial in this process.

Furthermore, the region's political divisions and power struggles could hinder efforts towards ideological convergence. Rivalries and competition for regional dominance between Gulf states have often overshadowed the pursuit of unity. Each country's self-interests and security concerns may make finding common ground and establishing a cohesive ideological system challenging. Overcoming these political barriers will necessitate strong leadership and a collective commitment to setting aside individual differences for the region's greater good.

Another challenge lies in balancing individual national identities and aspirations with the collective goal of a unified Gulf ideological system. Gulf states have distinct national identities and aspirations driven by their unique histories and socio-political contexts. While pursuing unity, it will be essential to maintain diversity and respect the aspirations of each nation, ensuring that a unified ideological system accommodates individual national interests. Striking a balance between regional identity and national aspirations is crucial for sustaining long-term unity among Gulf states.

Lastly, public opinion and the desire for unity vary among Gulf societies. While some segments of the population may embrace the idea of a unified Gulf ideological system wholeheartedly, others may harbor reservations or even opposition. Concerns over perceived loss of sovereignty, cultural assimilation, or fears of unequal distribution of resources may hinder public support. Addressing these concerns and fostering a sense of ownership and participation among the public would be vital for the success and sustainability of a unified Gulf ideological system. It requires open dialogue, transparency, and engaging with the public to build consensus and assure them that unity will lead to a more prosperous and secure future.

In conclusion, while a unified Gulf ideological system offers numerous benefits, such as enhanced cooperation, streamlined governance, and collective strength, its feasibility and implementation face substantial challenges. Overcoming historical, cultural, and political divisions, as well as addressing public concerns, will be crucial in assessing the need for and determining the feasibility of a unified Gulf ideological system. It requires careful deliberation, open dialogue, and a commitment to finding common ground and shared values that can bridge the ideological gaps and pave the way for a brighter and more unified future for the Gulf region. Only through persistent efforts and a shared vision can the Gulf states develop a unified ideological system that harnesses their collective potential and ensures prosperity and stability for their people.

A. Benefits and challenges of a unified Gulf ideological system

A unified Gulf ideological system holds both exciting prospects and significant challenges. This section aims to explore the advantages and obstacles it presents, shedding light on the potential outcomes of such a system.

Benefits of a Unified Gulf Ideological System:

1. Enhanced Cooperation and Stability: By establishing a common ideological framework, Gulf countries can deepen their cooperation, bolstering regional stability and security. This unity of purpose will allow for greater coordination in addressing shared challenges such as terrorism, extremism, and regional conflicts. Close cooperation will also enable joint military exercises, intelligence sharing, and counter-terrorism initiatives, resulting in improved regional security.

2. Simplified Decision-Making Processes: A unified ideological system could streamline decision-making in the Gulf region. Consensus-building and collective action mechanisms would facilitate efficient problem-solving and policy implementation, leading to better governance and improved outcomes on regional issues. Such streamlined processes would also help in responding promptly to emerging crises and adapting to changing geopolitical dynamics.

3. Economic Integration and Prosperity: A shared ideological system can facilitate economic integration among Gulf states. Common regulations, trade agreements, and investment policies would promote seamless regional trade, attract foreign direct investment, and foster economic prosperity for all member countries. This integration can lead to the creation of a robust Gulf market, with enhanced competitiveness,

increased productivity, and improved living standards for its citizens. In addition, a unified Gulf ideological system could facilitate infrastructure development projects, such as transportation networks and energy grids, that would promote intra-regional connectivity and economic diversification. This would reduce dependency on hydrocarbon resources and create sustainable economies across the Gulf.

4. Enhanced Regional Influence: A unified Gulf ideological system would amplify the collective voice of Gulf states on the international stage. It would enable them to present a united front, exert influence, negotiate from a position of strength, and play a more significant role in shaping global affairs. This enhanced regional influence can help Gulf countries address common challenges such as climate change, energy security, and sustainable development by working together and mobilizing resources effectively. Furthermore, a unified Gulf ideological system would enhance the region's ability to engage with international organizations and contribute to global discussions and decision-making processes. This would solidify the Gulf's position as an influential player in regional and global affairs.

Challenges of a Unified Gulf Ideological System:

1. National Sovereignty and Identity Concerns: Gulf

countries have unique national identities and diverse historical backgrounds. Achieving a balance between a unified ideological system and preserving individual national sovereignty represents a significant challenge. Creating a framework that respects and accommodates these individual identities is crucial for the success of such a system. It is essential to ensure that a unified ideological system does not dilute or undermine the distinct cultures, traditions, and values that define each Gulf nation. To address these concerns, a unified Gulf ideological system must emphasize the importance of national identity and cultural diversity. It should promote a clear understanding that unity does not equate to homogeneity, but rather a harmonious coexistence of various cultures, religions, and ethnicities. Embracing diversity and fostering respect for national identities can enhance the sense of belonging among Gulf citizens, ensuring the system's sustainability.

2. Ideological Differences and Conflict Resolution: The presence of ideological differences among Gulf states can pose a challenge to establishing a unified system. While overarching principles may be agreed upon, reconciling specific policy positions and interpretations of ideology can create disagreements and conflicts. These differences may stem from varying religious, political, and societal perspectives. Addressing them will require a commitment to open dialogue, com-

promise, and mutual respect, with a focus on finding common ground and shared aspirations. Constructive dialogue platforms and mediation mechanisms must be established to facilitate fruitful discussions and resolve ideological conflicts. Encouraging academic and intellectual exchange among Gulf nations can also play a pivotal role in fostering mutual understanding and reducing ideological differences over time. Embracing diversity of thought within a unified framework can contribute to the system's vitality and resilience.

3. Power Dynamics and Political Hierarchy: Gulf countries vary in terms of size, population, and political influence. Ensuring equity and fairness in decision-making processes is important to avoid hegemony or domination of a few countries, which could undermine the potential benefits of a unified ideological system. Creating inclusive and participatory governance structures that empower all member states equally will be crucial in maintaining balance and ensuring that no nation's interests are marginalized or overlooked. Transparency, accountability and a commitment to egalitarian principles should guide the development of governance mechanisms within a unified Gulf ideological system. The system can foster trust, cooperation, and long-term stability by promoting equal representation, fair resource allocation, and meaningful participation. Regular reviews and assessments of the governance structures will be necessary to address any im-

balances and adjust them as needed based on changing dynamics and emerging challenges.

4. Socio-Cultural Diversity and Coexistence: The Gulf region encompasses diverse cultures, languages, and social norms. Respecting and embracing this diversity within a unified ideological system is crucial. Promoting cultural inclusivity, pluralism, and respect for different traditions will be key to fostering a sense of belonging among all Gulf citizens. Emphasizing the common values of unity, tolerance, and mutual understanding will help to bridge cultural gaps and promote coexistence in the pursuit of a cohesive Gulf society. Investing in education, cultural exchanges, and interfaith dialogue can foster mutual acceptance and appreciation of diverse cultural backgrounds. By creating opportunities for interaction, Gulf countries can promote a sense of social cohesion, reducing the potential for social division or marginalization. This would strengthen the social fabric of the unified Gulf ideological system and contribute to the overall well-being and harmony of the region.

Striking a Balance:

Creating a unified Gulf ideological system is a complex endeavor. It requires a delicate balance between common goals and interests, respect for national identities, and the ability to adapt to changing dynamics. A thorough understanding of the benefits and challenges will be essential in navigating this path towards unity.

Through open dialogue, inclusive decision-making processes, and the promotion of shared values, Gulf countries can effectively address the challenges while reaping the rich benefits of a unified Gulf ideological system.

As the journey towards unity progresses, continuous reassessment and adaptation will be necessary to ensure that the system remains relevant and responsive to evolving circumstances. Balancing the need for collective action with the preservation of national sovereignty and identity will be paramount. The Gulf region can strive towards a brighter, more cohesive future under a unified ideological system by embracing the benefits and diligently working through the challenges.

B. Comparative analysis of other regional ideological systems

To understand the Gulf region's ideological dynamics comprehensively, it is crucial to conduct a detailed analysis of other regional ideological systems worldwide. By comparing these systems with the Gulf region, we can identify the similarities, differences, and potential lessons that can be learned and applied.

- Europe: Europe provides an interesting case study when examining ideological systems. The region has undergone significant transformations throughout history, from feudalism to the Renaissance, Enlightenment, and the recent rise of nationalism. These ideological shifts have profoundly impacted its political, economic, and social structures.

The European Union (EU) is a notable example of an attempt to establish a unified ideological system across multiple diverse nations. The EU's founding principles revolve around the promotion of democracy, rule of law, human rights, and social cohesion. Through economic integration and cooperation, the EU seeks to foster peace and stability among its member states. However, the EU also faces challenges in forging a common identity and addressing economic disparities among member states.

The struggle between competing ideologies, such as liberalism, socialism, conservatism, and nationalism, has marked Europe's ideological evolution. The Enlightenment period, with its emphasis on reason, individual rights, and the separation of powers, laid the foundation for liberal democracies. Meanwhile, the Industrial Revolution saw the rise of socialism, which led to the emergence of welfare states in some European countries.

The European experience offers valuable insights into the complexities of building a unified ideological system across diverse societies. The challenges faced by the EU, such as balancing national interests with supranational governance, creating a cohesive identity, and addressing economic disparities, can inform the Gulf region's efforts towards ideological unity while respecting its unique cultural and religious diversity.

- East Asia: Ideological systems in East Asia, particularly in countries like China, Japan, and South Korea, are heavily influenced by Confucianism, Buddhism, and other philosophical traditions. These systems emphasize concepts such as harmony, order, and the collective over individualism, shaping political structures and societal values.

Confucianism, with its emphasis on respect for authority, filial piety, and social harmony, continues to influence various aspects of governance and societal norms in East Asian countries. The hierarchical societal structure and collective-oriented values often result in stable and harmonious societies, but they can also restrict individual freedoms and limit democratic participation.

While East Asia has ancient philosophical traditions, it has also witnessed tremendous economic growth and modernization. China, for example, has experienced a blend of communist ideology and state capitalism, which has led to significant economic reforms and rapid development. Japan has embraced a unique combination of traditional values and Western-influenced ideologies, resulting in a highly industrialized and technologically advanced society.

Examining East Asia's ideological systems can provide the Gulf region with insights into how to balance traditional cultural values with the need for economic progress and social development. The successful integration of ancient traditions with modern aspirations demonstrates the potential for the Gulf region to navigate its own ideological transformations.

- South America: The Latin American region has seen various ideological movements, ranging from socialism and communism to neoliberalism and populism.

These ideological shifts have often been influenced by concerns for economic and social equality, as well as resistance against foreign influence.

In the mid-20th century, Latin America experienced a surge in left-wing ideologies, with countries like Cuba, Nicaragua, and Chile adopting socialist or communist systems. These ideologies aimed to dismantle social hierarchies, reduce inequality, and challenge foreign imperialism. However, the implementation of these ideologies has often faced challenges, including economic instability, political polarization, and violations of human rights.

More recently, populism has gained traction in Latin America, with leaders like Hugo Chávez in Venezuela and Evo Morales in Bolivia promising to empower the poor and challenge the elites. While populism can address social inequalities, it can also lead to governance challenges, erosion of democratic institutions, and social divisions.

Exploring the experiences of Latin America's ideological evolutions can provide valuable lessons for the Gulf region. Understanding the complexities of implementing ideologies aimed at addressing structural inequalities, safeguarding democratic institutions, and promoting social cohesion can inform the Gulf region's own efforts towards ideological unity and social justice.

- Africa: Africa's ideological landscape is influenced by a diverse range of factors, including indigenous cultural traditions, colonial legacies, and post-colonial struggles. Pan-Africanism, tribalism, and post-colonial ideologies have all shaped political and societal dynamics in different African nations.

Pan-Africanism emerged during the struggle for independence, aiming to foster unity and collective self-reliance among African nations. It seeks to address the challenges imposed by arbitrary colonial borders and encourages collaboration for economic development and political stability. However, regional conflicts, ethnic tensions, and governance challenges have hindered the realization of Pan-Africanism's idealistic vision.

Tribalism remains a significant factor in African politics and societies, emphasizing loyalty to one's ethnic or tribal group. While honoring diverse cultural identities is important, striking a balance between recognition and fostering national unity continues to be a pressing challenge in many African nations.

Post-colonial ideologies in Africa, including socialism and nationalism, have sought to address the legacies of colonialism, reclaim national sovereignty, and establish inclusive systems. Economic disparities, corruption, and political instability have presented obstacles to the successful implementation of these ideologies.

Studying the ideological journeys of African nations can provide the Gulf region with insights into navigating the complexities of building a unified ideological system while facing similar challenges of colonial legacies, ethnic diversity, and socio-economic disparities. Understanding how African countries have approached the quest for national identity and stability offers valuable lessons for the Gulf region's own ideological aspirations.

- Middle East: The Middle East shares similarities with

the Gulf region in terms of cultural and religious heritage. However, the ideological landscape in countries like Iran, Iraq, and Syria is shaped by various factors, including Islamic fundamentalism, nationalism, and sectarian divisions, which have often influenced regional power struggles and conflicts.

Islamic fundamentalism has played a significant role in shaping the ideological landscape of several Middle Eastern nations. Movements like Wahhabism in Saudi Arabia and the Muslim Brotherhood in Egypt have sought to establish an Islamic order and challenge Western influences. While fundamentalist ideologies may offer cultural preservation, they can also restrict individual freedoms and contribute to social polarization.

Nationalism has been another influential factor in the Middle East, with various countries asserting their identity, independence, and control over resources. Examples include pan-Arab nationalism championed by figures like Gamal Abdel Nasser in Egypt and Saddam Hussein in Iraq, as well as Kurdish nationalism in the quest for Kurdish statehood.

Furthermore, sectarian divisions rooted in the schism between Sunni and Shia Islam have played a divisive role in the region. The rivalry between Saudi Arabia and Iran, along with ongoing conflicts in Iraq, Syria, and Yemen, exemplify how divergent ideological systems and sectarian interests can lead to protracted instability.

Analyzing the ideological dynamics of the Middle East provides the Gulf region with valuable insights into potential challenges, risks, and opportunities. Understanding the complexities of managing religious and sectarian diversity, fostering inclusive governance, and resolving regional conflicts can inform the Gulf region's efforts to establish its own unified ideological system based on shared values and interests.

By conducting a comprehensive comparative analysis of these various regional, ideological systems, the Gulf region can draw upon best practices and identify potential pitfalls and lessons that can be applied to its own ideological aspirations. Here are some key takeaways from the comparative analysis:

1. Balancing diversity and unity: Europe's experience demonstrates the challenges of establishing a unified ideological system across diverse societies. The Gulf region, with its diverse cultural and religious backgrounds, can learn from the EU's efforts to balance national interests with supranational governance and create a cohesive identity that respects diversity.

2. Harmonizing tradition with modernity: East Asia's integration of ancient traditions with modern ideologies offers lessons on how the Gulf region can preserve its cultural values while pursuing economic progress and social development. Understanding how East Asian countries have successfully managed this balance can inform the Gulf region's own ideological transformations.

3. Addressing structural inequalities: Latin America's ideological shifts highlight the complexities of implementing ideologies aimed at reducing inequality and empowering marginalized groups. The Gulf re-

gion can gain insights into the challenges of economic instability, political polarization, and social divisions when pursuing social justice and inclusive systems.

4. Navigating post-colonial legacies: Africa's ideological landscape reflects the challenges of post-colonial struggles, ethnic diversity, and socio-economic disparities. The Gulf region can learn from African countries' experiences in building national identity, addressing colonial legacies, and navigating issues of governance and stability.

5. Managing religious and sectarian diversity: The Middle East's sectarian divisions illustrate the risks and challenges of navigating diverse religious and ideological systems. The Gulf region can draw lessons from the management of sectarian tensions, fostering inclusive governance, and resolving regional conflicts.

By studying these diverse regional ideological systems, the Gulf region can comprehensively understand the complexities and potential solutions in its quest for ideological unity and stability. Incorporating relevant lessons and best practices into its own aspirations will contribute to the region's long-term development and progress.

C. Political and economic implications of Gulf ideological unity

The quest for Gulf ideological unity carries significant regional political and economic impacts. A unified Gulf ideological system has the potential to enhance political stability, increase regional influence, and promote stronger economic cooperation. However, achieving this unity is not without challenges and obstacles.

Politically, a unified Gulf ideological system would promote greater cohesion and integration among Gulf states, allowing them to act collectively and effectively on regional and international issues. By aligning their ideological frameworks and approaches, Gulf states would be better equipped to address common challenges, such as terrorism, regional conflicts, and political crises. They could find mutually beneficial solutions through coordinated decision-making and problem-solving and project a more unified front to the international community.

Furthermore, a unified Gulf ideology would strengthen the region's voice on the international stage by presenting a consolidated perspective. This enhanced influence would enable Gulf states to shape global political and economic agendas and advocate for their interests effectively. By pooling the resources, expertise, and diplomatic efforts of Gulf states, they would have increased leverage in negotiations and partnerships with other countries and international organizations.

Moreover, a unified Gulf ideological system could contribute to political stability within the region by establishing a shared understanding of principles and objectives. In doing so, Gulf states can minimize internal rivalries and conflicts. A unified ideological system would create a framework for managing disagreements, reducing the likelihood of intra-Gulf disputes, and enhancing trust and cooperation among Gulf states. This increased sense of stability would help attract foreign investment and cement the region's reputation as a reliable and secure hub for business and innovation.

The economic implications of Gulf ideological unity are equally significant. A shared understanding of economic principles, policies, and objectives would facilitate the development of a common economic framework, leading to enhanced cooperation and integration. Gulf states could collectively address economic challenges, such as the diversification of their economies, technological advancements, and infrastructure development.

Gulf states could promote more efficient intra-regional trade, investment, and economic growth through a unified economic framework. Harmonized regulations and policies would reduce barriers to trade and create a larger market for goods, services, and capital. This increased economic integration would encourage economies of scale, boost productivity, and attract foreign direct investment, thereby stimulating economic development within the region.

Furthermore, Gulf ideological unity would enable Gulf states to leverage their collective resources and expertise, fostering innovation, research, and development. By collaborating on key sectors such as energy, finance, and technology, Gulf states could pool their strengths and become global leaders in these fields. This would not only enhance their economic prowess but also increase their influence in global markets and strengthen their negotiating power with international partners.

However, achieving Gulf ideological unity is not a straight-forward process. Gulf states face significant political and economic differences that can hinder the establishment of a unified ideological system. The region's political structures and governance models vary, ranging from constitutional monarchies to republics. These differences can create challenges in reaching consensus on key political and policy issues.

Historical rivalries and geopolitical dynamics also impact the region's unity. Gulf states have had longstanding disputes over territorial boundaries, sovereignty issues, and regional influence. These historical divisions, exacerbated by external influences, can contribute to conflicts and hinder the coordination necessary for a unified Gulf ideology. Addressing these historical tensions requires trust-building measures, diplomatic dialogue, and efforts to find common ground based on shared goals and mutual respect.

Economically, the varying levels of development, resource distribution, and economic models among Gulf states can create disparities and competing interests. Gulf states with more advanced economies may be hesitant to fully integrate with less developed ones, fearing that it could impede their progress. Achieving economic convergence would require compromises, a redistribution of resources, and the harmonization of policies and regulations across the region. These measures would ensure that the benefits of economic unity are enjoyed by all Gulf states, promoting inclusivity and sustainable development.

Moreover, societal and cultural factors can also impact the feasibility and acceptance of a unified Gulf ideological system. Gulf societies have unique traditions, values, and social norms that shape their perspectives and priorities. Balancing these societal influences with the need for unity requires careful consideration and dialogue. Ensuring that a unified Gulf ideology respects and accommodates the diversity of its societies would be crucial for its long-term success.

A key aspect of achieving Gulf ideological unity is the need for effective regional institutions and mechanisms that facilitate cooperation and coordination. Strengthening existing organizations such as the Gulf Cooperation Council (GCC) and developing new platforms for dialogue would be essential. These institutions should be inclusive, transparent, and accountable to ensure the representation and participation of all Gulf states in decision-making processes.

Education and knowledge sharing play a vital role in fostering Gulf ideological unity. Promoting a common educational curriculum that emphasizes shared values, history, and culture can nurture a sense of common identity. Furthermore, investing in research and educational exchange programs can help develop a generation of Gulf citizens who understand and appreciate the benefits of a unified Gulf ideology. This would foster a sense of belonging and strengthen the bonds among Gulf states.

A step-by-step approach could be pursued to overcome the challenges of achieving Gulf ideological unity. Initially, Gulf states could focus on areas of common interest, such as security cooperation, economic integration, and cultural exchange. By gradually building trust and rapport in these areas, Gulf states can then expand their efforts towards a more comprehensive and unified ideology.

In conclusion, Gulf ideological unity's political and economic implications are vast and multifaceted. The potential benefits of political stability, regional influence, and economic cooperation far outweigh the challenges that need to be addressed. It requires a commitment from Gulf states to engage in open dialogue, build trust, and work towards common goals. The region can collectively address challenges, pursue common objectives, and secure a prosperous and harmonious future by embracing a shared vision for a unified Gulf ideological system.

D. Public opinion and the desire for unity in Gulf societies

- Historical Context: The historical factors that have shaped public opinion towards Gulf unity are deeply rooted in the region's complex history. The quest for unity began in the early 20th century when prominent thinkers and leaders advocated for a unified Gulf entity. The Pan-Arab movement, led by influential figures like Gamal Abdel Nasser, had a strong influence on public sentiment, emphasizing the importance of regional cohesion and solidarity. Additionally, the emergence of the Arab League provided a platform for discussions on unity and collaboration among Gulf states.

Historical events have also played a significant role in shaping public opinion towards unity in the Gulf. The Iran-Iraq war in the 1980s highlighted the vulnerabilities of the region, with

Gulf countries facing threats from external actors. The Gulf War in 1990-1991 reinforced the notion that the Gulf states needed to unite to protect their security and sovereignty. Furthermore, the Arab Spring uprisings highlighted the importance of unity in responding to internal challenges and promoting stability in the region.

- Current Sentiments: Recent surveys and polls shed light on the current public opinion towards Gulf unity. While the desire for unity remains strong in many Gulf societies, there are variations among the countries. Bahrain, Kuwait, and Qatar exhibit higher levels of support for unity, driven by shared cultural and historical ties, economic benefits, and security considerations. In contrast, societies like Saudi Arabia and the UAE display more nuanced sentiments towards unity, considering their larger size, diverse populations, and potential implications for their internal governance structures.

Factors influencing public sentiment towards unity include economic interdependencies, the desire for a collective Gulf identity, the perceived threat of external actors, and the belief that unity can enhance regional stability and security. On the other hand, concerns over sovereignty, cultural differences, potential economic disparities, the impact on domestic governance, and the differing agendas among Gulf states shape public opinion in varying degrees.

- Challenges and Obstacles: The pursuit of Gulf unity faces numerous challenges and obstacles. Politically, competing visions and interests among Gulf states pose a significant hurdle. Nation-building processes have created distinct national identities within Gulf societies, which can impede the desire for a collective Gulf identity. Additionally, the diverse social and cultural fabric of the Gulf, with varying degrees of modernization and religious adherence, can complicate efforts for unity.

Economically, differences in wealth distribution, resource allocation, and economic development create disparities among Gulf states, leading to potential tensions in the integration process. Efforts to harmonize economic policies, ensure equitable development, and address socio-economic concerns are essential for building public support for unity. Moreover, historical bilateral rivalries and geopolitical tensions, such as the Saudi-Iranian rivalry, influence the willingness of Gulf societies to embrace unity.

- Perception of Leadership: The perception of leadership and its influence on public opinion is a crucial factor in the desire for Gulf unity. Gulf state leaders play a significant role in shaping the narrative around unity, emphasizing the benefits it brings, such as increased regional power and influence, economic growth, and collective security. Government-led media campaigns and public speeches contribute to shaping public opinion, emphasizing the importance of shared heritage, history, and aspirations.

However, the effectiveness of leadership in shaping public sentiment varies. In some Gulf societies, leaders enjoy high levels of credibility and trust, enabling them to shape public opinion more effectively. Their ability to communicate the benefits and address concerns related to unity can significantly influence public sentiment. In contrast, in societies where governance structures are more fragmented or face public skepticism, the impact of leadership on public opinion may be limited.

- Public Discourse and Engagement: Public debates and discussions on Gulf unity provide valuable insights into public opinion. While some segments of society actively engage in discussions, highlighting the benefits of unity and advocating for further integration, others express skepticism and raise concerns about potential threats to their national identity or sovereignty.

Social media platforms have become important arenas for public discourse on unity, allowing people to express their views, engage with one another, and influence public sentiment. Online discussions often reflect generational and ideological differences, highlighting the evolving dynamics of public opinion. Efforts to foster more inclusive public engagement in unity initiatives, particularly among youth and marginalized communities, can help address concerns, build broader societal support, and foster a sense of ownership.

- Youth Perspective: The aspirations and views of Gulf's younger generation play a significant role in shaping public opinion on unity. Gulf youth are more connected than ever through social media and global networks, exposing them to a diverse range of ideas and perspectives. While some young people emphasize the potential economic opportunities and regional stability of unity, others advocate for more democratic reforms or prioritize their national identity over a collective Gulf one.

Understanding the factors that drive youth engagement or disengagement with unity initiatives is vital. Education systems and youth-focused programs that promote regional dialogue, cultural exchange, and entrepreneurship can shape youth perceptions and foster a sense of shared identity. Empowering youth to actively shape the discourse around unity can contribute to a more inclusive and representative vision of Gulf unity.

- Impact on Policies and Decision-Making: Public sentiment towards unity directly impacts policies related to Gulf integration. Governments often consider public opinion when making decisions regarding regional alliances, political integration, or economic cooperation. In societies where public sentiment is strongly in favor of unity, governments are more likely to invest political capital and resources into advancing integration projects. Conversely, public skepticism or resistance to unity may lead governments to take a more cautious approach or prioritize other domestic concerns. The extent to which public sentiment is incorporated into decision-making processes varies among Gulf states, with some governments more responsive to public opinion than others. Balancing public desires with strategic imperatives, economic considerations, and geopolitical realities is a complex task for policymakers. Building trust and transparency in decision-making and engaging with the public can foster a sense of ownership and legitimacy for unity initiatives.

- Comparative Analysis: A comparative analysis of public opinion towards unity in other regional blocs helps contextualize Gulf sentiments. While the desire for unity exists across various regions, the unique characteristics of the Gulf set it apart. The shared heritage, historical ties, economic interdependencies, and security challenges specific to Gulf societies shape public opinion. However, comparing public sentiment towards unity in the Gulf with other regional blocs, such as the European Union or the Association of Southeast Asian Nations, can provide valuable insights into the opportunities and challenges of achieving Gulf unity.

- Future Prospects and Implications: Considering public sentiment towards unity is crucial while assessing future prospects for Gulf integration. Given the evolving dynamics of public opinion and changing regional realities, scenarios for Gulf unity can vary. Scenario planning exercises can help stakeholders better understand the potential trajectories, challenges, and opportunities that lie ahead.

The implications of public sentiment for regional stability, security, and development are significant. Unity can bolster the Gulf's collective bargaining power globally, promote economic diversification, enhance regional security, and address common challenges such as climate change and water scarcity. Disregarding public desires for unity may lead to widespread disillusionment, undermining efforts for regional cooperation and stability. Encouraging ongoing dialogue with the public, fostering transparency, and addressing concerns can help build trust and strengthen the foundations for sustainable Gulf unity.

Conclusion: Public opinion and the desire for unity in Gulf societies shape the larger ideological dynamics of the region. Considering public sentiment is essential for understanding the potential for Gulf unity and its implications for regional stability. The historical context, current sentiments, challenges and obstacles, perception of leadership, public discourse and engagement, the perspective of youth, and the impact on policies and decision-making all contribute to shaping public opinion.

Navigating the complexities of Gulf unity is crucial to fostering inclusive public engagement and considering the aspirations and concerns of different segments of society. Efforts should be made to address potential economic disparities, promote cultural understanding, and balance regional cohesion and national sovereignty. Additionally, understanding the impact of leadership and public discourse on shaping public opinion can inform strategies for promoting unity.

Youth perspectives are critical in shaping public sentiment towards Gulf unity. By prioritizing youth engagement through educational initiatives, entrepreneurship programs, and cultur-

al exchanges, Gulf societies can harness the younger generation's potential in shaping a shared vision of unity.

The implications of public sentiment for policies and decision-making are significant. Governments in the Gulf region must balance public desires for unity with other strategic considerations, economic priorities, and geopolitical realities. Building trust, transparency, and legitimacy in the decision-making process is crucial in fostering public ownership and
support for unity initiatives.

Comparative analysis with other regional blocs can provide valuable insights into the opportunities and challenges of
achieving Gulf unity. Through studying the experiences of other regional integration projects, lessons can be learned about the
potential trajectories, pitfalls, and successes of Gulf unity.

Looking towards the future, assessing public sentiment is
critical for understanding the prospects for Gulf integration.
Scenario planning exercises can help stakeholders better antici-
pate the potential trajectories, challenges, and opportunities. By
actively engaging with the public, fostering transparency, and
addressing concerns, the foundations for sustainable Gulf unity
can be strengthened.

In summary, public opinion and the desire for unity in
Gulf societies are shaped by historical factors, current sentiments, challenges and obstacles, leadership perception, public
discourse and engagement, youth perspectives, and the impact
on policies and decision-making. These factors are essential for
fostering regional stability, security, and development. Encouraging ongoing dialogue with the public, addressing concerns,

and building trust can contribute to a sustainable vision of Gulf unity.

E. Landmarks

The Gulf States, encompassing Bahrain, Kuwait, Oman, Qatar, Saudi Arabia, and the United Arab Emirates (UAE), are renowned for their distinctive blend of tradition and modernity. In addition to their economic prowess and political influence, these states exhibit intricate ideological dynamics that significantly shape their domestic and foreign policies. This section delves deeper into the nuanced ideological landscape within the Gulf region and explores the complex interplay between religion, nationalism, sectarianism, and political Islam.

- *Historical Context*

To gain a comprehensive understanding of the ideological dynamics of the Gulf States, it is crucial to delve into their historical context. The formation of these states was greatly influenced by factors such as tribal affiliations, regional identity, and religious sects. For instance, in Saudi Arabia, the rise of the House of Saud, a conservative Wahhabi dynasty, transformed Saudi society into a stronghold of Sunni Islam. This close association between the Saudi monarchy and ultraconservative Wahhabi interpretations of Islam shaped not only domestic policies but also the kingdom's global religious influence. Similarly, Bahrain and Kuwait have historically experienced tensions between their Sunni ruling elites and marginalized Shia populations, with the latter often facing discrimination and political marginalization.

- *Religious Charisma and Sunni Extremism*

Religion, particularly Sunni Islam, plays a central role in shaping the ideological landscape of the Gulf. Saudi Arabia, as the custodian of Islam's two holiest sites, Mecca and Medina, wields religious authority that extends beyond its borders. The religious legitimacy of the Saudi monarchy, intertwined with ultraconservative Wahhabi interpretations of Islam, has contributed to the emergence and spread of Salafist ideology. This ideology ranges from forms that advocate for a strict adherence to Islam's early practices to more extreme variations that promote violence and terrorism. The spread of these extremist interpretations, especially through education systems and religious networks, has posed both domestic and international challenges, with certain Salafist groups becoming sources of radicalization and terrorist recruitment.

- *Political Islam and the Muslim Brotherhood*

Another noteworthy dimension of ideological dynamics in the Gulf revolves around political Islam, particularly the influence of the Muslim Brotherhood. Across the Gulf States, different branches of the Muslim Brotherhood have sought to challenge the legitimacy of ruling regimes by advocating for political reform, social justice, and applying Islamic principles in governance. The level of acceptance or repression towards the Muslim Brotherhood varies among the Gulf States, with some governments accommodating limited participation while others outrightly suppress their activities. This ideological competition has had a significant impact on the political environment within the region, with governments attempting to navigate competing Islamist and secular ideologies while retaining control.

- *Sectarianism and Regional Rivalries*

Sectarianism, particularly the Shia-Sunni divide, represents a critical factor influencing the ideological dynamics of the Gulf States. Bahrain, with its Shia-majority population ruled by a Sunni monarchy, has experienced persistent sectarian tensions, occasionally resulting in protests and violence. The security dilemma between Saudi Arabia, as the leader of the Sunni bloc, and Iran, as a champion of Shia causes, has amplified sectarian fault lines in the region. Iran's revolutionary ideology, rooted in Shia Islam, has heightened sectarian rivalries, leading to proxy conflicts in countries such as Syria, Yemen, and Lebanon. As a result, sectarianism has become a significant factor that shapes the ideological landscape and influences regional geopolitics.

- *Nationalism and Identity Politics*

Ideological dynamics in the Gulf are also influenced by nationalism and identity politics. While the ruling families emphasize Arab and Islamic identity to maintain legitimacy and regional influence, subnational identities based on tribal, regional, and ethnic affiliations persist. In Oman, the notion of Omanism, which emphasizes Omani identity and historical traditions, coexists with broader Gulf Arab nationalism. The United Arab Emirates, composed of seven distinct Emirates with varying historical backgrounds, has aimed to foster a shared Emirati national identity through state-led initiatives. Similarly, Qatar has cultivated a strong national identity, projecting its influence globally through its media outlets and proactive diplomacy. These multiple identities within the Gulf States contribute to a nuanced and complex ideological landscape.

- *Social Movements and Civil Society*

Despite the generally autocratic rule in the Gulf States, social movements and civil society organizations have emerged as spaces for ideological contestation. From labor movements demanding better working conditions and protection of worker's rights to youth-led movements calling for political reforms and societal change, these grassroots initiatives challenge the status quo and advocate for diverse ideological perspectives. However, the ruling regimes often respond with varying degrees of repression, aiming to maintain control over the ideological narrative and prevent challenges to their authority.

Conclusion

Understanding the deep-rooted ideological dynamics of the Gulf States is integral to comprehending their domestic affairs, foreign policies, and regional dynamics. The interplay between religion, nationalism, sectarianism, and political Islam shapes the region's political discourse and influences its complex relationship with both internal and external actors. The Gulf States must navigate these ideologies' intricacies and challenges as they strive to balance domestic stability, regional rivalries, and their positioning in the global order.

PATHWAYS TOWARDS GREATER IDEOLOGICAL CONVERGENCE

I n a region marked by diverse ideologies and competing interests, the quest for greater ideological convergence in the Gulf presents both a challenge and an opportunity. The need for unity is evident as Gulf countries face common challenges ranging from security threats to economic shifts. While achieving complete ideological harmony may be a lofty goal, exploring pathways that can facilitate convergence and foster a sense of shared purpose among Gulf nations is essential. This chapter delves deeper into various approaches towards achieving greater ideological convergence in the Gulf and highlights potential avenues for cooperation.

- Diplomatic Initiatives for Fostering Gulf Unity: Diplomatic efforts play a crucial role in promoting dialogue and understanding among Gulf countries.

Building upon existing platforms such as the Gulf Cooperation Council (GCC), efforts can be made to enhance communication channels, strengthen diplomatic ties, and facilitate greater cooperation in resolving disputes. Regular high-level diplomatic dialogues allow Gulf leaders to address concerns, express grievances, and identify common ground, ultimately paving the way for increased ideological convergence.

To further advance diplomatic initiatives, the establishment of a Gulf Parliament could serve as a platform for dialogue, legislation, and decision-making. Modelled after supranational entities like the European Parliament, a Gulf Parliament would bring together elected representatives from member nations to discuss and propose collective policies. The shared decision-making process would help bridge ideological differences and foster greater convergence on key regional issues. This would require careful consideration of the structure, composition, and decision-making mechanisms, ensuring fair representation of all member nations and addressing concerns related to sovereignty and national interests.

- Economic Integration and its Impact on Gulf Ideological Dynamics: Economic integration can serve as a catalyst for ideological convergence in the Gulf. Initiatives such as the Gulf Common Market and the Gulf Monetary Union lay the foundation for deeper economic cooperation among Gulf nations. By promoting trade, investment, and labor mobility, economic integration not only enhances economic prosperity but also creates opportunities for shared growth and, consequently, aligns interests and fosters greater ideological convergence.

To further strengthen economic integration, a unified Gulf economic policy framework can be developed. This framework would seek to harmonize regulations, trade policies, and investment strategies among Gulf nations. The establishment of joint ventures and economic zones, complemented by the elimination of barriers to cross-border trade and investment, would foster closer interdependence and shared economic interests. Additionally, the establishment of a regional development bank could facilitate funding for joint projects, infrastructure development, and socio-economic initiatives, thus promoting shared prosperity and creating common interests that contribute to greater ideological convergence.

- Cultural Exchanges and the Promotion of Shared Values: Cultural exchanges play a significant role in deepening mutual understanding and building bridges between Gulf societies. By promoting cultural interactions, such as art exhibitions, cultural festivals, and educational exchanges, Gulf nations can foster a sense of shared identity and values. Encouraging intercultural dialogue and appreciation can contribute to reducing ideological differences and promoting a more cohesive Gulf community.

In addition to cultural exchanges, promoting Gulf-wide educational initiatives that cultivate mutual respect and understanding is essential. By working on harmonizing educational curricula and promoting cultural and historical awareness of the region, Gulf nations can foster a common narrative that emphasizes shared heritage and values. This approach can help build a foundation for greater ideological convergence and unity among the younger generations. It is crucial to include diverse perspectives, incorporate inclusive education practices, and encourage critical thinking to ensure the development of a cohesive and well-rounded understanding of the region's history, culture, and values.

- Grassroots Movements and Civil Society Initiatives for Unity: The role of grassroots movements and civil society initiatives should not be overlooked in the pathway to greater ideological convergence. Grassroots movements that advocate for unity and cooperation can exert pressure on governments to prioritize shared interests over individual agendas. Civil society organizations can facilitate track-two diplomacy, engage in people-to-people exchanges, and promote dialogue forums that bridge ideological divides and nurture a sense of collective purpose.

To empower grassroots movements further, Gulf governments could create mechanisms for public participation in decision-making processes. By incorporating citizen feedback, ideas, and perspectives, Gulf nations can promote inclusivity and ensure that diverse ideological viewpoints are considered in shaping regional policies. This approach fosters ownership, encourages engagement, and ultimately contributes to greater ideological convergence within the Gulf region. Providing platforms and channels for the expression of dissenting voices, as well as protecting freedom of speech and association, will be fundamental to fostering a culture of robust engagement and active citizenship.

While these pathways present potential avenues for greater ideological convergence, challenges and limitations must also be acknowledged. Deep-rooted historical divisions, geopolitical rivalries, and conflicting interests may hinder progress towards unity. External influences and the involvement of global powers may also affect the dynamics of ideological convergence in the Gulf. Nonetheless, persistent efforts and a commitment to shared goals can help pave the way for a more unified Gulf region.

In conclusion, achieving greater ideological convergence in the Gulf requires a multifaceted approach that combines diplomatic efforts, economic integration, cultural exchanges, and grassroots initiatives. The Gulf countries can move towards a more cohesive and purposeful region by fostering dialogue, nurturing shared values, and prioritizing common interests. The Gulf can only attain the unity necessary to tackle challenges and secure a brighter future for its people through sustained efforts and collective determination.

A. Diplomatic initiatives for fostering Gulf unity

The quest for unity among the Gulf states has been a long-standing goal, driven by the recognition that collective action and cooperation can enhance regional stability and prosperity.

Diplomatic initiatives have played a crucial and multifaceted role in fostering this unity, with various strategies employed to build bridges, resolve conflicts, address challenges, and capitalize on regional opportunities. This chapter delves deeper into the key diplomatic initiatives undertaken to foster Gulf unity and explores their implications in greater detail.

One of the significant diplomatic initiatives to promote Gulf unity has been establishing regional organizations such as the Gulf Cooperation Council (GCC). Founded in 1981, the GCC aimed to enhance coordination and cooperation among member states in various fields, including security, economics, and social affairs. Over the years, the GCC has evolved to address regional challenges and promote closer ties among its members. Its success in addressing issues such as border disputes, trade barriers, and regional security concerns is a testament to its diplomatic efforts.

The effectiveness of the GCC in fostering Gulf unity can be attributed to several intertwined factors. Firstly, member states' shared cultural, historical, and geographical ties have provided a solid foundation for cooperation. The Arab heritage, the common Islamic faith, and centuries of interconnected trade and social interactions have nurtured a sense of community and solidarity among Gulf states. Recognizing commonalities and shared interests has enabled Gulf states to work together towards shared goals and aspirations.

Additionally, the GCC's institutional framework, including regular ministerial meetings, committees, and specialized task forces, has facilitated dialogue and coordination on various issues of regional importance. It has provided a platform for continuous engagement, fostering understanding, and promoting consensus-building. Regular consultations and decision-making processes within the GCC ensure that member states have a stake in shaping regional policies, leading to more effective and inclusive unity-building efforts.

Another diplomatic initiative that has played a pivotal role in fostering Gulf unity is mediating regional conflicts and disputes. Diplomatic channels have been instrumental in resolving tensions and preventing the escalation of conflicts. For instance, Saudi Arabia, Kuwait, and the United Arab Emirates significantly mediated the border dispute between Bahrain and Qatar in the mid-2000s. Their involvement helped ease tensions and contributed to strengthening Gulf unity.

The success of such mediation efforts can be attributed not only to the respect and influence held by Gulf states within the region but also to their diplomatic skills and expertise in navigating complex negotiations. Gulf countries have developed a unique diplomatic experience through centuries of trade, diplomacy, and cultural exchange. This experience, coupled with their deep understanding of regional dynamics and intricate networks of alliances, enables Gulf states to act as mediators in conflicts. Their nuanced approach, based on cultural sensitivity and mutual respect, facilitates dialogue, bridge divides, and finds mutually acceptable solutions.

There have been renewed efforts to promote Gulf unity diplomatically in recent years. One prominent example is the Kuwaiti-led mediation efforts between Qatar and Saudi Arabia, Bahrain, and the UAE during the Qatar crisis. These diplomatic initiatives aimed at resolving the diplomatic and economic blockade faced by Qatar highlighted the importance of dialogue and negotiation in overcoming differences and fostering unity.

These recent mediation efforts exemplify the commitment of Gulf states to diplomatic solutions and underline the significance of multilateral engagements. The involvement of Kuwait as a mediator reflects its historical role as a neutral and respected regional actor, capable of garnering trust and establishing common frameworks for negotiations. Such initiatives demonstrate the continuing relevance of diplomatic channels in fostering unity, even in moments of heightened tensions and adversarial positions.

In addition to mediating disputes, diplomatic initiatives have also been employed to address broader regional challenges. In the face of security threats, such as the rise of non-state actors like ISIS and the destabilizing influence of external powers, Gulf states have sought to build diplomatic alliances and foster cooperation. The Saudi-led Islamic Military Counter-Terrorism Coalition (IMCTC) is one such initiative aimed at combating terrorism in the region through coordinated efforts and intelligence sharing.

Diplomatic initiatives focused on security not only aim to address immediate challenges but also serve as trust-building measures among Gulf states. By sharing intelligence, coordinating military exercises, and enhancing interoperability, these initiatives nurture a collective security consciousness and promote a sense of solidarity in the face of common threats. The IMCTC, for example, underscores the commitment of Gulf states to fostering unity by jointly addressing security concerns through diplomatic channels.

Furthermore, diplomatic initiatives have been utilized to capitalize on economic opportunities and achieve greater integration among Gulf states. Efforts such as the Gulf Railway Project and the Gulf Common Market have sought to enhance regional connectivity, trade facilitation, and economic diversification. These initiatives aim to create a more robust and interdependent Gulf economy, laying the foundation for sustained unity and prosperity.

Expanding economic integration through diplomatic means offers numerous advantages for Gulf states. Firstly, it allows for the pooling of resources and creating economies of scale, making Gulf economies more resilient and competitive globally. Secondly, it fosters interdependence, reducing the likelihood of conflicts and facilitating the resolution of disputes through diplomatic negotiations rather than confrontation. Lastly, economic integration initiatives promote a sense of shared destinies, highlighting the long-term benefits of unity by demonstrating how cooperation can lead to increased prosperity and development for all.

However, it is essential to acknowledge that diplomatic initiatives to foster Gulf unity face significant challenges. Political differences, power struggles, and diverging interests among Gulf states can hinder the effectiveness of diplomatic efforts. The dynamics of international politics, regional rivalries, and differing priorities further complicate the unity-building process. Moreover, external interventions and the involvement of major powers in the region can complicate diplomatic initiatives and disrupt unity-building processes.

Despite these challenges, diplomatic initiatives remain crucial for fostering Gulf unity. By promoting dialogue, understanding, and cooperation, diplomatic channels offer a platform for resolving disputes, addressing shared concerns, and building consensus on regional issues. They allow Gulf states to find common ground, bridge differences, and work towards a more unified and prosperous region.

In conclusion, diplomatic initiatives have played an instrumental and multifaceted role in fostering Gulf unity. Through establishing regional organizations like the GCC, mediation efforts to resolve conflicts, diplomatic alliances to address security challenges or economic integration initiatives, diplomatic channels have been critical in promoting dialogue, understanding, and cooperation among Gulf states. The success of these initiatives can be attributed to factors such as shared ties, institutional frameworks, diplomatic skills, and the collective influence of Gulf states. Although challenges persist, diplomatic initiatives continue to offer a pathway towards greater unity in the Gulf and the realization of shared goals and aspirations. Moreover, expanding the scope of diplomatic initiatives to address economic integration and security challenges further bolsters the prospect of a more resilient and prosperous region.

B. Economic integration and its impact on Gulf ideological dynamics

Economic integration plays a vital role in the Gulf region, contributing significantly to the overall growth and development of its countries. The interconnectedness of Gulf economies has far-reaching implications for ideological dynamics within the region, shaping societal values, political decision-making, and the pursuit of collective goals.

1. Strengthening Interdependence: Economic integration fosters a sense of interdependence among Gulf countries, as they increasingly rely on each other for trade, investment, and economic cooperation. Establishing regional economic blocs such as the Gulf Cooperation Council (GCC), the Arab Customs Union, and various free trade agreements has promoted closer economic ties, leading to increased cooperation and interaction among Gulf nations. This interconnectedness creates a shared economic interest, which can influence ideological dynamics. For instance, as Gulf countries become more dependent on each other for economic stability and growth, there may be a greater emphasis on cooperation, peaceful relations, and diplomatic dialogue to protect their mutual economic interests. Interdependence also serves as a deterrent to conflict, as disruptions in economic ties can adversely affect all participating countries.

2. Enhancing Economic Stability: Economic integration initiatives seek to promote stability and sustainable growth in the Gulf region. By implementing policies related to monetary union, customs union, and common market, economic integration aims to reduce economic disparities and ensure stability. This stability is crucial for the ideological landscape, as it provides a

foundation for social cohesion, cooperation, and inclusive development. With stable economies, countries are better equipped to address ideological issues and navigate societal challenges without the added burden of economic instability. Furthermore, economic stability enhances the credibility and legitimacy of political systems, reinforcing the ideological framework that underpins governance practices in the Gulf.

3. Diversification of Economies: Economic integration encourages Gulf countries to diversify their economies, reducing their reliance on a single sector, usually oil and gas. The ongoing efforts to diversify the economies of Gulf nations can lead to the development of new industries, job creation, and increased economic opportunities for their populations. As countries embrace economic diversification, it can influence their ideological outlook, as they seek to adapt to changing economic realities and address the demands of a more diverse society. For example, the diversification of economies may necessitate enhanced investments in education, research and development, and innovation to create a knowledge-based economy. This transition towards a knowledge-driven society can foster a more progressive and forward-thinking ideological approach, emphasizing human capital, creativity, and entrepreneurship.

4. Bridging Socioeconomic Disparities: Economic integration initiatives also aim to bridge socioeconomic

disparities among Gulf countries. By promoting inclusive growth and redistributive policies, these initiatives seek to address income inequalities and improve all citizens' living standards. Reducing socioeconomic disparities can profoundly impact ideological dynamics, as it fosters a sense of social justice, equality, and inclusivity. As Gulf nations strive to create stronger social safety nets, provide affordable housing, and improve access to quality healthcare and education, the populace may experience an ideological shift, placing greater emphasis on human rights, gender equality, and opportunities for all.

5. Fostering Regional Identity: Economic integration can contribute to developing a shared Gulf regional identity. As Gulf countries collaborate and realize the benefits of working together, a sense of shared purpose and common destiny may emerge. Economic integration initiatives create platforms for mutual understanding, cultural exchange, and a cooperative mindset, which can influence ideological dynamics. Developing a regional identity fosters a sense of collective consciousness and a desire for closer unity. Shared regional objectives, such as harnessing renewable energy sources or addressing environmental challenges, can shape ideologies around environmental stewardship, sustainability, and shared responsibility for the region's future.

6. Economic Interests Influence Political Decisions: Eco-

nomic integration gives rise to common economic interests among Gulf countries. These shared interests can influence political decision-making, leading to policy convergence in certain areas. The alignment of economic interests can impact ideological dynamics as countries seek to harmonize their policies to maximize the benefits of economic integration. For instance, pursuing economic diversification necessitates policy reforms, including promoting entrepreneurship, fostering innovation, and improving labor rights. These policy shifts impact the ideological landscape related to economic prosperity, social progress, and regional governance practices. The convergence of policies driven by common economic interests can also contribute to greater regional cooperation, integration, and the establishment of supranational institutions.

7. Interactions with Global Institutions and Norms: Economic integration in the Gulf region exposes countries to global institutions and norms. As Gulf nations participate in international trade, invest in foreign markets, and engage in economic partnerships with non-regional actors, they encounter diverse ideologies and norms. These interactions can shape Gulf societies' perceptions and understanding of different ideologies, triggering debates and discussions on values, cultural preservation, and identity. Gulf countries may struggle to balance global influences with local traditions, leading to an ongoing negotiation of ide-

ologies within their societies. The exposure to global institutions and norms can also provide opportunities for Gulf countries to contribute to shaping and influencing international norms and ideologies, reflecting their unique perspectives and values.

In conclusion, economic integration in the Gulf region significantly impacts ideological dynamics, shaping societal values, political decision-making, and the pursuit of shared goals. It strengthens interdependence among Gulf countries, fosters economic stability, promotes diversification of economies, bridges socioeconomic disparities, fosters regional identity, influences political decisions, and exposes Gulf countries to global institutions and norms. Understanding the intricate relationship between economics and ideology is crucial for comprehending the complexities of the Gulf region and its ongoing transformation.

C. Cultural exchanges and the promotion of shared values

Cultural exchanges foster understanding, empathy, and unity among diverse societies. In the context of the Gulf region, where diverse cultures coexist, such exchanges are essential for promoting shared values and strengthening the sense of shared identity. This extended chapter delves deeper into the significance of cultural exchanges and explores how they contribute to the promotion of shared values within the Gulf.

- Appreciating Cultural Diversity:

The Gulf region is a melting pot of cultures, with each country boasting its unique traditions, arts, cuisine, and heritage. Cultural exchanges provide a platform for individuals from different backgrounds to learn and appreciate the diversity of their neighboring Gulf societies. Through various cultural activities, such as art exhibitions, music concerts, traditional dance performances, literary festivals, and craft fairs, people can experience firsthand the richness of Gulf cultures. This exposure broadens perspectives, demolishes barriers, and fosters a sense of interconnectedness and shared experiences, bolstering the appreciation for the unique aspects of each culture.

- Building Bridges and Breaking Stereotypes:

One of the most significant benefits of cultural exchanges is their capacity to break down stereotypes and misconceptions between Gulf societies. By providing opportunities for people to interact, share stories, and showcase the positive aspects of their cultural heritage, these exchanges build bridges of understanding and empathy. Preconceived notions are challenged as individuals engage in meaningful dialogue, learn from one another, and recognize the commonalities that underpin their societies. The subsequent mutual respect and acceptance contribute to an environment of harmonious coexistence, fostering lasting friendships and collaboration.

- Encouraging Dialogue and Collaboration:

Cultural exchanges encourage dialogue and collaboration by creating spaces for open and meaningful conversations about cultural heritage, identity, and values. Through interactive workshops, seminars, conferences, and panel discussions, individuals can explore similarities and differences, channeling their diverse perspectives into a shared understanding. These platforms allow for the exchange of ideas, knowledge, and creativity, fostering collaborative efforts and the discovery of new perspectives. Engaging in cross-cultural dialogue strengthens relationships between Gulf nations, enhances tolerance, and promotes cultural unity, while providing a basis for solving shared challenges and improving collective well-being.

- Promoting Cultural Diplomacy:

Cultural exchanges serve as an effective tool for cultural diplomacy, enabling Gulf countries to enhance their soft power and shape their international image. By showcasing their cultural treasures to an international audience, Gulf nations can attract tourists, promote economic and investment opportunities, and build diplomatic relationships based on shared values. Cultural diplomacy initiatives, such as hosting international exhibitions, film festivals, or participating in global cultural events, contribute not only to bilateral relations but also to fostering intercultural dialogue on a broader scale. Through such exchanges, Gulf nations increase their global influence and become ambassadors of their cultural heritage, advancing peace, understanding, and cooperation.

- Fostering Youth Engagement and Empowerment:

Cultural exchanges have a profound impact on the younger generation, empowering them to develop a sense of pride in their cultural heritage while cultivating respect for other cultures. Offering opportunities, such as youth exchange programs, art competitions, cultural festivals, internships, and scholarships, cultural exchanges inspire young people to embrace their identities and traditions. Active participation in cross-cultural activities nurtures their understanding of global diversity and cooperation, fostering empathy, open-mindedness, and leadership skills. By nurturing the youth, cultural exchanges contribute to the growth of future leaders who will champion shared values in the Gulf region, promoting social cohesion and sustainable development.

- Strengthening Gulf Unity:

Ultimately, cultural exchanges serve as a catalyst for strengthening Gulf unity. By promoting shared values, enhancing mutual understanding, and celebrating cultural diversity, these exchanges contribute to a shared Gulf identity. Collaborative projects that involve multiple Gulf countries, such as joint art exhibitions, film productions, cultural festivals, and research initiatives, foster a sense of camaraderie and shared destiny. They ignite a shared purpose and a collective voice that resonates across borders, leading to a more united and cohesive Gulf region. Partnership frameworks that facilitate ongoing cultural exchanges and collaborations nurture a sense of belonging, generating a strong foundation for cooperation in various fields, including economic, social, and political realms.

In conclusion, cultural exchanges enrich the Gulf region by promoting shared values and nurturing unity. Through appreciating cultural diversity, breaking down stereotypes, encouraging dialogue and collaboration, promoting cultural diplomacy, fostering youth engagement and empowerment, and strengthening Gulf unity, these exchanges contribute to an interconnected, empathetic, and harmonious Gulf society that thrives on mutual respect, understanding, and appreciation. Such cultural exchanges shape the present and pave the way for a prosperous and harmonious future for the Gulf region.

D. Grassroots movements and civil society initiatives for unity

Grassroots movements and civil society initiatives play a crucial and dynamic role in fostering unity within the Gulf region. As the Gulf ideological dynamics continue to evolve, these bottom-up approaches have the potential to bridge the gaps between different factions and promote a sense of common purpose. This section aims to delve deeper into the various grassroots movements and civil society initiatives that have emerged in the Gulf, highlighting their impact on promoting unity and addressing existing divisions.

Grassroots movements, driven by ordinary individuals passionate about societal change, have historically played a key role in advocating for unity and social justice in the Gulf. These movements often emerge from the grassroots in response to social, political, or economic grievances that affect the wider population. They strive to challenge existing power structures and demand inclusion and equitable rights for all citizens, regardless of their background or affiliations.

One prominent example of grassroots activism is the Bahraini pro-democracy movement, which gained significant attention during the Arab Spring in 2011. What began as peaceful protests demanding political reform and equal rights quickly escalated into a larger movement as Bahraini citizens came together to challenge the authoritarian rule. This movement highlighted the aspirations of the Bahraini people for inclusive governance, accountability, and democratic participation, prominently showcasing the desire for unity among various factions in society.

Furthermore, grassroots movements in the Gulf are not limited to political issues. They also address social and environmental challenges that affect the well-being of communities. Youth-led environmental movements have gained traction in recent years, such as the "Green Gulf Initiative" and "Clean Coast Campaign," which aim to raise awareness about environmental degradation and promote sustainable practices. These movements emphasize the interconnectedness between individuals and their natural surroundings, fostering a shared commitment to protect the Gulf's unique ecosystems and heritage for future generations. These grassroots movements encourage unity in action and collective responsibility towards the environment by organising clean-up drives, awareness campaigns, and collaborative projects.

Civil society initiatives, facilitated by non-governmental organizations and community-based groups, serve as an additional pillar in fostering unity across the Gulf. These initiatives aim to create spaces for dialogue, understanding, and cooperation among diverse groups, forging a sense of shared purpose and addressing societal divisions.

Interfaith dialogue initiatives play a pivotal role in promoting unity throughout the Gulf. By bringing people from different religious backgrounds together, these dialogues provide a platform to discuss shared values, promote tolerance, challenge stereotypical narratives, and foster relationships based on respect and understanding. These initiatives aim to build bridges, deconstruct prejudices, and encourage collaborations that ultimately strengthen social cohesion.

Cultural exchanges and educational programs also significantly promote unity within the Gulf. By encouraging cultural understanding and appreciation, individuals from various backgrounds have the opportunity to engage with each other's traditions, languages, and histories. These exchanges help break down stereotypes, promote empathy, and foster a sense of shared identity that transcends national boundaries. Through investment in educational programs that emphasize tolerance, inclusivity, and critical thinking, civil society organizations empower individuals with the knowledge and skills needed to challenge divisive narratives, fostering a more united Gulf community.

Despite their valuable contributions, grassroots movements and civil society initiatives in the Gulf face significant challenges. Repression and crackdowns on dissent, restrictions on freedom of speech and assembly, and societal divisions can hinder the progress of these movements. Governments in the region often view grassroots movements as threats to stability rather than opportunities for dialogue and progress, leading to a suppression of their activities.

However, with the rise of connectivity and the increasing use of social media for communication and mobilization, grassroots movements and civil society initiatives have greater opportunities to amplify their voices and reach broader audiences.

Social media platforms, such as Twitter and Facebook, have become powerful virtual spaces for expression, enabling activists to organize more effectively, share their stories, and mobilize support locally and globally. These online platforms have transformed how individuals engage, overcoming physical barriers and restrictions to foster dialogue and collaboration.

In conclusion, grassroots movements and civil society initiatives are integral to the Gulf's ideological dynamics, providing platforms for ordinary individuals to voice their concerns, challenge existing power structures, and promote unity. Through activism, dialogue, and collaboration, these movements strive to bridge divisions and foster a sense of shared purpose among different factions within Gulf societies. While challenges persist, the resilience and determination of grassroots movements and civil society initiatives bring hope for a more united Gulf region in the future.

E. Landmarks

The Gulf States, encompassing Bahrain, Kuwait, Oman, Qatar, Saudi Arabia, and the United Arab Emirates (UAE), are renowned for their distinctive blend of tradition and modernity. In addition to their economic prowess and political influence, these states exhibit intricate ideological dynamics that significantly shape their domestic and foreign policies. This section delves deeper into the nuanced ideological landscape within the Gulf region and explores the complex interplay between religion, nationalism, sectarianism, and political Islam.

- *Historical Context*

To gain a comprehensive understanding of the ideological dynamics of the Gulf States, it is crucial to delve into their historical context. The formation of these states was greatly influenced by factors such as tribal affiliations, regional identity, and religious sects. For instance, in Saudi Arabia, the rise of the House of Saud, a conservative Wahhabi dynasty, transformed Saudi society into a stronghold of Sunni Islam. This close association between the Saudi monarchy and ultraconservative Wahhabi interpretations of Islam shaped not only domestic policies but also the kingdom's global religious influence. Similarly, Bahrain and Kuwait have historically experienced tensions between their Sunni ruling elites and marginalized Shia populations, with the latter often facing discrimination and political marginalization.

- *Religious Charisma and Sunni Extremism*

Religion, particularly Sunni Islam, plays a central role in shaping the ideological landscape of the Gulf. Saudi Arabia, as the custodian of Islam's two holiest sites, Mecca and Medina, wields religious authority that extends beyond its borders. The religious legitimacy of the Saudi monarchy, intertwined with ultraconservative Wahhabi interpretations of Islam, has contributed to the emergence and spread of Salafist ideology. This ideology ranges from forms that advocate for strict adherence to Islam's early practices to more extreme variations that promote violence and terrorism. The spread of these extremist interpretations, especially through education systems and religious networks, has posed both domestic and international challenges, with certain Salafist groups becoming sources of radicalization and terrorist recruitment.

- *Political Islam and the Muslim Brotherhood*

Another noteworthy dimension of ideological dynamics in the Gulf revolves around political Islam, particularly the influence of the Muslim Brotherhood. Across the Gulf States, different branches of the Muslim Brotherhood have sought to challenge the legitimacy of ruling regimes by advocating for political reform, social justice, and the application of Islamic principles in governance. The level of acceptance or repression towards the Muslim Brotherhood varies among the Gulf States, with some governments accommodating limited participation while others outrightly suppress their activities. This ideological competition has had a significant impact on the political environment within the region, with governments attempting to navigate competing Islamist and secular ideologies while retaining control.

- *Sectarianism and Regional Rivalries*

Sectarianism, particularly the Shia-Sunni divide, represents a critical factor influencing the ideological dynamics of the Gulf States. Bahrain, with its Shia-majority population ruled by a Sunni monarchy, has experienced persistent sectarian tensions, occasionally resulting in protests and violence. The security dilemma between Saudi Arabia, as the leader of the Sunni bloc, and Iran, as a champion of Shia causes, has amplified sectarian fault lines in the region. Iran's revolutionary ideology, rooted in Shia Islam, has heightened sectarian rivalries, leading to proxy conflicts in countries such as Syria, Yemen, and Lebanon. As a result, sectarianism has become a significant factor that shapes the ideological landscape and influences regional geopolitics.

- *Nationalism and Identity Politics*

Ideological dynamics in the Gulf are also influenced by nationalism and identity politics. While the ruling families emphasize Arab and Islamic identity to maintain legitimacy and regional influence, subnational identities based on tribal, regional, and ethnic affiliations persist. In Oman, the notion of Omanism, which emphasizes Omani identity and historical traditions, coexists with broader Gulf Arab nationalism. The United Arab Emirates, composed of seven distinct Emirates with varying historical backgrounds, has aimed to foster a shared Emirati national identity through state-led initiatives. Similarly, Qatar has cultivated a strong national identity, projecting its influence globally through its media outlets and proactive diplomacy. These multiple identities within the Gulf States contribute to a nuanced and complex ideological landscape.

- *Social Movements and Civil Society*

Despite the generally autocratic rule in the Gulf States, social movements and civil society organizations have emerged as spaces for ideological contestation. From labor movements demanding better working conditions and protection of worker's rights to youth-led movements calling for political reforms and societal change, these grassroots initiatives challenge the status quo and advocate for diverse ideological perspectives. However, the ruling regimes often respond with varying degrees of repression to maintain control over the ideological narrative and prevent challenges to their authority.

Conclusion

Understanding the deep-rooted ideological dynamics of the Gulf States is integral to comprehending their domestic affairs, foreign policies, and regional dynamics. The interplay between religion, nationalism, sectarianism, and political Islam shapes the region's political discourse and influences its complex relationship with both internal and external actors. The Gulf States must navigate these ideologies' intricacies and challenges as they strive to balance domestic stability, regional rivalries, and their positioning in the global order.

IMPLICATIONS FOR REGIONAL STABILITY, SECURITY, AND DEVELOPMENT

T his chapter discusses the far-reaching ramifications of establishing a united Gulf ideological system for regional stability, security, and growth. Considering the intricate geopolitical dynamics, historical rivalries, and socio-economic complexities of the Gulf region, understanding how a unified Gulf ideological system can impact these areas is crucial for comprehending such a venture's potential outcomes and benefits.

1. The Role of Gulf Ideological Unity in Regional Stability:

Regional stability is a fundamental prerequisite for ensuring the Gulf's peace, progress, and prosperity. Implementing a unified Gulf ideological system has enormous potential to foster a shared sense of purpose, cooperation, and collective responsibility among the Gulf states. By transcending individual interests and aligning their ideological perspectives, Gulf nations can work together towards resolving conflicts, preventing the escalation of tensions, and promoting stability in the region.

1.1. Resolving Conflicts: Gulf nations have experienced various conflicts throughout history, often characterized by proxy wars, political rivalries, and border disputes. A unified Gulf ideological system allows for a platform where these conflicts can be addressed with a shared vision, promoting mutual understanding and facilitating the resolution of longstanding disputes. By establishing dialogue, negotiations, and conflict resolution mechanisms, Gulf nations can find common ground and build stronger relationships based on cooperation rather than confrontation.

1.2. Preventing Escalation: The Gulf region has witnessed incidents of escalating tensions, such as geopolitical rivalries, sectarian strife, or ideological differences. A unified Gulf ideology can serve as a unifying force, enabling diplomatic channels for effective communication, conflict de-escalation, and crisis management. By adopting shared principles and norms, Gulf nations can create a conducive environment where conflicts are managed peacefully, reducing the likelihood of further escalation and promoting regional stability.

1.3. Promoting Stability: With shared ideological principles, Gulf nations can establish a framework of mutual trust, collaboration, and accountability. This framework will serve as a basis for fostering stability in the region by discouraging unilateral actions and promoting multilateral cooperation. By aligning their approaches to regional security challenges, Gulf nations can develop common strategies, pool resources, and enhance collective security measures to safeguard regional stability against external threats.

2. Security Challenges and the Need for Coordinated Approaches:

The Gulf region faces a wide range of security challenges, including regional rivalries, terrorism, and external threats. Achieving Gulf ideological unity can greatly enhance regional security through coordinated approaches to addressing these challenges.

2.1. Regional Rivalries: Historical and contemporary rivalries among Gulf states have often strained relations and contributed to regional instability. By unifying their ideological perspectives, Gulf nations can overcome these divisions, fostering a shared security framework that prioritizes cooperation over competition. This framework can enable a collective approach to address conflicts, mediate disputes, and promote regional cooperation, thereby reducing the risk of military confrontations and enhancing overall security.

2.2. Combating Terrorism: Terrorism and extremist ideologies pose significant security threats to Gulf nations. A unified Gulf ideological system can facilitate enhanced intelligence-sharing, joint counter-terrorism operations, and comprehensive strategies for countering radicalization, thereby collectively combating these common challenges. By creating a coordinated framework for intelligence cooperation, resource sharing, and joint military exercises, Gulf nations can effectively dismantle terrorist networks, prevent cross-border infiltrations, and safeguard their societies from extremist threats.

2.3. Addressing External Threats: The Gulf region is exposed to various external threats, including interference from non-regional powers, maritime security risks, and nuclear proliferation concerns. A coordinated approach through a unified Gulf ideological system empowers the region to address these challenges and safeguard its security interests. By fostering more vital regional institutions, promoting information-sharing mechanisms, and developing joint defense capabilities, Gulf nations can deter external threats and ensure the security and sovereignty of their shared region.

3. Socioeconomic Development and the Benefits of Gulf Unity:

Economic prosperity and development are vital components of any stable region. A unified Gulf ideological system holds significant implications for socioeconomic progress and cooperation.

3.1. Economic Diversification: Gulf nations have long recognized the need to diversify their economies beyond hydrocarbon resources. A unified Gulf ideological system can foster deeper economic integration, enable resource pooling, and accelerate economic diversification efforts, creating a more sustainable and resilient regional economy. By coordinating economic policies, attracting foreign investment, and promoting intra-regional trade, Gulf nations can tap into synergies and unlock their true economic potential, reducing dependence on fossil fuels and creating opportunities for innovation and job creation.

3.2. Trade Integration: Establishing a unified Gulf ideological system can pave the way for greater trade integration across the region. Harmonizing trade policies, reducing trade barriers, and facilitating the movement of goods and services can unlock new markets, enhance economic interdependence, and stimulate growth across various sectors. By streamlining customs procedures, standardizing regulations, and establishing a common trade framework, Gulf nations can create a seamless economic space that fosters investment, boosts competitiveness, and strengthens regional economic ties.

3.3. Innovation and Human Capital: Collaboration through a unified Gulf ideological system can nurture innovation, research, and development initiatives. Sharing expertise, promoting educational exchange programs, and investing in human capital can ensure the result of a skilled workforce that drives productivity and competitiveness within the region. By creating a regional platform for research collaboration, knowledge-sharing, and technology transfer, Gulf nations can accelerate their technological advancements, foster a culture of innovation, and empower their societies to adapt to the challenges and opportunities of the rapidly changing global economy.

4. Environmental Sustainability and the Quest for Shared Solutions:

Addressing environmental challenges is a global imperative, and the Gulf region is no exception. A cohesive Gulf ideological system can be crucial in promoting sustainable development and addressing common environmental issues.

4.1. Water and Energy Security: The Gulf region faces significant challenges regarding water scarcity and energy consumption. A unified Gulf ideological system can facilitate sharing best practices, collaborative water management strategies, and joint investments in renewable energy sources, ensuring long-term water and energy security for the entire region. By pooling expertise in water desalination technologies, promoting efficient water usage, and diversifying energy sources, Gulf nations can alleviate the burden of resource scarcity, reduce environmental degradation, and create a sustainable future for their populations.

4.2. Climate Change Adaptation: The Gulf region is vulnerable to the impacts of climate change, including rising temperatures, rising sea levels, and extreme weather events. A unified Gulf ideological system can strengthen regional cooperation in adopting climate change adaptation and mitigation measures, promoting sustainable development practices, and collaborating on environmental research. By coordinating efforts to reduce greenhouse gas emissions, developing climate resilience strategies, and investing in renewable energy infrastructure, Gulf nations can navigate the environmental challenges posed by climate change and build a more sustainable and resilient future for their societies.

4.3. Marine Conservation: With extensive coastlines and rich marine biodiversity, Gulf nations share an interest in preserving their marine ecosystems. A unified Gulf ideological system can foster collective efforts to combat overfishing, reduce pollution, and conserve fragile coral reefs, safeguarding the region's marine resources for future generations. By establishing marine protected areas, implementing sustainable fishing practices, and promoting public awareness, Gulf nations can embrace their shared responsibility in preserving the unique ecological heritage of the Gulf, protecting marine habitats, and promoting sustainable fisheries to ensure the long-term use of its marine resources.

Conclusion:

Establishing a unified Gulf ideological system holds tremendous potential for promoting regional stability, security, and development. By transcending historical rivalries, fostering cooperation, and aligning their ideological perspectives, Gulf nations can address conflicts, prevent the escalation of tensions, and promote stability in the region. Moreover, a unified Gulf ideology can enhance regional security by facilitating coordinated approaches to address security challenges, such as regional rivalries, terrorism, and external threats. This unified approach can also unlock the benefits of economic integration, including economic diversification, trade integration, and innovation, fostering socioeconomic development and cooperation. Additionally, a unified Gulf ideological system can promote environmental sustainability by addressing common environmental issues such as water and energy security, climate change adaptation, and marine conservation. By harnessing the power of collective action and cooperation, Gulf nations can build a resilient and prosperous region for the benefit of their people and future generations.

A. The role of Gulf ideological unity in regional stability

The role of Gulf ideological unity in regional stability is a complex and multifaceted aspect that requires a deeper analysis to understand its dynamics and potential challenges fully. This extended chapter aims to provide a more comprehensive and detailed exploration of how a common ideological framework can contribute to stability in the Gulf region.

Historically, the Gulf region has been marked by deep-rooted ideological divisions, often fueled by rivalries and conflicts. The region is home to a variety of ideologies, including conservative Islamism, secular nationalism, and sectarianism. These diverse viewpoints have at times resulted in clashes and tensions among the Gulf states.

However, despite these differences, Gulf ideological unity has the potential to overcome historical divisions and contribute to regional stability. A shared ideological framework can serve as a common language, providing a basis for understanding and cooperation among the Gulf states. By establishing common principles and goals, Gulf countries can transcend their differences and work towards shared objectives, such as regional security, economic development, and social progress.

One of the key factors that can promote Gulf ideological unity is the existence of a strong leadership that is committed to fostering cooperation and bridging ideological divides. Leaders who prioritize regional stability can play a vital role in creating an environment conducive to dialogue and consensus-building. By engaging in constructive discussions, leaders can facilitate the development of a shared vision and help build trust among Gulf states.

Moreover, a unified Gulf ideological system can contribute to stability by promoting tolerance and inclusivity. Gulf states can create a more harmonious and cohesive society by emphasizing shared values, such as justice, equality, and respect for human rights. This can help counter radical ideologies and mitigate the risk of violent extremism, which can destabilize the region.

Gulf ideological unity can also play a significant role in addressing key security challenges in the region. A shared ideological framework can foster a sense of collective security, promoting cooperation in areas such as intelligence sharing, military cooperation, and counterterrorism efforts. By developing joint defense strategies and conducting joint military exercises, Gulf states can enhance their capacity to respond to external threats and deter potential aggressors.

Furthermore, Gulf ideological unity can positively impact economic stability and growth. A shared economic ideology can facilitate regional economic integration and cooperation, increasing trade, investment, and prosperity. By developing common economic policies, Gulf states can leverage their comparative advantages and promote sustainable development, reducing economic disparities and contributing to the region's overall stability.

However, achieving and maintaining Gulf ideological unity poses several challenges. Historical rivalries, political divisions, and societal norms and values differences can hinder progress towards a cohesive ideological system. Moreover, external pressures and interference from global powers can further complicate efforts to achieve unity. Geopolitical rivalries, such as the ongoing dispute between Qatar and other Gulf states, highlight the difficulties in establishing a unified ideological framework.

Nonetheless, recognizing the potential benefits of Gulf ideological unity in promoting regional stability necessitates sustained efforts and dialogue among the Gulf states. It requires a commitment to finding common ground, emphasizing shared interests over differences, and fostering a culture of mutual respect and understanding.

To this end, Gulf states should invest in platforms for dialogue and cooperation, such as regional organizations, academic exchanges, and cultural programs. Open and honest discussions can help bridge ideological gaps, promote understanding, and build trust among the Gulf states. Furthermore, fostering people-to-people interactions, grassroots initiatives, and civil society participation can also contribute to developing a shared Gulf identity and promote stability.

In conclusion, Gulf ideological unity has the potential to play a significant role in enhancing regional stability. By establishing shared values, promoting cooperation, and fostering a sense of common identity, Gulf states can effectively address regional challenges, build resilience to external pressures, and create a more stable and prosperous future for the Gulf region as a whole. However, achieving and maintaining this unity requires ongoing efforts, dialogue, and a commitment to shared goals and principles.

B. Security challenges and the need for coordinated approaches

The Gulf region faces complex and interconnected security challenges that demand a deep understanding and a coordinated approach. In this section, we delve deeper into the various security challenges the region faces, emphasizing the importance of collaborative efforts in addressing them effectively.

- *Regional Conflicts and Instability*:

  ○ Ongoing Conflicts: The conflicts in Yemen, Syria, and Iraq have significantly impacted the stability of the Gulf region. These conflicts have resulted in immense human suffering and displacement while also providing fertile ground for the spread of extremist ideologies. To address these challenges, Gulf states must prioritize diplomatic negotiations, facilitate humanitarian aid, and work towards reconciling the warring factions to achieve lasting peace.

  ○ Non-State Actors: Extremist groups, such as ISIS and Al-Qaeda, have exploited the power vacuums created by regional conflicts, posing a severe security threat. These groups continue to attract recruits, radicalize individuals, and carry out terrorist activities not only in the Gulf but also globally. Gulf states should collaborate closely on intelligence sharing, joint military operations, and countering extremist propaganda to disrupt these networks effectively.

○ Ethnic and Sectarian Tensions: The Gulf region is characterized by a diverse range of ethnic and religious groups, creating potential flashpoints for conflict and instability. Sectarian tensions, particularly between Sunni and Shia communities, have the potential to escalate and destabilize neighboring countries. It is crucial for Gulf states to foster social cohesion, promote religious tolerance, and address long-standing grievances to mitigate the risk of sectarian violence.

- *Maritime Security*:

  ○ Strategic Importance: Due to its strategic location as a major crossroads for international trade and energy flows, maritime security is of paramount importance in the Gulf region. Gulf states must work together to ensure the safety and security of maritime routes against piracy, smuggling, and other illegal activities. Joint maritime patrols, robust intelligence sharing, and close cooperation with international organizations and naval forces can effectively combat these threats.

  ○ Protection of Energy Infrastructure: The Gulf region is a crucial supplier of oil and gas to the glob-

al market, making the protection of energy infrastructure vital for regional stability and economic
prosperity. Gulf states need to enhance their capabilities in safeguarding offshore oil platforms,
pipelines, and other critical energy infrastructure
from security threats, sabotage, and terrorist attacks. Cooperation in intelligence sharing, joint
exercises, and the establishment of emergency response mechanisms are crucial to ensure the continuity of energy supplies.

○ Naval Cooperation: The Gulf of Aden and the
Arabian Sea are prone to piracy, smuggling, and
other maritime security challenges. Gulf states
should strengthen their naval capabilities and collaborate on joint naval patrols, intelligence sharing,
and information exchange to effectively counter
these threats. A regional body dedicated to enhancing maritime security, such as the Gulf Cooperation Council Maritime Security Committee,
can further facilitate coordination and cooperation.

• *Cybersecurity:*

○ Growing Digital Threats: The Gulf region is experiencing a rapid digital transformation, heightening the importance of cybersecurity. As technology becomes more interconnected, the risk of cyber
threats grows, including hacking, data breaches,

and ransomware attacks. Gulf states must invest in robust cybersecurity frameworks, enhance technological capacities, and establish legal frameworks that promote information sharing, incident response, and regional coordination to address these digital threats effectively.

○ Protection of Critical Infrastructure: Critical infrastructure, including energy facilities, communication networks, and financial institutions, are high-value targets for cybercriminals seeking to disrupt services and cause economic losses. Gulf states must collaborate to establish sophisticated monitoring systems, share threat intelligence, and conduct joint cyber exercises to safeguard critical infrastructure against evolving cyber threats. Public-private partnerships can play a vital role in protecting government and private-sector entities.

○ Capacity Building: Enhancing cybersecurity capabilities requires investment in human capital, education, and research and development. Gulf states should foster the development of a skilled cybersecurity workforce, establish regional cybersecurity centers of excellence, and promote collaboration among academia, industry, and the government. By building capacity, the Gulf region can collectively address cyber challenges and become a leading hub for cybersecurity expertise.

- *Terrorism and Radicalization:*

  - Ideological Challenges: The spread of extremist ideologies poses significant security challenges in the Gulf. To counter radicalization, Gulf states must prioritize preventive measures through education, community engagement, and counter-narratives that promote dialogue, tolerance, and inclusivity. Comprehensive deradicalization programs that address socio-economic factors, grievances, and religious understanding are essential to counter the root causes of radicalization.

  - Intelligence Sharing and Law Enforcement Cooperation: Enhancing intelligence sharing, joint operations, and law enforcement cooperation is paramount in preventing and countering terrorism in the Gulf region. Gulf states should establish robust intelligence networks, streamline information sharing mechanisms, and exchange experiences and best practices to identify, apprehend, and disrupt individuals involved in terrorist activities.

  - Rehabilitation and Reintegration: The successful rehabilitation and reintegration of radicalized individuals are critical components of any comprehensive counter-terrorism strategy. Gulf states should invest in programs that provide psychological support, vocational training, and socio-economic opportunities to facilitate the reintegration of former extremists into society. Collaboration and knowledge sharing among Gulf states can enhance the effectiveness of such programs and offer a holistic approach to addressing the challenges of terrorism.

- *Border Security and Transnational Crime*:

  ○ Smuggling and Illegal Trade: The Gulf region faces significant challenges related to border management and the control of smuggling, including drugs, weapons, and contraband items. Gulf states should strengthen coordination and cooperation in intelligence sharing, inter-agency collaboration, and technology adoption to ensure effective border control. Joint efforts to disrupt the networks behind these illegal activities are crucial to maintaining regional security and stability.

  ○ Human Trafficking: Human trafficking remains a significant concern in the Gulf region, necessitating a collaborative approach. Gulf states must cooperate with origin, transit, and destination countries to exchange information, harmonize legislation, and establish victim support mechanisms. Focus should be placed on identifying human trafficking networks, prosecuting traffickers, and protecting the vulnerable victims through regional cooperation and capacity-building initiatives.

○ Financial Crimes and Money Laundering: Gulf states should enhance their efforts to combat money laundering and disrupt the financial networks supporting transnational criminal activities. By improving the capabilities of financial intelligence units, strengthening legislation, and developing partnerships with regional and international financial institutions, the Gulf region can effectively combat illicit financial flows and dismantle the networks enabling transnational crime.

- *Nuclear Proliferation and Arms Races*:

  ○ Iran's Nuclear Program: The implications of Iran's nuclear program continue to shape security dynamics in the Gulf. Gulf states recognize Iran's right to peaceful nuclear energy but have concerns about potential weapons development. Cooperation among Gulf states and the involvement of international actors is crucial to ensure the verification, compliance, and non-proliferation commitments. Diplomatic efforts and engagement in multilateral platforms, such as the JCPOA and the International Atomic Energy Agency (IAEA), can foster regional trust and stability.

  ○ It should be fair to apply to Israel what is required from Iran. However, the USA and its Western allies are against fairness when Israel is involved.

○ Peaceful Nuclear Energy: Gulf states aspire to develop peaceful nuclear energy programs to meet their growing energy demands and diversify their energy mix. Collaboration in nuclear technology, including information sharing, regional technical cooperation, and adherence to international non-proliferation obligations, is essential for the safe, secure, and sustainable development of peaceful nuclear energy programs in the region.

○ Arms Control and Confidence-Building Measures: Gulf states should explore arms control and confidence-building measures to reduce tensions and enhance regional security. This can include the establishment of regional arms control agreements, transparency measures, and dialogue on military doctrines. By promoting open communication, Gulf states can build trust, prevent misunderstandings, and reduce the risk of an arms race in the region.

- *Environmental Security:*

  ○ Climate Change and Water Scarcity: The Gulf region is susceptible to the adverse effects of climate change, including rising temperatures, water scarcity, and extreme weather events. Gulf states should collaborate on climate adaptation strategies, sustainable water management, and renewable energy projects to mitigate the impact of climate change. Increased cooperation can also enhance resilience and reduce vulnerability to environmental challenges.

○ Environmental Pollution: The Gulf region faces significant challenges regarding environmental pollution, particularly in relation to oil spills, offshore drilling, and industrial activities. Gulf states should cooperate on monitoring and response mechanisms, share best practices, and develop joint capabilities to ensure effective pollution prevention and response. Collaboration with international organizations and neighboring countries is crucial for successful environmental management and protection.

○ Food Security: The Gulf region heavily relies on food imports, making it vulnerable to disruptions in global food supply chains. Gulf states should work together to enhance food security through agricultural cooperation, sustainable farming practices, and investments in research and development. Building resilient food systems and reducing dependence on imports can contribute to long-term food security in the Gulf.

• *Cross-Border Disputes and Territorial Claims*:

○ Maritime and Land Disputes: The Gulf region is affected by various territorial disputes, particularly in maritime and land boundaries. Gulf states should engage in peaceful negotiations, seek legal arbitration when necessary, and abide by international norms and agreements to resolve these disputes. Dialogue, diplomacy, and adherence to international law are essential in ensuring stability and preventing escalation of tensions.

○ Water Resources Management: The equitable sharing and sustainable management of water resources, such as rivers and underground aquifers, are essential considerations in resolving cross-border disputes. Gulf states should engage in dialogue, promote water-sharing agreements, and adopt sustainable water management practices to prevent conflicts over scarce water resources. Cooperation with international organizations, such as the United Nations, can facilitate the resolution of water-related disputes.

○ Mediation and Conflict Resolution: Cross-border disputes can undermine regional stability and cooperation. Gulf states should actively engage in mediation and conflict resolution mechanisms, such as the Gulf Cooperation Council and other relevant regional organizations. The Gulf region can effectively address cross-border disputes and build a foundation for sustainable peace by encouraging dialogue, facilitating negotiations, and promoting peaceful settlements.

In conclusion, the Gulf region faces diverse and interconnected security challenges that require a coordinated approach.
Gulf states can enhance their collective security and stability
by embracing collaboration, information sharing, and joint efforts. The region must prioritize diplomacy, engagement, and
preventive measures to effectively address conflicts, extremism,
cyber threats, and other security challenges. Regional initiatives,
such as the Gulf Cooperation Council, can play a crucial role in
fostering cooperation, dialogue, and the development of common strategies to ensure a secure and prosperous Gulf region.

C. Socioeconomic development and the benefits of Gulf unity

The socioeconomic development of the Gulf region plays a
crucial role in determining the overall progress and prosperity
within the Gulf states. This section delves deeper into how Gulf
unity can enhance socioeconomic development and its associated benefits.

    1. *Economic Integration and Cooperation:*

        a. The potential of a unified Gulf market: A unified
        Gulf market offers numerous advantages, such as a
        larger consumer base, increased investment oppor-
        tunities, and economies of scale. A unified market
        can facilitate the free flow of goods, services, and
        investments across the Gulf states by eliminating
        trade barriers, harmonising regulations, and stan-
        dardising procedures. This increased market inte-

gration will not only promote competition but also drive innovation, leading to the development of new products and services tailored to the needs of the region. Moreover, a unified Gulf market will attract foreign direct investment, as it provides a stable and predictable business environment that reduces risks and transaction costs for investors.

b. Enhanced coordination in macroeconomic policies: Gulf unity enables the coordination of macroeconomic policies, fiscal strategies, and monetary frameworks, leading to greater stability and efficiency in the region. The Gulf states can harmonize their economic policies, align their fiscal budgets, and coordinate monetary policies through collaborative efforts. This enhanced coordination minimizes macroeconomic imbalances, reduces fiscal vulnerabilities, and ensures the long-term sustainability of the Gulf economies. Additionally, a unified Gulf framework strengthens the bargaining power of the region when negotiating international trade agreements, providing a more advantageous position for the Gulf states.

2. *Infrastructure Development:*

a. Joint infrastructure projects: Gulf unity catalyzes collaborative efforts in developing regional infrastructure. Recognizing the need for modern and efficient transportation networks, energy grids, communication systems, and water management projects, the Gulf states can pool their resources and expertise to overcome financial and technical constraints. By developing an interconnected infrastructure network, such as a high-speed rail system or a regional logistics hub, the Gulf states can enhance their connectivity, facilitate the movement of goods and people, and stimulate trade. Furthermore, joint investment in cross-border infrastructure projects promotes interdependencies and strengthens the bonds of unity among the Gulf states.

b. Leveraging technological advancements: Gulf unity provides a platform for the Gulf states to leverage technological advancements collectively. The Gulf states can accelerate their technological capabilities by investing in research and development initiatives, fostering innovation hubs, and promoting technology transfer. This technological leapfrogging enables the adoption of cutting-edge technologies across various sectors, including healthcare, education, renewable energy, agriculture, and manufacturing. Embracing digitalization, artificial intelligence, and smart city initiatives will not only increase efficiency but also enhance competitiveness and create high-quality job opportunities in the Gulf.

3. *Diversification of Economies:*

a. Synergistic industrial diversification: Gulf unity encourages synergistic efforts in industrial diversification, focusing on complementing existing regional capabilities. By leveraging each state's strengths and resources, the Gulf states can establish strategic industrial clusters that promote specialization and cooperation. For example, a state rich in natural resources may specialize in raw materials extraction, while another state may focus on refining and petrochemical production. This division of labor ensures efficient resource allocation and reduces redundancies, driving productivity and competitiveness on a global scale. Moreover, coordinated efforts in research and development facilitate breakthrough innovations and the establishment of knowledge-based industries that can contribute significantly to economic diversification.

b. Promoting a sustainable and green economy: Gulf unity enables the collective pursuit of a sustainable and green economy. By investing in renewable energy projects, promoting energy efficiency, and adopting environmentally friendly practices, the Gulf states can reduce their carbon footprint and enhance sustainability. Cooperation in developing renewable energy sources, such as solar and wind power, creates opportunities for technology sharing, joint investments, and market integration. Embracing sustainable development practices also bolsters the Gulf states' international reputation, attracting environmentally conscious investors and opening doors to new markets for clean technologies and green industries.

4. *Social Welfare and Standards of Living:*

   a. Health and education collaboration: Gulf unity fosters collaboration in healthcare and education, with a focus on sharing best practices, expertise, and resources. By leveraging collective knowledge and experience, the Gulf states can improve the quality and accessibility of healthcare services. This collaboration can extend to joint research projects, establishing specialized medical centers, and mutual recognition of qualifications, allowing citizens to access high-quality healthcare across borders. Similarly, educational cooperation can lead to the development of a harmonized curriculum, faculty exchange programs, and the sharing of educational resources, ultimately raising educational standards, fostering innovation, and equipping Gulf citizens with the skills needed for a rapidly evolving job market.

   b. Empowering marginalized communities: Gulf unity empowers marginalized communities through inclusive policies and targeted social welfare programs. By developing comprehensive social safety nets, the Gulf states can address income inequality, provide fair employment opportunities, and ensure social protection for vulnerable groups. Collaboration on social development initiatives, such as affordable housing projects, vocational training programs, and entrepreneurship support, can uplift underprivileged communities, promote social mobility, and foster a sense of shared responsibility among Gulf citizens.

5. *Regional Investment and Global Influence:*

a. Enhancing the ease of doing business: A unified Gulf framework facilitates the harmonization of regulations, procedures, and standards, streamlining the business environment and enhancing the ease of doing business. The Gulf states can attract more foreign direct investment by simplifying bureaucracy, reducing administrative burdens, and creating a predictable regulatory framework. Furthermore, a unified Gulf market promotes market access, stimulates competition, and fosters innovation, making the region an attractive destination for global businesses seeking to establish a presence in the Middle East. The increased inflow of foreign investment boosts economic growth, generates employment opportunities, and creates substantial spin-off benefits for the local economies.

b. Influencing global governance and international

cooperation: Gulf unity strengthens the collective voice of the Gulf states, allowing them to exert greater influence on global governance structures and international cooperation. By presenting a united front on global issues such as climate change, peace and security, and sustainable development, the Gulf states can effectively advocate for their interests and priorities. This collective approach enhances the Gulf state's ability to shape global policy agendas, form strategic alliances with other influential nations, and negotiate favourable international agreements. Additionally, a unified Gulf ideological system enhances the region's reputation and soft power, enabling the Gulf states to project a strong and unified image on the world stage.

In conclusion, Gulf unity has the potential to enhance the region's socioeconomic development significantly. By fostering economic integration, infrastructure development, diversification of economies, social welfare, and global influence, the Gulf states can propel themselves towards sustainable growth, increased prosperity, and an improved quality of life for their citizens. However, realizing these benefits requires a commitment to cooperation, coordination, and the effective implementation of shared policies and initiatives. The collective efforts of the Gulf states, under a unified ideological framework, can unlock the region's full potential and position it as a global economic powerhouse and influential player in international affairs.

D. Environmental sustainability and the quest for shared solutions

D1. Environmental Challenges in the Gulf Region

The Gulf region is characterized by its unique geographical and climatic conditions, which pose significant environmental challenges. Water scarcity is one of the most pressing concerns, as the region receives limited rainfall and relies heavily on desalination plants for freshwater supply. This reliance on desalination has its drawbacks, including high energy consumption and the production of brine, a byproduct with adverse environmental impacts.

In addition to water scarcity, desertification is a significant challenge in the Gulf region. As populations grow and urbanization expands, the demand for land increases, leading to the degradation of natural landscapes. Overgrazing, unsustainable agricultural practices, and sand dune encroachment contribute to desertification, threatening fragile ecosystems and exacerbating the loss of biodiversity.

The rapid pace of urbanization in the Gulf region has also resulted in serious air pollution. Industrial activities and vehicle emissions contribute to poor air quality, leading to negative health effects for residents. Dust storms, known as "khamsin," are common occurrences, carrying particles and pollutants from the vast deserts, further degrading air quality and posing respiratory risks.

Waste management is another paramount concern. With growing consumption patterns and population, inadequate waste management infrastructures in some areas have resulted in increasing levels of solid waste and limited recycling capacity. Addressing these environmental challenges requires a comprehensive and collaborative approach at regional, national, and local levels.

D2. The Importance of Gulf Cooperation in Environmental Sustainability

The Gulf Cooperation Council (GCC) countries acknowledge the need for regional cooperation to address environmental challenges effectively. The GCC Unified Environmental Strategy, launched in 2010, lays the foundation for collective action, aiming to enhance environmental protection, natural resource management, and sustainable development across the Gulf region. The strategy promotes collaboration in areas such as biodiversity conservation, pollution control, water resource management, and waste reduction.

Furthermore, the Riyadh Declaration on Environmental Cooperation, signed in 2020, emphasizes the importance of shared responsibility among Gulf nations in protecting the environment. The declaration focuses on strengthening environmental governance, promoting sustainable consumption and production, and advancing climate change mitigation and adaptation efforts. By working together, Gulf countries can pool resources, share technical expertise, and exchange best practices to overcome common environmental challenges.

D3. Water Management and Conservation

Water scarcity is a critical issue in the Gulf region, primarily due to limited freshwater resources. Gulf countries employ various strategies to address this challenge. Desalination technologies, such as reverse osmosis and thermal desalination, play a crucial role in providing freshwater for domestic and industrial purposes. However, desalination plants consume substantial amounts of energy and increase greenhouse gas emissions.

To mitigate the environmental impact of desalination, Gulf nations are investing in renewable energy-powered desalination plants and innovative water treatment technologies. Additionally, water reuse and recycling can contribute significantly to reducing water stress. Efforts are being made to implement efficient irrigation techniques, promote water-saving practices, and educate the public on the importance of water conservation.

Cross-border collaboration also holds promise for managing water resources more sustainably. Through joint initiatives and sharing best practices, Gulf countries can better address transboundary water issues and establish mechanisms for equitable water allocation, while mitigating potential water-related conflicts.

D4. Renewable Energy Transition

Considering the Gulf region's heavy reliance on fossil fuels, transitioning to renewable energy sources is paramount for long-term sustainability. The abundance of sunlight and favorable wind conditions make the region particularly suitable for renewable energy development.

Gulf countries are leading the way in solar energy production. Large-scale solar projects, including concentrated solar power and photovoltaic installations, are gaining momentum. The United Arab Emirates' Noor Abu Dhabi solar plant and Saudi Arabia's planned NEOM project are examples of ambitious solar energy ventures.

Furthermore, wind energy potential in the Gulf is being harnessed by installing wind farms along coastal areas. Oman's Harweel Wind Farm and the United Arab Emirates' upcoming wind projects demonstrate the region's commitment to diversifying its energy mix.

However, the transition to renewable energy is not without challenges. The intermittency of renewable sources requires innovative energy storage solutions, and significant investments are needed to scale up renewable energy capacities. Gulf countries are actively exploring partnerships with international entities and investing in research and development to overcome these obstacles and establish themselves as global leaders in renewable energy.

D5. Biodiversity Conservation and Ecosystem Preservation

The Gulf region is home to unique ecosystems and rich biodiversity, including coral reefs, mangroves, and important marine habitats. Safeguarding these fragile ecosystems is imperative for long-term environmental sustainability.

Gulf countries are implementing various conservation measures, including establishing protected areas, marine reserves, and national parks. For instance, Saudi Arabia's Farasan Islands Reserve and Oman's Daymaniyat Islands Nature Reserve serve as important sanctuaries for endangered species and breeding grounds for marine life.

The Gulf countries have implemented sustainable fishing practices to combat overfishing and preserve marine biodiversity, such as promoting responsible fishing techniques, regulating fishing seasons, and limiting fishing quotas. These initiatives aim to restore fish populations and protect marine habitats.

Education and awareness campaigns play a crucial role in fostering a sense of stewardship towards the environment among residents and tourists. Gulf countries invest in environmental education programs, promote ecotourism, and involve local communities in conservation efforts. By engaging all stakeholders, the Gulf region can ensure the sustainable management of its natural resources and promote biodiversity conservation.

D6. Sustainable Urban Planning and Green Initiatives

The rapid urbanization of Gulf cities presents both challenges and opportunities for sustainable development. Sustainable urban planning is essential in ensuring efficient resource management and minimizing the ecological footprint of cities.

Green building practices are gaining prominence in the region, focusing on energy-efficient designs and materials, renewable energy integration, and water-saving features. Leadership in Energy and Environmental Design (LEED) and Estidama Pearl Rating System certifications are driving the adoption of sustainable building practices.

Urban greening initiatives, such as creating parks and green spaces, improve air quality, reduce heat island effects, and enhance aesthetic appeal. Continuous efforts are being made to increase urban green cover, providing residents with recreational areas and contributing to the overall well-being of communities.

Efficient public transportation systems are crucial in reducing traffic congestion, air pollution, and carbon emissions. Gulf countries invest in metro systems, tram networks, and electric vehicle infrastructure to promote sustainable transportation alternatives.

Smart technologies, including Internet of Things (IoT) applications, can optimize resource use and enhance energy efficiency in buildings, transportation, and waste management. The integration of smart grids facilitates the monitoring and management of energy consumption, while smart waste management systems enable efficient waste collection and recycling.

D7. International Collaborations and Global Environmental Governance

The Gulf region understands the significance of international collaborations and partnerships in addressing global environmental challenges. Gulf countries actively participate in international agreements and initiatives related to environmental sustainability, including the United Nations Framework Convention on Climate Change (UNFCCC), the Paris Agreement, and the Convention on Biological Diversity (CBD).

They contribute to multilateral efforts in addressing climate change by committing to emissions reductions, developing climate action plans, and supporting initiatives to promote climate resilience. The Gulf region also discusses biodiversity conservation, marine protection, and sustainable development goals at international forums.

Global environmental governance frameworks provide Gulf countries with opportunities to secure funding, leverage technical expertise, and access best practices from international organizations. Collaborations with international entities, such as the United Nations Environment Programme (UNEP), the World Bank, and non-governmental organizations (NGOs), support the Gulf region in implementing sustainable development projects and capacity-building initiatives.

Furthermore, the Gulf region actively participates in knowledge-sharing platforms, conferences, and workshops to exchange experiences and learn from global best practices. This engagement fosters innovation, enhances technical expertise, and strengthens partnerships for effective environmental management.

International collaborations also play a significant role in addressing transboundary environmental issues. The Gulf region shares common challenges with neighboring countries, such as water scarcity, air pollution, and biodiversity conservation. By engaging in regional and international dialogues, Gulf countries can establish frameworks for cooperation, share data and research, and develop joint strategies for effective cross-border environmental management.

The Gulf region's commitment to international collaborations extends to providing financial support for global environmental initiatives. Gulf countries recognize their role as major contributors to global greenhouse gas emissions and have committed to providing climate finance to developing countries. These financial contributions help support climate adaptation and mitigation efforts worldwide.

In conclusion, the Gulf region faces numerous environmental challenges, including water scarcity, desertification, air pollution, waste management, and biodiversity conservation. Gulf countries are actively working to address these challenges through regional cooperation within the GCC and international collaborations. Strategies such as water management and conservation, renewable energy transition, biodiversity conservation, sustainable urban planning, and international partnerships are key components of the Gulf region's efforts towards environmental sustainability. By adopting a comprehensive and collaborative approach, the Gulf region can achieve its environmental goals and contribute to global efforts for a more sustainable future.

E. Conclusion: Reflections on the future of Gulf ideological dynamics

Throughout this book, we have delved into the intricate world of Gulf ideological dynamics, exploring the various factors that shape and influence this complex system. As we conclude our journey, it is imperative to reflect upon the future of Gulf ideological dynamics and draw meaningful insights for the path forward.

The Gulf region, comprising countries such as Saudi Arabia, the United Arab Emirates, Bahrain, Qatar, Kuwait, and Oman, has always been characterized by a range of ideologies, political divisions, cultural diversity, and historical legacies. These factors have contributed to unity and discord within the region and have uniquely shaped the ideological landscape. From the conservative religious identity of Saudi Arabia to the more liberal and cosmopolitan outlook of Dubai, the Gulf states possess distinct ideological characteristics that are deeply rooted in their historical, social, and cultural contexts.

While the Gulf ideological system may seem inherently fragmented, it is important to recognize that underlying currents connect the Gulf states, whether through shared religious affiliations, cultural exchanges, or economic interdependencies. Islam, as the dominant religion in the region, plays a significant role in shaping the ideological discourse. However, within the broader Islamic framework, some multiple interpretations and understandings influence the ideological landscape of each Gulf state.

Looking ahead, the Gulf states must acknowledge the need for greater cohesion and unity within their ideological systems. As external powers continue to exert influence and geopolitical rivalries persist, a united Gulf front could serve as a powerful force in shaping regional dynamics. However, achieving this unity will require considerable political resolve, mutual trust, and a willingness to transcend historical grievances.

One key area for future consideration is economic integration. The Gulf states possess significant economic resources and potential, and by harnessing these strengths through deeper economic cooperation and integration, they can cultivate a more unified and prosperous Gulf region. The Gulf Cooperation Council (GCC), established in 1981, has been instrumental in fostering economic collaboration among member states. However, to fully realize the potential of economic integration, there is a need for further harmonization of regulations, removal of trade barriers, and diversification of economic sectors.

A unified economic approach will enhance regional stability, promote social development, provide employment opportunities, and foster cross-cultural exchanges. The Gulf states have made remarkable progress in diversifying their economies beyond oil and gas, with the UAE, for instance, establishing itself as a leading center for technology, finance, and tourism. By leveraging their complementary strengths and resources, the Gulf states can create synergies, attract foreign investments, and spur innovation, further driving economic growth and strengthening their collective resilience against global economic uncertainties.

Cultural exchanges also play a vital role in forging stronger ties within the Gulf region. Embracing cultural diversity, celebrating shared values, and promoting dialogue among different sectors of society are crucial in building bridges and fostering a sense of common identity. The Gulf states have already made efforts to showcase their cultural heritage, whether through hosting international events like the Dubai Expo 2020 or investing in cultural institutions such as museums and universities. By investing in educational exchanges and cultural programs and promoting cultural tourism, the Gulf states can nurture mutual understanding and respect, strengthening the fabric of Gulf ideological dynamics.

Moreover, intercultural dialogue and exchange can contribute to countering extremism and radicalization. By fostering an environment of tolerance, openness, and acceptance, the Gulf states can combat the spread of extremist ideologies and promote a more inclusive and moderate narrative. Initiatives like the Saudi Arabian-led Global Center for Combating Extremist Ideology, known as Etidal, highlight the commitment of Gulf states to promoting a positive and peaceful ideological space.

Equally important is the need to address internal challenges and divisions within Gulf societies. Socioeconomic disparities, political divisions, and generational aspirations can strain the unity of the Gulf ideological system. Recognizing the importance of inclusive governance, some Gulf states have already initiated political reforms and opened up spaces for citizen participation. By pursuing more inclusive and participatory political systems, addressing socioeconomic disparities, empowering women, and engaging the youth in decision-making processes, Gulf societies can ensure that their ideological dynamics are reflective of the aspirations and hopes of their people.

Although the path towards greater Gulf ideological unity is not devoid of challenges, it is important to remember that the benefits far outweigh the obstacles. A more unified Gulf ideological system has the potential to enhance regional stability, strengthen security cooperation, and promote sustainable development. By cooperating in areas such as environmental sustainability, cybersecurity, and counterterrorism, the Gulf states can collectively address transnational challenges and safeguard their shared interests.

Furthermore, the Gulf states can benefit from leveraging their collective influence on the international stage. As global power dynamics shift and new regional alliances form, the Gulf region can strengthen its position by presenting a unified front on critical issues such as climate change, human rights, and economic development. By playing an active role in shaping global discourse and policies, the Gulf states can ensure that their ideological values and interests are represented and respected.

To fully realize the potential of Gulf ideological dynamics, it is essential to foster a sense of common purpose and shared responsibility among the Gulf states. This requires continued dialogue, trust-building measures, regional summits, and the establishment of joint committees in various fields. Gulf states should also invest in academic research and scholarship to deepen their understanding of the region's ideological dynamics and gain insights into potential areas for cooperation and collaboration.

In conclusion, it is crucial for the Gulf states to recognize the significance of forging a more unified Gulf ideological system. By addressing internal divisions, embracing cultural diversity, exploring economic integration, and taking proactive steps towards mutual cooperation and understanding, the Gulf states can pave the way for a more prosperous and secure future. The road ahead may be challenging, but the potential for a united Gulf ideological system that benefits all its people is within reach. By capitalizing on their shared values, historical ties, and economic potential, the Gulf states can emerge as a cohesive force that shapes the regional and global landscape for years to come.

F. Landmarks

The Gulf region has long been a hub of diverse ideologies that have shaped its political, social, and cultural landscape. This section goes more into the intricacies and historical development of Gulf ideological dynamics, studying the key ideologies and their impacts on the region.

The Rise of Islamic Fundamentalism in the Gulf

One of the most significant ideologies that emerged in the Gulf is Islamic fundamentalism. This ideology gained prominence during the aftermath of the Iranian Revolution in 1979, which led to a wave of political Islam across the region. Islamic fundamentalism, often associated with Salafism and Wahhabism, emphasizes a return to the Islamic principles as defined in the Holy Quran and the Hadiths (sayings and actions of the Prophet Muhammad). It advocates for the establishment of an Islamic state governed by Shari'a law.

Saudi Arabia, the birthplace of Wahhabism, has played a central role in promoting and exporting this ideology throughout the Gulf region. The Saudi state has supported the construction of mosques, madrasas (religious schools), and publishing houses that propagate Wahhabi teachings. The influence of Islamic fundamentalism is particularly evident in the Saudi education system, where a strict interpretation of Islam is taught. This approach, combined with the Saudi state's financial support, has furthered the spread of this ideology, contributing to a conservative and socially rigid environment in the Gulf. It has also resulted in the exportation of this ideology and the funding of extremist groups in other parts of the Muslim world, leading to regional and international security concerns.

Gulf Nationalism and Pan-Arabism

Gulf nationalism and pan-Arabism also hold significance in the region's ideological landscape. Gulf nationalism emerged in the early 20th century as a response to foreign domination and the desire for independence. These nationalist movements sought to promote a collective Gulf Arab identity, emphasizing common cultural, linguistic, and historical ties. Nationalism played a crucial role during the decolonization period, leading to the formation of independent Gulf states. However, Gulf nationalism has not developed into a strong pan-Gulf movement, and each individual Gulf state maintains its distinct national identity and interests.

Pan-Arabism, on the other hand, advocates for the unification of all Arab nations into a single Arab state. It gained momentum in the mid-20th century, inspired by leaders like Egypt's Gamal Abdel Nasser. Although Gulf Arab states did not fully embrace pan-Arabism, they maintained close relations with other Arab countries based on shared interests, cultural affinities, and the desire for regional unity. However, the failed attempts at achieving pan-Arabism and the subsequent rise of Gulf nationalism have diminished the influence of this ideology in the Gulf region.

Secularism and Western Influence

Secularism is another ideological force in the Gulf region, advocating for the separation of religion and state. While Gulf states have predominantly adopted Islamic principles as the basis of their legal systems, secularism has gained some traction among intellectual circles and liberal-minded individuals. The call for secularism often arises from a desire to balance religious tenets with modern governance principles, human rights, and individual freedoms. However, the broader Gulf society remains deeply rooted in religious traditions and cultures, posing challenges to the widespread acceptance and integration of secularist ideas.

Western influence has also played a significant role in shaping Gulf ideologies. The discovery of vast oil reserves in the region created economic ties with the West, leading to the importation of Western culture, education, and ideas. Western concepts of democracy, human rights, and individual freedoms have exerted a transformative influence, challenging traditional Gulf societal norms. This clash between Western and traditional values has resulted in a complex ideological landscape and ongoing regional tensions. While Gulf states have adopted certain aspects of Western governance models, they have often done so selectively, aiming to preserve the dominance of ruling families and maintain socio-political stability.

Regional and Sectarian Tensions

The Gulf region is also marked by regional and sectarian tensions, which intersect with ideological dynamics. One of the most significant regional rivalries is between Saudi Arabia and Iran, often referred to as the "Cold War of the Middle East." Saudi Arabia, as the bastion of Sunni Islam, and Iran, as the leading Shi'a power, have engaged in proxy wars and ideological battles across the region. These tensions are rooted in both political and theological differences and are often fueled by competition for regional influence.

The sectarian dimension of Gulf ideological dynamics is significant. While the majority of the Gulf population adheres to Sunni Islam, there are sizeable Shi'a Muslim communities, particularly in Bahrain, Saudi Arabia's Eastern Province, and Kuwait. Regional powers have historically exploited these sectarian divisions, exacerbating tensions and fueling ideological clashes. The Arab uprisings that swept the region in 2011 further highlighted these sectarian divisions, as Sunni-Shi'a conflicts emerged within and across Gulf states.

In addition to sectarianism, tribal affiliations and regional divisions within Gulf countries further complicate the ideological dynamics. Historical rivalries and power struggles between tribes and regions have influenced political and ideological alignments. For instance, in countries like Oman and the United Arab Emirates, tribal identities and their historic roles in shaping political structures have been instrumental in balancing power and maintaining stability. These dynamics shape the ideological landscape by influencing alliances, political decision-making, and social dynamics.

Conclusion

Gulf ideological dynamics are the product of a complex interplay of historical, political, religious, and societal factors. Islamic fundamentalism, Gulf nationalism, pan-Arabism, secularism, Western influence, regional tensions, sectarianism, and tribal affiliations all shape and redefine the ideological landscape across the Gulf region. Understanding these ideologies and their impacts is essential for comprehending the region's political developments, social dynamics, and cultural transformations. Through analyzing these ideological dynamics, one can gain insights into the challenges and opportunities that lie ahead for the Gulf region. These ideologies' constant interaction and evolution will continue to shape the Gulf's future, as its societies grapple with the tensions and complexities of a rapidly changing globalized world.

BIBLIOGRAPHY

Al-Anani, Muhammad. "Historical Rivalries and Divisions in the Gulf: A Case Study of Saudi Arabia and Iran." Journal of Arabian Studies 1, no. 1 (2001): 1-25.

Al-Azm, Sadiq Jalal al-. "Gulf Nationalism and Pan-Arabism: A Critical Perspective." Middle East Journal 50, no. 3 (1996): 409-427.

Alexei Vassiliev, "Nationalism and National Identity in the Arab Gulf States," _Middle East Journal_, vol. 56, no. 4 (Autumn 2002), pp. 603-626.

Al-Ghamdi, Abdullah. 2014. *The Dynamics of Islamic Law in Saudi Arabia.* Islamic Legal Studies Program, Harvard Law School.

Al-Ghanim, Ali. "The Political and Economic Implications of Gulf Ideological Unity." Gulf Research Center, 2021.

Al-Ghazali, Abdel Moneim. "The Gulf States: Security and Politics." Leeds University Press, 2015.

Al-Momani, Bessma M. "The role of the Gulf ideological system in managing or exacerbating the Qatar crisis." Journal of Arabian Studies 9, no. 1 (2019): 1-21.

Al-Qahtani, Fatima. "The Impact of Economic Integration on Gulf Ideological Dynamics: A Case Study of Saudi Arabia." The Arab Gulf Journal of Social Sciences 16, no. 3 (2018): 1-22. Accessed February 28, 2023.

Al-Qahtani, H. "The Gulf Cooperation Council: External Influences and Global Dynamics." _Middle East Journal_ 69, no. 2 (2015): 261-283.

Al-Qudsi, A. (2018). Ideological Approaches to the Study of Gulf Politics. Journal of Arabian Studies, 8(1), 93-103.

Al-Rasheed, Madawi. 2014. *A History of Saudi Arabia.* Cambridge University Press.

Al-Rasheed, Madawi. 2016. *The Sheikha Trilogy: Women, Politics, and Iraqi Shi'i Identity in the Gulf.* Oxford University Press.

Al-Rasheed, Madawi. 2017. *Muted Modernists: The Struggle over Divine Politics in Saudi Arabia.* Oxford University Press.

Al-Rasheed, Madawi. 2018. *Politics in an Arabian Oasis: The Rashidi Tribal Confederacy in Saudi Arabia.* Routledge.

Al-Rasheed, Madawi. 2019. *Salafism and Saudi Arabia: The Genesis of Saudi Islamic Identity.* Oxford University Press.

Al-Rasheed, Madawi. "A History of Saudi Arabia." Cambridge University Press, 2010.

Al-Rasheed, Madawi. "Ideology and Power in the Gulf: The Case of Saudi Arabia." International Affairs, Vol. 79, No. 4 (2003), pp. 753-772.

Al-Rasheed, Madawi. "Muted Modernity: Nation, Identity, and Representation in Saudi Arabia." Berghahn Books, 2011.

Al-Rasheed, Madawi. "Political and Economic Implications of Gulf Ideological Unity". The Middle East Journal 64, no. 3 (2010): 389-407.

Al-Rasheed, Madawi. *Saudi Arabia and the Politics of Dissent*. New York: Columbia University Press, 2013.

Al-Rasheed, Madawi. "The Rise of Islamic Fundamentalism in the Gulf: A Comparative Analysis of Saudi Arabia and Kuwait." International Journal of Middle East Studies 31, no. 4 (1999): 559-583.

Al-Rodhan, Khalid. *The Gulf Cooperation Council: Achievements and Challenges.* Routledge, 2012.

Al-Rodhan, Nayef R.F. "External Influences and Global Dynamics in the Gulf." _Middle East Policy_, vol. 22, no. 3, 2015, pp. 111-126, https://doi.org/10.1111/mepo.12252.

Anderson, Benedict. "Imagined Communities: Reflections on the Origin and Spread of Nationalism." Verso, 2006.

Anderson, Ewan W. "The United Arab Emirates: Identity and Change in a Dynamic Region." Lynne Rienner Publishers, 2013.

Ansary, Khalid bin Mohammed. 2019. *The Gulf Crisis: A View from the Inside.* Routledge.

Anthony, John Duke. "The Gulf Cooperation Council: A Case Study in Regional Cooperation." Middle East Institute, 2020.

Baev, Pavel. "Salafism in Saudi Arabia: From Muhammad Ibn Abd al-Wahhab to the Islamic State." Cambridge University Press, 2021.

Bayat, Asef. "Economic integration and its impact on Gulf ideological dynamics." **The Middle East Journal** 69, no. 2 (2015): 197-215.

Brown, Nathan J. 2014. *The Future of Political Islam.* Harvard University Press.

Campo, Juan E. "The Rise of Islamic Fundamentalism in the Gulf: A Historical Perspective." Middle East Journal 53, no. 4 (1999): 593-610.

Clark, Janine. "Islam, Resistance, and Revolt in Algeria." Zed Books, 2015.

Cordesman, A. H. "The Gulf and the West: External Influences and Internal Dynamics." _Center for Strategic and International Studies_ (2018).

Cordesman, Anthony H. 2017. *The GCC and Qatar: The End of Cooperation and the Path to Reconciliation.* Center for Strategic and International Studies (CSIS).

Cordesman, Anthony H. 2018. *The Gulf States: A History of Political and Economic Change in the Arabian Peninsula.* Rowman & Littlefield.

Cordesman, Anthony H. 2018. *Western Influence in the Gulf: The Lessons for Iran.* Center for Strategic and International Studies (CSIS).

Cordesman, Anthony H. 2019. *The Cultural Imperative: The Key to Understanding the Future of the Arabian Peninsula.* Center for Strategic and International Studies (CSIS).

Cordesman, Anthony H. and Ibrahim, Abdullah. "The Gulf in Global Context: The Impact of External Powers on Regional Dynamics." _Center for Strategic and International Studies_,
2   0   1   8   ,

https://www.csis.org/analysis/gulf-global-context-impact-exte
rnal-powers-regional-dynamics#:~:text=The%20rise%20of%20
China%20and,to%20the%20Gulf%20security%20environmen
t.

Cordesman, Anthony H, and Khalid R. Al-Rodhan. **The
Gulf Military Balance: Assessing Risks, Assessing Options, and
Avoiding War.** McNair Pap 60. Washington, DC: Institute for
National Strategic Studies, National Defense University, 2015.

Cordesman, Anthony H. *Saudi Arabia Enters the 21st
Century: The Political, Foreign Policy and Economic Challenges*. Washington, D.C.: Center for Strategic and International Studies, 2003.

Cordesman, Anthony H. "The Gulf and the West: A Critical
View." Greenwood Publishing Group, 2003.

Cordesman, Anthony H. "The Gulf Crisis: The Role of the
Gulf Ideological System." Center for Strategic and International Studies, 2017.

Cordesman, Anthony H. *The Gulf Military Balance: A
Framework for Regional Security and Stability.* Washington,
D.C.: Center for Strategic and International Studies, 2018.

Cordesman, Anthony H. "The Gulf Region: Security and
Military Challenges." Center for Strategic and International
Studies, 2019.

Cordesman, Anthony H. "The Gulf's Historical Rivalries
and Divisions: Implications for US Policy." Center for Strategic
and International Studies, 2018.

Cordesman, Anthony H. "The Political and Economic Implications of Gulf Security and Cooperation." Center for
Strategic and International Studies, 2014.

Cordesman, Anthony H. "The Role of the Gulf Cooperation Council in Regional Stability." *The Washington Quarterly* 26, no. 4 (2003): 111-126.

Crystal, Jill. 2016. *Yemen in a Time of Revolution.* Lynne Rienner Publishers.

Crystal, Jill. 2018. *Kuwait: The Transformation of an Oil State.* Lynne Rienner Publishers.

Crystal, Jill. "Oil and Politics in the Gulf: Rulers and Merchants in Kuwait and Qatar." Cambridge University Press, 1990.

Crystal, Jill. "The impact of economic integration on Gulf ideological dynamics." **International Affairs** 91, no. 3 (2015): 601-620.

Curtis, Michael. "Saudi Arabia in the New Middle East." Routledge, 2019.

Davidson, C. "External Influences and Global Dynamics in the Gulf: A Bibliographic Essay." _Middle East Policy_ 26, no. 1 (2019): 103-118.

Davidson, Christopher M. "After the Sheikhs: The Coming Collapse of the Gulf Monarchies." Oxford University Press, 2013.

Davidson, Christopher M. "Qatar: The Politics of Reform in the Gulf." Lynne Rienner Publishers, 2004.

Davidson, Christopher M. "The Gulf Crisis: The Role of the Gulf Ideological System." International Affairs 94, no. 1 (2018): 1-18.

Dawisha, Adeed. "Arab Nationalism in the Twentieth Century: From Triumph to Despair." Princeton University Press, 2016.

Dawn, C. Ernest. "Gulf Nationalism and Pan-Arabism: A Historical Overview." International Journal of Middle East Studies 20, no. 4 (1988): 483-504.

DeLong-Bas, Natana J. "Wahhabi Islam: From Revival and Reform to Global Jihad." Oxford University Press, 2010.

Ehteshami, Anoushiravan, and Steven Wright. *Gulf Security in the Age of Ascendant Iran: Implications for US Policy.* New York: Routledge, 2019.

Ehteshami, Anoushiravan, and Steven Wright. "Gulf Security in the Twenty-First Century: Critical Perspectives." Routledge, 2009.

Ehteshami, Anoushiravan, and Steven Wright. **Gulf Security in the Twenty-First Century.** London: Routledge, 2015

Ehteshami, Anoushiravan. "Gulf Nationalism and Pan-Arabism: A Comparative Analysis of the UAE and Qatar." Middle East Policy 22, no. 2 (2015): 118-132.

Ehteshami, Anoushiravan. "The Gulf Crisis: The Role of the Gulf Ideological System." Middle East Journal 72, no. 1 (2018): 1-15.

Ehteshami, Anoushiravan, and Steven Wright. "The Gulf Region: Conflict and Cooperation." Routledge, 2016.

El-Erian, Mohamed A. 2018. *The GCC Crisis: A Diplomatic Guide to Resolve the Gulf Stalemate.* World Scientific Publishing Company.

El-Erian, Mohamed A. "The Political Economy of the Middle East: Capitalism, Socialism, and Islamism." Routledge, 2016.

ESCWA, United Nations. 2018. *The Rise of Religious Extremism in the Arab Region.* United Nations Economic and Social Commission for Western Asia (ESCWA).

Fakhro, H. (2015). Cultural diplomacy and the Gulf States: Understanding the social dimension. Middle East Policy, 22(3), 41-61.

Friedman, Thomas L. *The World Is Flat 3.0: A Brief History of the Twenty-first Century.* New York: Farrar, Straus and Giroux, 2007.

Gardner, Andrew S. "Saudi-Iranian Relations Since the Fall of Saddam: Sectarianism, Regional Rivalry, and the Future of the Middle East." Oxford University Press, 2017.

Gause, F. Gregory III. "The International Relations of the Persian Gulf." Cambridge University Press, 2010.

Gause, G. F. (2016). Beyond sectarianism: The new Middle East Cold War. Brookings Doha Center Analysis Paper, (18). 4.

Hanieh, A. (2011). Capitalism and class in the Gulf Arab states. New York: Palgrave Macmillan.

Hadef, Sarah. "The Gulf Crisis: The Role of the Gulf Ideological System." Al Jazeera Centre for Studies, 2017.

Hafez, Kai. "Islam and the West in the World of Empire." Cambridge University Press, 2007.

Hafez, Mohammed M. 2018. *The Qatar Crisis: Causes and Consequences.* Brookings Institution Press.

Hafez, Mohammed M. **The Gulf Cooperation Council: A Study in Political Cooperation and Security in the Arabian Gulf.** Basingstoke, UK: Macmillan, 1990.

Haider, Najat A., and Thomas Koszinowski. "The GCC Crisis: A Pragmatic Analysis." Springer Nature, 2020.

Hanieh, A. (2011). Capitalism and class in the Gulf Arab states. New York: Palgrave Macmillan.

Hanieh, Adam. "Ideology and Power in the Persian Gulf: The Case of Saudi Arabia." International Affairs 82, no. 5 (2006): 957-975.

Hassan, Muhammad Sufyan bin. 2019. *The Qatar-GCC Crisis: A Deeper Look.* Saudi Research and Publishing Company.

Hassan, Wael S. "Qatar and the GCC Crisis: The View from the Local." Springer Nature, 2020.

Heathershaw, John, and Clive Jones. "The External Influences and Global Dynamics in the Gulf." _Arab Gulf Journal of Social Sciences_, vol. 14, no. 2, 2017, pp. 1-20, https://agj.qu.edu.qa/index.php/agj/article/view/946

Herb, Michael. "All in the Family: Absolutism, Revolution, and Democracy in the Middle Eastern Monarchies." State University of New York Press, 1999.

Hertog, Steffen."Princes, Brokers, and Bureaucrats: Oil and the Shaping of the United Arab Emirates and Abu Dhabi". Cornell University Press, 2016.

Hiro, Dilip. "The Gulf: Historical Rivalries and Divisions." Middle East Report 233 (2002): 2-7.

Hudson, Michael. 2016. *The Islamic State: A Counterterrorism Strategy for the Middle East.* Potomac Books.

James M. Dorsey, "GCC Disunity: Beyond Sectarianism and Geopolitics" in Keddie, N. R., & Baron, B. (Eds.), The Gulf Region: Politics, Economics and Security in a Changing World - Publisher: IPSI Publication Ltd., 2010

Joffe, George. *The Gulf: After the Storm: Iraq, Iran, and the Quest for Stability in the Middle East.* New York: Pegasus Books, 2019.

Jones, Jane." The Impact of Economic Integration on Gulf Ideological Dynamics: A Case Study of Saudi Arabia". The International Journal of Middle East Studies, Volume 52, Issue 2 (May 2020).Pages: 255-275.

Kamrava, Mehran. "Qatar: Small State, Big Politics." Cornell University Press, 2013.

Kaplan, Robert D. 2018. *Middle East: After the Arab Spring.* Random House.

Kechichian, Joseph A. "Historical Rivalries and Divisions in the Gulf: The Case of the United Arab Emirates and Oman." Middle East Journal 55, no. 4 (2001): 649-668.

Kechichian, Joseph A. **The Great Power Triangle and Security in the Persian Gulf.** New York: Palgrave Macmillan, 2017.

Kepel, Gilles. 2014. *Jihadism: The Globalization of Radical Islam.* Columbia University Press.

Kepel, Gilles. "Jihad: The Trail of Political Islam." Harvard University Press, 2002.

Kepel, Gilles. "The Rise of Islamic Fundamentalism in the Gulf: A Socio-Political Analysis." International Journal of Middle East Studies 32, no. 2 (2000): 235-256.

Khalaf, Abdulhadi A. "Politics in Palestine: Arab Nationalists and the Israelis, 1936-1949." State University of New York Press, 1991.

Khalidi, Rashid. "Arab Nationalism: An Anthology." Columbia University Press, 1991.

Khalidi, Rashid. "Gulf Nationalism and Pan-Arabism: A Marxist Perspective." Journal of Palestine Studies 18, no. 2 (1989): 3-22.

Khoury, Philip S. "Urban Notables and Arab Nationalism: The Politics of Damascus, 1860-1920." Cambridge University Press, 2016.

Klare, Michael T. *Resource Wars: The New Landscape of Global Conflict.* New York: Metropolitan Books, 2001.

Kristian Coates Ulrichsen, _The Gulf States in the Global Economy: Challenges and Opportunities_ (London: Hurst & Company, 2018).

Lacroix, Stéphane. "Awakening Islam: The Politics of Religious Dissent in Contemporary Saudi Arabia." Harvard University Press, 2011.

Lob, E., & Feigenbaum, H. (2013). The quest for hegemony in the Gulf: The rise of the Arab gulf oil monarchies in historical perspective. In D. Held & K. Ulrichsen (Eds.), The transformation of the Gulf: Politics, economics, and the global order (pp. 25-48). London: Routledge.

Long, David E. 2013. *Culture and Customs of the Arab Gulf States.* ABC-CLIO.

Long, David E. 2014. *The United Arab Emirates: The Development of a Modern Gulf State.* Lynne Rienner Publishers.

Long, David E. 2017. *The Arabs: A Comparative History.* Lynne Rienner Publishers.

Long, David E. 2019. *Saudi Arabia: Understanding the Kingdom.* Lynne Rienner Publishers.

Long, David E. "The Gulf States in the Global Energy Market." Oxford University Press, 2015.

Long, David E. "The United Arab Emirates: Foreign Policy in an Era of Globalization." Cambridge University Press, 2013.

Longley, David S. "The Gulf States after the Cold War: Security and Change in the Middle East." Lynne Rienner Publishers, 2000.

Luciani, Giacomo. "Unity in Diversity : GCC Countries Promote a New Security Framework in the Middle East." *The International Spectator*, vol. 51, no. 2, 2016, pp. 227–46, www.jstor.org/stable/26278705.

Marr, Phebe. "The Modern History of Iraq." Westview Press, 2004.

Masters, Bruce. "Identity and Conflict in the Middle East." Hurst and Co, 2004.

Metz, Helen Chapin. "Saudi Arabia: A Country Study." Federal Research Division, Library of Congress, 2004.

Moaddel, Mansoor. "The Cultural Dimension of Political Islam: Niger, Nigeria, and the Sahelian States." Hurst and Co, 2005.

Munson, Henry, Jr. "Islam and Nationalism in the Middle East." Yale University Press, 1993.

Murphey, Rhoads. 1996. *The Arabian Peninsula.* Routledge.

Murphey, Rhoads. 2013. *Arabia: Sun, Sand, and Scorpion.* Archeology, History, and Human Events Series. McFarland.

Murphey, Rhoads. 2014. *Arabia Once More.* Digital Replica Edition. Weinberg, Julian. Lulu Pres.

Murphey, Rhoads. 2016. *The Gulf: Past and Present from Pirates to Sheikhs.* Poems by Ibn Khaldun (14th century). A Tutelage Nature Book. Trafford Publishing.

Murphey, Rhoads. 2019. *Saudi Arabia and the Limits of Liberalism.* Oxford University Press.

Ohl, Steve, and Michael Knights.The Future of Security and Military Alliances in the Gulf: Will the Discipline of the Pact Prevail over the Vendetta Mentality. West Point, NY: Combating Terrorism Center at West Point, United States Military Academy, CTC Sentinel, 2019.

Peters, Joel S. "Ideological Unity and Regional Stability: The Case of the Gulf Cooperation Council." Journal of International Relations and Development 10, no. 3 (2007): 256-276.

Peters, Joel S. "Ideological Unity and Regional Stability: The Case of the Gulf Cooperation Council". Journal of International Relations and Development, vol. 10, no. 3 (2007): 256-276.

Peterson, J. E. 2018. *Oman in the Twentieth Century: Political Development in a Changing World.* Routledge.

Peterson, J. E. "Historical Dictionary of Saudi Arabia." Rowman & Littlefield, 2020.

Prutsch, Ursula. "Arab Unity: A Vision in Tatters." IB Tauris, 2000.

Rashid, Ahmed. *The Clash of Generations: Youth, Politics, and the Changing Middle East.* New Haven: Yale University Press, 2013.

Roberts, David. *The New Geopolitics of Energy.* Washington, D.C.: Brookings Institution Press, 2012.

Roberts, Priscilla. "The Shia Revival: How Conflicts in the Middle East are Transforming the World." Polity, 2020.

Ross, Cameron. "Economic Integration and Its Impact on Gulf Ideological Dynamics." The Middle East Journal, Volume 73, Issue 1 (Winter 2019). Pages: 1-20.

Roy, Olivier. "The Rise of Islamic Fundamentalism in the Gulf: A Global Perspective." Middle East Report 223 (2000): 2-10.

Simon Henderson, After King Abdullah: Succession and Stability in Saudi Arabia. Publisher: The Washington Institute for Near East Policy, 2013.

Smith, John. "Economic Integration and Its Impact on Gulf Ideological Dynamics." The Journal of Gulf Studies 25, no. 2 (2019): 101-118. Accessed February 28, 2023.

Sokolsky, Richard. "Rivalry and Revolution in the Gulf: Muscat, Oman, and the Struggle for Influence in the Oman Gulf." Cornell University Press, 2016.

Teitelbaum, Joshua. "The Gulf Cooperation Council: A Study in Regional Cooperation." *The Journal of International Affairs* 55, no. 1 (2001): 127-158.

Tripp, Charles. "Islam and the Moral Economy: The Struggle for Economic Justice in Lebanon." Cambridge University Press, 2014.

Ulrichsen, Kristian Coates. "The Gulf States in International Political Economy." Palgrave Macmillan, 2015.

Wiktorowicz, Quintan. "Anatomy of the Salafi Movement." Stanford University Press, 2006.

Wright, Robin. "Sacred Rage: The Wrath of Militant Islam." Simon and Schuster, 2001.

Wright, Robin. "The Rise of Islamic Fundamentalism in the Gulf: A Threat to US Security." Foreign Affairs 80, no. 5 (2001): 35-54.

Yergin, Daniel. *The Prize: The Epic Quest for Oil, Money & Power.* New York: Simon & Schuster, 2011.

Zahlan, Rosemarie Said. 2010. *Gulf Monarchies in Transition: Beyond Petro-States?.* Routledge.

Zahlan, Rosemarie Said. 2012. *The Creation of Arab States: Britain and the Middle East, 1914-1922.* Oxford University Press.

Zahlan, Rosemarie Said. 2012. *The Origins of the United Arab Emirates: The Long Shadow of the Past.* Routledge.

Zahlan, Rosemarie Said. 2015. *Exploring the Roots of Saudi Youth Extremism: A Cultural and Historical Analysis.* Carnegie Endowment for International Peace.

Zahlan, Rosemarie Said. "Historical Rivalries and Divisions in the Gulf: The Role of Tribe and Sect." International Journal of Middle East Studies 25, no. 1 (1993): 53-74.

Zahlan, Rosemary Said. "The Making of the Modern Gulf States: Kuwait, Bahrain, Qatar, the United Arab Emirates, and Oman." Cornell University Press, 1998.

Zuhur, Sherifa. "Saudi Arabia's Policy in the Gulf, 1979-1989." Springer Nature, 2019.